NORTHERN
CALIFORNIA

MICHAEL'S GUIDE SERIES INCLUDES:

MICHAEL'S GUIDE ARGENTINA, CHILE, PARAGUAY
                      & URUGUAY
MICHAEL'S GUIDE BOLIVIA & PERU
MICHAEL'S GUIDE ECUADOR, COLOMBIA & VENEZUELA
MICHAEL'S GUIDE BRAZIL
MICHAEL'S GUIDE SOUTH AMERICA (Continental)

MICHAEL'S GUIDE NORTHERN CALIFORNIA
MICHAEL'S GUIDE SOUTHERN CALIFORNIA
MICHAEL'S GUIDE CALIFORNIA

MICHAEL'S GUIDE SCANDINAVIA
MICHAEL'S GUIDE SCOTLAND
MICHAEL'S GUIDE SWITZERLAND
MICHAEL'S GUIDE HUNGARY
MICHAEL'S GUIDE TURKEY

MICHAEL'S GUIDE NEW YORK CITY
MICHAEL'S GUIDE LONDON
MICHAEL'S GUIDE PARIS
MICHAEL'S GUIDE AMSTERDAM
MICHAEL'S GUIDE BRUSSELS & ANTWERP
MICHAEL'S GUIDE FRANKFURT
MICHAEL'S GUIDE ROME
MICHAEL'S GUIDE MADRID
MICHAEL'S GUIDE BARCELONA
MICHAEL'S GUIDE JERUSALEM

NORTHERN CALIFORNIA

Series editor:
Michael Shichor

I $\dfrac{N\,B\,A\,L}{\textit{Travel Information Ltd.}}$

Inbal Travel Information Ltd.
P.O.Box 39090 Tel Aviv Israel 61390

Intl. ISBN 965-288-060-4

Photos: The Californias
Michelle Menna

Distributed in the United Kingdom by:
Kuperard (London) Ltd.
30 Cliff Rd.
London NW1 9AG

U.K. ISBN 1-870668-34-0

CONTENTS

Preface 9
Using this Guide 10

INTRODUCTION 13

Part One - A First Taste of What's to Come 13
History and population (14), Geography (18), California literature (20), Pop architecture (21)

Part Two - Setting Out 23
How to get there (23), Safety precautions (24), When to come; National holidays (25), What to wear (25), How much will it cost (26)

Part Three - Easing the Shock: Where Have We Landed? 29
Transportation (29), Accommodation (37), Food (40), Parks and reserves (42), Practical tips for getting around (43), Important addresses and phone numbers (46)

CALIFORNIA 49

Monterey Peninsula 49

Santa Cruz 63

San Francisco 70
How to get there (74), Local transportation (78), Accommodations (81), Food (84)

Financial District 90
Downtown 92
Chinatown 94
North Beach 95
Fisherman's Wharf 98
Exploratorium 102
Civic Center 104
SOMA 105
Japantown 106

Union Street	106
Clement Street	107
The Mission	107
Castro Street	108
Haight-Ashbury	108
Golden Gate Park	110
The City's Coast	112
San Francisco Bay	114

Around San Francisco — **118**
The Peninsula	118
Berkeley	119
Main County	125
Marine World	130

Wine Country — **131**
Napa Valley	131
Sonoma Valley	136
Russian River and Sonoma Coast	139

Inland Northern California — **145**
Sacramento	145
Davis	151
Gold Country	152
Lake Tahoe	161
Toward Reno	167

Yosemite — **170**

The North Coast — **183**
Mendocino Coast	183
Redwood Country	186

Shasta and Lassen — **191**

*I*NDEX 198

*N*OTES 201

TABLE OF MAPS

CALIFORNIA	48
SAN FRANCISCO	72
DOWNTOWN SAN FRANCISCO	93
RUSSIAN RIVER	141
SACRAMENTO CITY CENTER	148
YOSEMITE NATIONAL PARK	172

Preface

California, the 'Golden State' of America, is a legendary land of promise where anything is possible. It has attracted gold-hunters. nature lovers, loners and revolutionaries, radical reformers, refugees, waves of immigarants. and a perennial stream of tourists wanting to taste the good life.

California's extraordinary beauty and pleasant climate are no doubt part of the attraction. California was the ultimate Western frontier, and today connections extend west beyond the Pacific to the Far East. It is a land rich in resources, and the most populaous state in the U.S.A, with a population of more than 23 million. Ninety-three percent of these people live in the metropolitan centers, but California also has some of the richest agricultural land in the U.S.A and the most productive economy. The clear. The clear skies, sunny climate and wide open spaces provide ideal conditions for the aerospace industry. and 'Silicon Valley' is a leading center for high technology. Hoolywood, the cradle of the film industry is still Mecca for thousands of actors, scripwriters, directors and comedians. The music industry also thrives here.

For the millions of tourists who visit California every year, the big attractions are the big inspiring natural wonders of the national parks, dramatic coastlines, golden beaches, haunting desert landscapes and misty cool forests, plus the excitement of metropolitan Los Angeles and San Francisco, and the magic of Disneyland.

We hope to introduce you to the many facets of California, and a variety of attractions in each area are presented, allowing the traveler to choose a choice, according to personal interest.

Our aim is to give you a deeper understanding of California, to help you plan a ideal trip, to lead you to the best and most exciting attractions, and to ensure that you derive maximum pleasure from your trip. We are sure that the effort invested in the compiling of this guide will be justiffied by your enhanced enjoyment.

Using this Guide

In order to reap maximum benefit from the information concentrated in this Guide, we advise the traveler to carefully read the following advice. The facts contained in this book are meant to help the tourist find his or her way around, and to assure that he see the most, with maximum savings of money, time and effort.

The information contained in the Introduction should be read in its entirety as it has details which will help in making the earlh decisions and arrangements regarding hour trip. Reviewing the material thoroughly means that you will be better organized and set for your visit. Upon arrival in California you will already feel familiar and comfortable, more so than otherwise might have been the case.

The basic guideline in all MICHAEL'S GUIDE publications is to survey places in a primarily geographical sequence and not a thematic one. The logic behind it is that a geographical plan not only ensures the most efficient time use, but also contributes dramatically to getting to know an area and its different aspects as well as acquiring a feeling for it. Furthermore, you will be directed from a museum to a historical place, incorporating in your visit to one site several other locations which you may not have thought or heard of nor planned to visit.

The sections are accompanied by maps, especially designed to ease your way. Each chapter also includes a list of useful addresses and telephone numbers.

To further facilitate the use of this Guide, we have included an index, which includes all the major locations mentoned throughout the book. Consult the index to find something by name and it will refer you to the place where it is described in greatest detail.

Because times and places do change, an important rule when traveling in general, and when visitin California in particular, should be to consult the local sources of information. We have therefore accompanied nearly every place with a phone number for last minute checks and suggest you consult the hotel concierge, the local publications and newpapers, the tourist information offices, etc. All of them can advise you of the latest updated information at the specific time of your visit.

As for updating, a guide to a place like California cannot afford to march in place, and up to the time that the Guide went to press, we attempted to confim its relevance and up-to-dateness.

However, it is only natural that due to frequent changes which occur, travelers will find certain time-related facts somewhat less than precise when they arrive at their destination, and for this we apologize in advance.

To this end, cooperation and assistance is necessary and vital from those of you have enjoyed the information contained in this Guide. It ensures, first and foremost, that those who travel in your wake will also enjoy and succeed in their ventures as much as you have. For this purpose, we have included a short questionnaire at the end of this Guide and we will be most grateful to those who complete it and send it to us. A **complimentary copy** of the new edition will be forwardedto those of you who take the time, and whose contribution will apear in the updated edition.

During your visit you will see and experience many things — we have therefore left several blank pages at the back of this Guide. These are for you; to jot down those special experiences of people and places, feelings you may have had, or any other significant happenings along the way. You will always be able to look back on those words and remember.

Have a pleasant and exciting trip — Bon Voyage!

*I*NTRODUCTION

Part One — A First Taste of What's to Come

California is a multi-faceted gem. The gleam of each facet is only partial, yet together they create a strange, enticing and unique aura. This is a land of great physical beauty and contrasts, but the physical extremes are mild compared to the social, cultural and political ones. It is a land where the freedom of life-style can verge on the hedonistic, yet where religious sects with strict codes of behaviour flourish. It is a society generally tolerant of ethnic diversity, yet is marred by a history of vicious racial outbursts. It contains the agricultural heart of the nation, just an hour away from the nerve center of the microelectronics industry. It witnessed the birth of the modern conservation movement and shows a high degree of sensitivity to the environment, yet untempered greed and rampant exploitation have been driving forces in the growth of California. The land of bean sprouts and tofu, it also sustains the most gimmicky and greasy fast-food stands. Although the cauldron of the radicalism of the 1960s, California also gave the nation Richard Nixon and Ronald Reagan, two deeply conservative presidents. It is a land that has attracted dreamers, outcasts, desperate hopefuls, fugitives, artists, rebels, ambitious achievers and more than its share of swindlers and conmen. Somehow they all managed to find a place in the cultural circus of California, as do those who arrive as casual visitors and never leave.

INTRODUCTION

History and Population

For thousands of years, various Indian tribes found a foothold within every niche of California's diverse environment. In 1542, Juan Rodriguez Cabrillo, a Portuguese seaman in the service of Spain, set forth to explore the completely unknown coast north of Mexico, and to claim any lands possible for Spain. Cabrillo's expedition set out because of the Spanish empire's desire for expansion in the New World. It really was a new world, promising endless riches, but vastness and mystery as well. Only 50 years had passed since Columbus discovered America, and less than 25 since Cortes had vanquished Aztec Mexico. Cabrillo himself had marched with the famed *conquistador*. Mexico brimmed with rumors of vast fortunes piled in the northern hinterland. Antonio de Mendoza, Viceroy of Mexico and rival of Cortez for power, had only two years earlier dispatched Francisco Coronado to seek the fabled Seven Cities of Cibola in the region of New Mexico. Now he sent out Cabrillo, a skilled navigator, determined to break through the known limits of the earth. His quest was inspired by the legend of an island kingdom whose huge warriors carried swords of gold, as well as by hopes of discovering a secret passage to the Orient.

Cabrillo set sail in June with two small ships from the Mexican port of Navidad, and reached San Diego Bay in late September. He pushed northward along the coast, observing the plains and mountains of the interior, toward the island of **Santa Catalina**. He named the landmarks he passed (most of the names have been forgotten today) and claimed each for the King of Spain. His ships hugged the coast, trailed by Indians in canoes eager to barter.

In November, Cabrillo landed in the Channel Island archipelago, probably on **San Miguel Island**. As he rushed to help some soldiers who were scuffling with Indians ashore, he fell and broke a leg. Infection set in, and Cabrillo's condition deteriorated over the next six weeks. Amazingly, he retained command and steered his ships north through battering storms off the coast of **Big Sur**.

Cabrillo sailed northward as far as present-day **Fort Ross**, then returned to what was probably San Miguel Island where he finally died and was buried. His grave has not been found. Under the chief pilot, the expedition continued as far north as southern Oregon before it finally returned south.

The expedition reached Navidad in April, 1543, ten months after it departed. It brought back a wealth of information about the bays, inlets, natives and rich potential of the northern coast, and made claims to California for Spain that were not challenged for almost three hundred years. However, it found no golden swords, or passage to China, and it left behind the remains of an intrepid explorer.

Cabrillo's exploration of the Pacific Coast opened California to the

INTRODUCTION

European world, but there was little settlement on the part of the Spanish or anyone else. In 1579 Sir Francis Drake claimed the **San Francisco** area for the Queen of England. Various explorers made forays along the coast, but it was only when the Russians began to move down from Alaska and establish hunting and trading outposts as far south as the Sonoma coast, that the Spanish began to initiate settlement.

The first settlement was established in 1769 in **San Diego**, as a joint military-religious enterprise, with Father Junipero Serra overseeing the construction of a mission intended for the conversion of the local Indians. San Diego was the first of a chain of missions which Serra built, in an effort which was continued by others after his death.

A mission often appeared first with a presidio, and only later did a pueblo — a secular civilian settlement — grow near it. This was a common pattern. The San Gabriel Mission, for example, established in 1771, provided the impetus for the construction of a small village nine miles away, called **Los Angeles**.

The missions were all built along the coast, about a day's journey apart. The paths and dirt roads worn between the missions were eventually spliced into a main coastal road, called El Camino Real, still marked by roadside signs today.

The padres of the far-flung Franciscan missions were immersed as much in physical labor as in spiritual. They were pioneers and settlers, as well as padres. It must have been an amazing time to be in California; everything was new, untouched, open, and the surrounding land so deeply beautiful.

The missions prospered. The padres tilled the fertile valleys. They planted grain crops as well as olives, figs, grape vines, and fruits and vegetables from Spain and Mexico. Their large herds of livestock grazed in the virgin grasslands. In some missions the padres built sophisticated and extensive water systems. The tracts under Franciscan ownership and tillage were immense. By the time the last mission was completed in 1823, the missions controlled one sixth of the total land in California.

But much of this physical progress rested on the backs of local Indians. Conversion was massive and rapid. Many Indians drew toward the missions and the new way of life, while others were pressed into service. There were many forced conversions, resulting in rebellion and consequent repression and punishment. The urge to hasten the Indians' enlightenment might have been intensified if they happened to dwell upon a particularly fertile stretch of land. About 2,000 Chumash Indians were removed en masse from Santa Cruz Island to the Santa Barbara mission.

Written testimony from the early 19th century details regular whippings of Indians in some missions. Even the much-praised

INTRODUCTION

Father Serra was reprimanded by the Spanish governor for implementing excessively heavy punishments. Moreover, the changing of age-old life patterns and sexual molestation by local soldiers, exposed the mission Indians to epidemics. In the sixty years of Spanish control, the Indian population in those areas dropped from about 130 thousand to 83 thousand, with a much higher death rate among the mission Indians.

Rebellion in the 1820's was anti-clerical as well as anti-Spanish. With independence won in 1833, the Mexican congress wrested the missions from Franciscan control. The missions were secularized and stripped of their vast tracts of land. They went into decline, and some into deep decay. Various parties found ways to claim title to land parcels. Later, some of the missions were restored and returned to Franciscan auspices.

The missions left a legacy for Mexican and American rule. They were the first to experiment with California's tremendous agricultural potential. They bequeathed a style of architecture harmonious with the landscape, and several mission names now belong to major cities. The missions gave local Indians new skills for the new world that was fast approaching. They also reduced and deeply scarred the Indian population, but that was but a prelude to future actions. A fiew dacades later, when Mexico won her independence from Spain in 1882 and California was not Mexican anymore, the missions were secularized and efforts were made to expand and solidify settlement.

Meanwhile, an increasing number of American settlers and sailors moved into California. By the mid-1840s there was a call in the east for the annexation of California, as part of the American philosophy of "Manifest Destiny"; the establishment of a republic from coast to coast. In 1848 the mexican war, between Mexico and U.S., came to its end after three years of fighting. One of its consequences — California was ceded to the U.S.

At this year of its turnover to the United States, gold was discovered in California in the Sierra foothills of **Sutter's Mill**. Within a few years the population escalated by about 1000%, and California became the main attraction for American settlers who dreamed of striking it rich.

Gold-hungry immigrants used the local Indian population to work the mines. The Indians were enormously abused. California historian Josian Royce describes how some miners used Indian villages as "targets for rifle-practice, or to destroy wholesale with fire, outrage and murder, as if they had been so many wasps' nests in our gardens at home". The 100,000 Indians in California in 1846 were reduced to 31,000 by 1852. Those left were humiliated, uprooted and exposed to epidemic diseases and alcohol. Over 7 million acres were left to the California Indians by signed treaty in 1850, but this was whittled down to a pitiful 500,000 acres. It was only in 1963 that the California Indians were awarded $27 million by the federal government as long overdue compensation for the lands they lost.

After the Civil War, the national economy and industry boomed, and in 1869 California was linked to the east by the first trans-continental railroad.

California's history has been a record of booms and depressions; of land sales, land grabs and land frauds; of the discovery of new resources and the sudden influx of people to exploit them. The discovery of oil in **Los Angeles** and **Long Beach** at the end of the 19th century created an economic boom in Los Angeles.

With the creation of the movie industry in Hollywood, a new kind of wealth was created in California, and there was suddenly a large number of self-made millionaires. A glamorous "royalty" of movie stars was created, and in their wake thousands of hopefuls flocked to Los Angeles seeking glory in celluloid, but finding instead jobs as cooks, waitresses and cops.

During the Great Depression, more hordes crossed the eastern hills into the valleys seeking not fame and fortune but work, bread or a little land. With this influx of "Oakies" came an ideological clash between radicalism and conservative, land-holding interests. Labor protests, which were violently supressed, burst forth everywhere.

In the 1940s fear of the Japanese replaced fear of the "Reds". In anticipation of the Japanese invasion that never came, thousands of American citizens of Japanese descent were interned in isolated camps, and much of their property was confiscated or looted.

In the 1950s post-war prosperity, the attraction of California became even stronger. The aeronautics industry drew thousands of workers and became the state's industrial and technological mainstay, which it remained until the recent surge in microelectronics took hold in the **Silicon Valley** (at **San Jose**) and revolutionized technology. A steady stream of residents still flows to California. By 1964, California had surpassed New York as the country's most populous state, and today the population exceeds 25 million.

People are attracted to the "sunbelt" of the west and southwest, including an influx of foreign immigrants. California has always attracted a variety of ethnic groups with its multitudinous economic opportunities. Today's immigrants do not come from European countries, but from the Pacific areas and Latin America.

California has been in flux from the moment of statehood. For over a hundred years, the population doubled every twenty years. Although that rate has slowed slightly, the change in the ethnic fabric of the state has accelerated. In the last 15 years, the percentage of Hispanics has almost doubled and the percentage of Asians has almost tripled, while the Caucasian population has dropped considerably. Immigration is becoming one of the key issues of California's future as, in a sense, it has been for over 150 years. The number of children growing up speaking a first language other than English is rapidly growing, yet English has been voted as the single official language of the state.

Meanwhile California's breakneck development and technological advancement continues, swelling its population, taking over rich farmland and exploiting natural resources. Some demographers predict that the population could reach 35 million by the year 2000. Whatever the future holds, no doubt California will face it in its typically dynamic, experimental and completely individual way.

Geography

The coast of California is about 900 miles (1440 km) long, from **Crescent City** at the Oregan border to **San Diego** at the Mexican border. The north coast has endless acres of tall pines and redwoods. The coast is rocky and studded with cliffs, and just beyond the beach area there are ranges of coastal mountains.

The mountain ranges stretch east, reaching towering Mt. Shasta at the southern tip of the Cascade Mountains. Beyond the Cascades, in the northeastern corner of the state, is a strange, weathered and pockmarked world of ancient lava. Below this mountainous cap, which spans the width of California, many of the state's topographical features run parallel to the coast.

Along the northern border, down past the Golden Gate and **San Francisco**, past **Monterey Bay** to the cliffs of **Big Sur**, the coast is stark, and the weather is foggy due to cold currents. Further south, however, near **Santa Barbara**, the ocean currents are warm, and the weather is gentler. The beaches are also softer. The land becomes drier and scrubbier towards the Los Angeles basin which is surrounded by mountains. South of this point the land basks in a hot, constant, semi-tropical sun.

A range of hills runs along the coast from the north, almost all the way down to Mexico. They extend towards the east and in the central part of the state, reach into the rich San Joaquin Valley. This valley is a 400-mile (640 km) long fertile furrow running through the heart of the state. It stretches from the foot of the Cascades in the north, (as the Sacramento Valley), past **Sacramento** to **Bakersfield**, stopping before the thin barrier of the Tehachapi range that separates it from Los Angeles. This great valley is paralled on the east by the long granite massif of the **Sierra Nevada**. The mountain slopes rise gently from the west, in round compact hills where the discovery of gold launched the mad rush of the 1850s. The sequoia trees, the largest living things on earth, grow higher up on the slopes of these hills.

INTRODUCTION

Numerous westward-flowing rivers, with the assistance of ancient glaciers, carved the cliffs, domes and cascades of the Yosemite Valley and other canyons. Yosemite National Park, Lake Tahoe, and King's Canyon/Sequoia National Parks are the main sights of the Sierras. Through the whole range runs a majestic spine of craggy and snow-covered peaks, which is superb backpacking country.

The eastern slope drops like a sheer granite wall, into a high semi arid plateau. This is the great Basin, with isolated mountain peaks, alkaline flats and ancient bristlecone pines 4,000 years old. The Basin extends as far as the desert.

The desert forms the state's largest geographical entity. East of the Sierras, it extends south towards Mexico and stretches across the border. In the east, it extends to the Colorado River and into Nevada and Arizona, and in the west towards Los Angeles.

Climate

The climate in California varies greatly according to the region. In the south, the summers are hot and dry and the sun shines most of the year. The rains usually come in winter, though interspersed with sunshine. Near the beaches especially, it may be tempered by refreshing breezes, but summer in the L.A. urban area can also bring on smog alerts, when the sky is hazy not from fog but from the brown clouds of pollution, and venturing forth in such conditions can actually be hazardous. Winter temperatures of 40 degrees Fahrenheit (4.5 degrees Centigrade) are considered cold enough here to wear minks and down jackets.

The deserts can be comfortable during most of the year but broiling in the summer. The dry heat, however, is more bearable than humidity. Desert summer nights are warm and comfortable, but temperatures can sometimes drop sharply at sunset. An occasional summer rain in the desert is a welcome relief. The clouds swirl and gleam, and the rain churns up delicious fresh smells from the desert floor. In winter the desert can be quite windy and cold.

Seasons in the California mountains are more sharply demarcated than along the coast. Summers can be hot, punctuated by rains, and summer evenings can turn breezy and cool. In the immense areas of conifers, autumn can barely be distinguished, but in some areas where deciduous trees follow the course of stream, the autumnal mountains are etched with rivers of blazing gold.

The first snows can fall as early as late September, and they fall not only in soft white flutterings but in full-fledged blizzards. Snow can pile up to 20 feet (7 m) or more, and last well into spring. In the mountains in late spring the many streams are turbulent and swollen with melted snow.

In the San Joaquin Valley, the summer heat is humid, and extremely unpleasant. That's when you'll want to press your foot on the

*I*NTRODUCTION

accelerator and buzz along that super-highway as fast as possible.

Northern California, along the coast, is characterised by wet winters, often with very heavy rainfall. Nevertheless, there are plenty of fresh and blue-skied winter days as well. The summers can be cool, foggy and overcast, but generally not for long durations. Inland, the winters are a bit drier.

California Literature

California, as a physical reality and state of mind, has attracted both American and foreign writers since before the Gold Rush days. A number of books will give you a feel for the unique texture of California.

Raymond Chandler, mysteries: Corruption and murder in a young Los Angeles, as seen through the eyes of private eye Philip Marlowe.

Richard Henry Dana, *Two Years Before the Mast*: A vivid and detailed travelogue in the 19th-century tradition. With tremendous accuracy he describes the coast of what was then a new and wide-open world.

Joan Didion, *Slouching Towards Bethlehem*: Well-known essays on modern California life and manners.

Allen Ginsberg, *Howl*: Ginsberg's unleashing of this powerful poem became a literary turning point in San Francisco. With Jack Kerouac he helped create a literary movement.

Dashiell Hammett, mysteries: The San Francisco bars frequented by his hard-boiled detective Sam Spade still stand today. Hammett's tough and laconic style greatly influenced many other mystery writers, particularly Raymond Chandler.

Bret Hart, *The Outcast of Poker Flat*: An American story writer and journalist, Hart was the first to depict life in the gold-mining days.

Robinson Jeffers, poetry: Jeffers spent years on the Big Sur coast, and uses the cliffs and waves as powerful metaphors.

Jack Kerouac, *On the Road*: This, the most sincere of Kerouac's writing, preached a "spontaneous" way of life. This work helped launch the beatnik generation.

Henry Miller, *Big Sur and the Oranges of Hieronymous Bosch*: After exploring the alleys and brothels of Paris, Miller stumbled into the wild coast where he found a sense of peace and a focus for his prose.

John Muir, various writings. Elegant descriptions of nature and the wilderness.

John Steinbeck, *The Grapes of Wrath*, *Of Mice and Men*, *East of Eden*, *Cannery Row*, *Tortilla Flat*, *In Dubious Battle*: The *Grapes of Wrath* is Steinbeck's masterpiece about the odyssey of a migrant

*I*NTRODUCTION

family to the farmlands of California. Virtually all of his best writing concerns California. No one writes of the state, and its less shining characters, with more wisdom, warmth and compassion.

Mark Twain, *Roughing It*: No one is more hilarious, or shrewdly observant in capturing the frontier and the Gold Rush.

Evelyn Waugh, *The Loved One*: A biting satire on the American undertaking industry, based around a gaudy and pretentious Los Angeles cemetery.

Pop Architecture

Weird and wonderful architectural forms are as much a part of California's heritage as the rambling Victorian buildings and stucco cottages with red tile roofs. Giant donuts, ice cream cones, owls and hearts, big hats and tractors, towering cowboys, lumberjacks and dinosaurs decorate the California landscape.

Imaginative architecture, which served as advertising, sprang up in the 1920s, with the advent of the automobile, a growing highway system and a newly-mobile middle class. Even during the Depression years, such building continued. It became the expression of hundreds of small private dreams and fantasies.

California soil seemed fertile for such imaginative advertising. Space was wide open, land was available, and already the state was becoming based on the automobile. There was relatively little existing architectural tradition, and the commercial and imaginative climate was right for a bit of profitable whimsy. Any commercial gimmick that might turn a buck had a fighting chance in California. You might say that scattered along the highways of southern California were the precursors of Disneyland. Igloos and castles, southern manors and quaint thatched-roof villages became landmarks. The *Tail o' the Pup*, on the 300 block of La Cienega in Los Angeles, was clever play on the word "hot dog". An L. A. institution, it has appeared in many movies including the relatively recent *Ruthless People*. In Castroville, during a public-relations effort to get the local artichokes on the map, a 16-foot (5 m) artichoke, complete with spikes, was planted in the ground.

The king of pop art architecture in California must be *Dinny the Dinosaur*, at the Cabazon exit off I-10 on the way to Palm Springs. It is the creation of Claude Bell, who was inspired as a boy by a giant elephant-shaped hotel in the New Jersey resort of Margate. He designed many sculptures and buildings for fairs and parks.

When he moved to California and bought a desert plot on which he opened a restaurant, his dream evolved in the shape of a brontosaurus three times the size of a real one! Dinny was a labor of love that took ten years to build. His belly houses a museum and small apartment, reached by a stairway through the tail. He surpasses other roadside models not only in size but through the graceful proportions and meticulous detail, down to the wrinkles and lumps in his hide. Bell was still busy working on his primeval pets into his nineties, having added a tyrannosaurus (with a viewing platform on its head and a slide down its back) to keep Dinny company. The two prehistoric reptiles are clearly visible from the highway and look poised to gobble up the trucks lined up outside the restaurant.

*I*NTRODUCTION

Part Two — Setting Out

How to get there

By air: The two major airports in California are **Los Angeles International Airport (LAX)** and the **San Francisco Airport (SFO)**. Both airports are served by major international and domestic airlines. San Diego airport also serves an increasing amount of national and international air traffic. Special offers of air tickets are worth investigating.

By land: Main train routes to California run from Seattle to San Francisco, Chicago to San Francisco and Chicago to Los Angeles. Major bus companies are *Greyhound* and *Trailways*, which both have special offers and various travel options. Car rental is probably the best way of getting around California.

Documents and customs regulations

Visas

Foreign visitors must enter the United States with a valid passport and visa. Most B-2 tourist visas are valid for 6 months. A lost visa can be replaced through the embassy of the visitor's country. To apply for a visa extension, or to replace the arrival/departure form received on arrival, a foreign citizen must go to the nearest U.S. Immigration and Naturalization Service office.

If you have any problems, it is advisable to contact the nearest consulate of your country. Many countries have consular offices in Los Angeles and/or San Francisco.

A foreign visitor can bring in $100 worth of gifts into the U.S. duty-free, up to 200 cigarettes, and a liter of alcohol. There is no limit on currency. Prescription drugs should be clearly visible and labeled, accompanied by a copy of the doctor's prescription.

International Driver's License

A driver's license valid for the U.S. should be obtained in the country of origin. It will not be issued in the U.S.

Student Cards

Students with proper identification can often receive considerable discount on transportation fares, hotel rates and admission prices. Proper identification includes either a valid university identification card, or an **International Student Identity Card (ISIC)**. The latter, which costs $8, can be obtained with proof of full-time student status. This could be a university identification card, a stamped letter from the registrar, a current grade report, etc. Students enrolled at school for the previous fall semester are eligible to receive the card. In certain cities, with junior colleges, full-time registration costs are negligible, and people have been known to register for a semester just to obtain a student card.

The Council of International Educational Exchange (CIEE) sponsors a special discount plan which, for a small sum, entitles the holder to 25% savings on room rates at various lodgings. Much additional advice on travel is available. To use these services, an ISIC is required, and is obtainable from the CIEE.

Insurance
Insurance is essential. Do not play games with health or medical emergency, even though most major centers do have crisis centers or public clinics that can and will offer immediate care to the uninsured. University hospitals will often do the same. Call the local emergency number, or the crisis center mentioned in this book.

The insuring of valuable objects, such as cameras, is obviously a personal choice. In the big cities especially, professional thieves abound and are very smooth. This is not meant to frighten you off, but it is best to be realistic. A moment's carelessness, a camera can disappear. Insurance can sometimes be purchased through a travel organization.

Safety Precautions

It is best to avoid bus terminals and train stations late at night, and it is not advisable to walk in deserted downtown neighborhoods at high. Avoid public restrooms in the cities.

It is advisable to keep some money separate from your wallet, and to keep a list of traveler's checks separate as well. Make a note of important numbers — driver's license, credit card, passport — and keep it somewhere safe.

Many travelers choose to carry money and important documents in a money belt that fits around the waist inside the shirt, or one that hangs around the neck. Some go so far as to carry a "decoy" wallet in a pocket, to draw attention away from the money belt. All this is a matter of personal choice. The most important thing is to take the steps necessary for your own peace of mind and maximum enjoyment.

When to come; National Holidays

California is a vacationland for all seasons. During every season of the year, there is at least one part of the state where the weather seems just perfect.

Most people flock to California in the summer, and in most tourist areas prices tend to rise accordingly. The exception to this is the desert resort of Palm Springs where prices actually go down in summer due to the intense heat. Winters in southern California are delightfully sunny and warm; summers in northern California are refreshingly cool. In the Sierra Nevada and the other mountain ranges, each season has its own beauty and activities. Some mountain passes are closed in winter, but the mountain ski resorts are popular.

Planning a time for your visit may be not so much a matter of weather, but rather a matter of crowds. There is no doubt that most tourist facilities are far more crowded in summer, with a commensurate rise in prices. If possible, try and avoid traveling on the following days:

Memorial Day weekend, around May 31st.
Independence Day weekend, around July 4th.
Labor Day weekend, at the beginning of September.

From Memorial Day onwards, there is a great increase in the number of vacationers on the roads, with a sharp decline following Labor Day. In fact, in terms of numbers, prices, and the accessibility of facilities, early fall is an ideal time to travel. Children are back at school and students are back at college.

The weeks surrounding Christmas and New Year's Day are also crowded with visitors. However, the rest of the winter is considered off-season, other than for ski resorts.

American public holidays include:
New Year's Day, January 1st.
President's Day, the third Monday in February.
Memorial Day, the last Monday in May.
Independence Day, July 4th (businesses close on the nearest Monday or Friday).
Labor Day, first Monday in September.
Columbus Day, second Monday in October.
Veteran's Day, November 11th.
Thanksgiving, last Thursday in November.
Christmas, December 25th.

What to wear

Clothing to be packed depends upon the region to be visited. For southern California, be sure to pack a heavy sweater and light waterproof coat for the winter. You will need these in summer in northern California. Style in California tends to be casual.

Ties are usually worn by businessmen, but this is not as strictly required as it is in the east. Colors for both men's and women's fashions are brighter in California than in some other regions, and also brighter in the south than in the north. Californian casualness has become a fashion in its own right, blending a bright, tailored tapered look with comfort. Shoes can also be casual. A good pair of walking shoes can serve in a number of situations. There always seems to be a sale at one or another of the numerous clothing stores, so it is easy to pick up what you need. For women, slacks are acceptable for most occasions, and are worn by many.

California is also the place for down-to-earth second-hand artistic funk. "Contemporary Salvation Army" is becoming so popular that charity and second-hand stores have begun to raise their prices, and some have turned downright chic.

If planning to enjoy California's natural wonders, be sure to include sturdy durable clothes and shoes. In southern California especially, a hat, preferably broad-brimmed, is advisable during the summer. Sandals are increasingly accepted as everyday summer footwear. Birkenstocks, though more expensive than some others, are sturdy, long-lasting, comfortable and popular. For hiking shoes, the new models made of light yet water resistant material, are gaining in popularity. These are suitable for California's diverse terrains.

How much will it cost

The amount of money a visitor will spend is, of course, a very subjective matter, depending on the individual's needs, tastes and style. The point to remember is that California, more than many other areas, provides enough variety in resources and alternatives for most people to relax and enjoy themselves within their means.

The main expense, besides the cost of getting to California, will naturally be **lodging**. The prices of average lodging has sky-rocketed in recent years. Even Motel 6, which made its name an advertisement of its price, would have to change its name to Motel 21.50 to be accurate today. For a standard basic motel room, expect to pay a minimum of $23-$30 per day. Most cost considerably more. For an average motel room or a room in a B&B a visitor could easily pay $50-$60 per day. Of course there are plenty of better hotels that charge up to $150 per day for their amenities; spending more is never a problem.

INTRODUCTION

Nevertheless, a person on a strict budget can definitely find cheap accommodation, and in some comfort, if he or she shows some flexibility. Hostels, for example, though not the last word in luxury or privacy, rarely cost more than $8 per day, and provide a unique traveling experience. YMCAs offer another inexpensive solution. The person determined to backpack can do so and still have access to the major cities. Car-camping is popular, and private and public campgrounds are numerous, ranging between $6-$15 per night, depending on the place, facilities, etc.

Transportation costs can also vary greatly. Car-rental can range from $20-$40 per day. Insurance is added on a daily basis (see "Car Rental"). Local bus systems may cost between 50 cents and $1, usually with some sort of transfer arrangement. Transportation between major cities is private. Buses cost approximately $14 between Los Angeles and San Diego, and $25-$40 between Los Angeles and San Francisco. Private vans, airport shuttles and so forth can start at about $7 and go up to $20.

Those preferring to work on a firm transportation budget may want to base costs on monthly car rentals ($400 and up, plus insurance), or monthly bus or train passes. These can be combined with local public transportation, daily car or bicycle rental (see "Transportation").

As for **food**, there is a wide range of budgeting possibilities, especially in the two major urban areas, where the choice and variety is enormous. Cheapest of all is to buy from grocery stores, delis and fast-food stands, but a good and filling meal in certain restaurants can be had for as little as $3-$5. Good breakfasts can cost from $1.50-$3.50. Many places, especially simple Chinese restaurants, have lunch specials costing $3-$5. Mexican restaurants cost slightly more, with large meals running from $4.50-$6. Salad bars start at about $3.50 and up.

Steak or fish meals in good restaurants start at about $10, but the same meal, during an "Early Bird Special" will cost about $6.95. (There is almost no upper limit.) At the lower limit, even a really inexpensive special will cost about $5, including beverage and tip.

California, especially southern California, is a shopper's and bargain-seeker's paradise. Discount houses proliferate and large drug-store chains sell merchandise at cut-rate prices.

Entertainment — night clubs, concerts and shows — can be expensive. Many clubs include a cover charge and a one or two-drink minimum. For a couple, that could reach approximately $20. First run movies cost about $5-6. Such attractions as amusement parks are especially expensive. Admission for some of these private tourist attractions is over $10 per person, with a parking fee slapped on top.

On the other hand, some of the top museums in the country are found in California, and are open to the public for nominal prices. Many museums, as mentioned throughout the book, set aside special hours or days when admission is free.

INTRODUCTION

Part Three — Easing the Shock: Where Have We Landed?

Transportation

Airports

The two major airports in California are the **Los Angeles (LAX)** and the **San Francisco (SFO)** airports. LAX is one of the busiest in the world. All major domestic and just about all major international and foreign lines serve the two airports. There is also an extremely busy commuter lane between SFO and LAX, in addition to numerous flights taking off to and from smaller airports within the same corridor.

The **San Diego** airport (SAN) also services flights along the coast and handles an increasing amount of national and international traffic.

There are several airlines that operate mainly in the west, and others that operate solely within California. It is possible to fly all around the state with small airlines such as Pacific Coast, Sky West, Mid Pacific, as well as on larger regional airlines such as PSA or Western. A number of smaller metropolitan airports handle major national carriers. This not only reduces the strain on the major airports, but allows the visitor greater flexibility. During high-season or on busy holiday weekends, it is sometimes wise to avoid a major center such as LAX and rather to land in a less frenetic local airport. The possibilities for direct air connections to the lesser-known areas of California are often much greater than visitors realize.

The following airports handle national airlines:
Arcata/Eureka: tel.707-445-7791.
Bakersfield (Meadows Field): tel. 805-393-7977.
Burbank-Glendale-Pasadena: tel. 818-840-8843.
Fresno: tel. 251-6051.
Long Beach: tel. 213-421-8293.
Los Angeles: tel. 213-646-5252 (also for international flights).
Monterey Peninsula: tel. 408-373-3731.
Oakland: tel. 415-577-4000 (also international flights).
Ontario: tel. 714-984-1207 (also international flights).
Palm Springs: tel. 619-323-8163.
Reno: tel. 702-785-2575.
Sacramento: tel. 916-929-5411.

San Francisco: tel. 415-761-0800 (also international flights).
San Diego: tel. 619-231-5220 (also international flights).
San Jose: tel. 408-277-5366.
Santa Barbara: tel. 805-967-1613 or 805-967-7111.

Since the deregulation of the airline industry a few years ago, and with new companies springing up and competition growing intense, the air traveler has been benefiting. If you shop around and are a bit flexible with your flying schedule, you can find some amazing flight deals, especially compared with what passengers paid some years back. Of course this could change. The airline industry, at least in America, is in great flux, but right now it is a flier's market.

When booking a flight, do not settle for the first answer you get, from either an airline or a travel agent. Try other airlines and other agents, until you have a good idea of the price range.

It might be up to you to ask the pertinent questions. Sometimes you must ferret out the details: they will not always be volunteered. Are there student fares? Stand-by fares? Midnight fares? Does a round-trip bought in advance cost less? Would the price be lower during another season? Airline officials often cannot answer all your questions because they do not know. With some special flight bargains, however, the deal comes with restrictions which will be made clear to you.

If you have purchased a round-trip ticket to the United States from abroad (some companies may require foreign residency), then you can buy a **VUSA** (Visit USA) ticket. This allows you to fly literally all over the United States for one set price — generally between $200-$400 — which is usually less than one standard cross-country flight. There are several similar types of VUSA tickets, based on a system whereby you pay a set price, and take an unlimited number of flights with the airline issuing the ticket, within a specific time limit. The only restriction is that you cannot leave from or enter the same terminal more than twice.

Even if you plan to stay within one region, such as California or the West Coast, a VUSA might still be worthwhile, as it may cost the same as one standard flight from the East Coast. Furthermore, some regional airlines have arrangements which honor the VUSA ticket of certain major airlines. If, for example, you buy a VUSA from Northwest Airlines, you can use it on PSA all through California and the West with no extra charge. Check this all out, because the arrangements can change periodically.

Many airlines have introduced, to the travelers' delight, a variety of **Frequent-Flyers** programs, in which the miles you fly can be used as credit toward free future flights. Business person who travel frequently can clock up enormous amounts of free mileage. The system is generally based on miles flown. Check these plans carefully, because with some companies you are given points only for the number of flights, regardless of the mileage of each flight. PSA seems to have the best frequent-flyer program in the West, more advantageous than that of Western, its major competitor.

There is also the new, unofficial "bumping game" that has taken over the airlines. Airlines now make a practice of overbooking certain, generally crowded, flights, to compensate for the number of people who make reservations and who do not turn up. If most or all passengers show up, however, then the airlines have more people than seats. Thanks to the efforts of consumer advocate Ralph Nader (after he himself was ignominiously "bumped" from an overbooked plane), government regulations require that passengers bumped involuntarily must be given cash payments, sometimes double the cost of the ticket; and they can still sue.

Financially ailing airlines, to avoid having to fork out cash, have come up with another solution. They ask for volunteers to give up their seat, and offer free tickets to various destinations in addition to a guaranteed seat on the next flight. This has become so commonplace that people make a sport of it. They've learned the angles and purposely book themselves on busy flights, their hands ready to shoot up the moment volunteers are requested. Businessmen have become pros. You may not be in their champion class, but if your schedule is flexible, the wrong flight may turn into the right flight, resulting in a voucher for a free trip somewhere.

Trains: Train travel is a throwback to a bygone world. The conductor rattles off the names of exotic-sounding frontier towns. The train pulls into an elegant Spanish-style station, or past a small smudged brick depot bordered by decrepit hotels and bars. People casually get acquainted in the lounge car. The countryside glides by at eye-level. The traveling becomes as rich an experience as the arrival.

Amtrak, the national passenger rail carrier, made a big push recently to encourage train travel by introducing extended routes, lower rates, package-tour deals, streamlined equipment and so forth. All this is geared to fill their trains, which were, for a while, pitifully empty.

The main train routes leading into California include:
Seattle to San Francisco (The Coast Starlight).
Chicago to San Francisco (The California Zephyr).
Chicago to Los Angeles, either directly through San Antonio, or through New Orleans (The Desert Wind).

An intricate system of buses and local commuter trains connects with *Amtrak* rail lines, greatly extending access by train.

There are several main routes within the state. The **Coast Starlight** takes ten-and-a+half hours between Los Angeles and San Francisco. This route affords a slow but pleasant way to travel between the major cities without the hassles of driving. Although it does not follow the rugged Big Sur Coast, the train passes some gorgeous shoreline.

In the San Francisco area, the actual departure station is in industrial Oakland. A special *Amtrak* bus connects to the San Francisco station, the trans-bay terminal, at 1st and Mission.

The California section of the **Zephyr** follows the route of the early transcontinental railroad, with access to the Truckee-Lake Tahoe area, as well as to Reno just across the Sierra Nevada.

The San Joaquin route runs through the main cities of the Central Valley. From Bakersfield in the south, a special *Amtrak* bus brings passengers to the *Amtrak* station in the Los Angeles area. In the north, the train connects with the main east-west line and with the train going north to Seattle. At various points along this route, there are connections with local and regional bus lines. At the **Merced** station, a private bus runs to Yosemite Park.

At the time of writing, *Amtrak* has a special scheme whereby for any regular ticket purchase of $60 or more, the return fare is only $7. In California, even some routes with fares less than $60 qualify for the special return fare, such as the routes between Los Angeles and San Diego, and between San Francisco and Bakersfield. You need to return by the same route, and there are no stopovers. The $7 fare is good for 45 days after the original trip. There are certain peak traveling seasons when the ticket is not valid, so check this out carefully.

Amtrak also has special fares for traveling within or between various regions of the country. If you are journeying to California from the east, a $250 fare allows you to weave towards the west along whatever route you want, with three stopovers within 45 days. Coming from the mid-west, the fare is $200. To zig-zag throughout the western region, from El Paso, Texas to Spokane, Washington including all of California, costs $150. As with the airlines, *Amtrak's* offers change often, so it is important to call for updated information.

Amtrak also offers total travel packages with hotels, tours, etc. There are such tours for Hearst Castle, the wine country, San Francisco and Disneyland. Trains have sleeping accommodation, ranging from a pillow for the seat to separate bedrooms, complete with bathroom. Some trains — or specific types of cars — require reservations, while others do not. If you buy your ticket on the train, when the station booth is open, you will be required to pay an additional $3. It is possible to bring bicycles aboard certain trains, without have to dismantle the bikes. For general *Amtrak* information and reservations: tel. 1-800-872-7245. This number will give you various local *Amtrak* numbers, if needed.

INTRODUCTION

Buses

The two major private bus companies are *Greyhound* and *Trailways*. Both companies offer special excursion fares, summer-travel fares and so forth. As with *Amtrak*, these rates and schedules change often, so it is always worth double-checking. *Greyhound* with its *Ameripass*, and Trailways with its *Eaglepass*, both offer unlimited travel for a fixed price, within a fixed number of days. Although most buses are stream-lined and comfortable, there is a limit to how long you can remain seated, especially when you push yourself, because you want to get the most for your money. Compare prices with *Amtrak*. In some cases, surprisingly, the train's bargain pass may actually be cheaper, and they are certainly more comfortable. For those wanting to reach California cheaply, both bus companies offer a 15-day one-way fare, in which travel in one direction for up to 15 days costs about $100. Stops are permitted.

Children between 12-16 ride for half-fare, and ages 11 and under ride free. Seniors receive a 10% discount except on special fares. Bicycles can be stowed in the baggage compartment. This opens the possibility for a hop-scotch travel schedule of bus rides and bike rides.

Bus stations almost always seem to be located in the bad part of town. If possible, avoid arriving late at night or having to wait around a dingy and depressing bus station in the wee hours.

Green Tortoise buses offer alternative tours which are adventurous (slightly), eccentric and cheap. The company once had a reputation as the "freak" bus line, but now it draws a wide variety of people, from hippies to foreigners to professionals and spunky seniors seeking an unusual travel experience. The buses have bunks (bring your own sleeping bag or bedding), and two drivers to allow night-time traveling and daytime excursions and diversions. For the lone traveler with a budget one notch above hitching, *Green Tortoise* provides a chance to meet similar travelers, to make contacts, to pick up traveling tips and just to have some company.

Green Tortoise conducts trips to Alaska, Vancouver and cross-country tours varying in duration and routes (one tour hits the major national parks). A cross-country to California costs about $200. There is also a strong schedule within California, including $25 trips between San Francisco and Los Angeles with stops for exploring. There are also trips to Yosemite ($49-$59). Communally-cooked vegetarian meals fuel the crew and the travelers. Each bus has a stereo, and you can volunteer your own cassettes.

Green Tortoise Main office: P.O.Box 24459, San Francisco, 94124. tel.415-821-0803. There are offices on the east coast and along the west coast, and a toll-free number, tel. 1-800-277-4766.

*I*NTRODUCTION

Car Rental

Renting a car can be the most convenient and the most expensive means of travel in California. It is worth calling up several agencies because rates and conditions vary widely. For a day, a car could cost from $16-$30, and per month between $450-$550. The larger agencies — *Hertz*, *Avis* and *National* — are available at airports and major tourist centers, but do not necessarily offer the best deals. Sometimes, the small agencies boast the best prices. Most major California cities have the equivalent of "rent-a+wreck" car rentals, giving just what the name applies, at commensurate prices, along with a certain distance radius.

3,000 miles (4,800 km) a month — the average amount given — may seem like sufficient distance, but that breaks down to just over one hundred miles per day, which, if you are a hard-pushing traveler, is not really very much. Los Angeles commuters easily cover that distance daily.

The real drawback to renting a car can be the insurance, which may cost $6-$8 per day. You can apply your own liability insurance, but only if you are an in-state driver with a California license. Of course, in that case there is less chance you would need to rent a car: one of life's little ironies. If you are entering California from outside the state and want to rent a car, you almost have no choice but to take the insurance as well. Some agencies might advise you to attach yourself to the insurance of a relative, but be very wary of this as it stands on shaky legal ground. When inquiring about the insurance, find out exactly what is covered. Agents have been known to quote insurance prices, only to reveal later that the coverage is only partial, and they then try to convince you to take on "extra" protection ("Perhaps you'd like your left tires covered as well?").

The larger agencies sometimes offer special weekend rates. These can start as early as Thursday, with a package deal for rental through Sunday.

Having access to a car makes all the difference in the world, especially in southern Califonia. For both the business traveler on a strict schedule, and the tourist, it may be best to fly between destinations and rent cars locally. California's excellent in-state and inter-region air connections allows this to be done with flexibility and ease.

A **drive-away** company offers a slightly uncertain but inexpensive way to travel, both to California and within the state. These companies find drivers to transport cars from one destination to another. It is usually easy to find cars being transported from coast to coast. Sometimes you may need to be a bit flexible and accept a car to Bakersfield even if you want to end up in Los Angeles. The driver leaves a deposit, usually around $100, and picks it up from the company's office at the other end of the line once the car is safely delivered. The time and mileage allowed is limited, but it is sometimes possible to squeeze in a short excursion to a nearby sight. Such transport is available within the state of California as well, but cars between Los Angeles and San Francisco are not easily found and are snapped up quickly. Major cities in the country have such offices. Check in the phonebook under car transport, auto transport or drive-away.

Roads

California has an excellent road system. Interstate and in-state freeways criss-cross the entire state. What they provide in directness, speed and convenience, however, is paid for by taking the boring route. Nothing can be more dangerously mesmerizing to a night driver than an endlessly flat and straight road with one white stripe after another passing in front of you. The driver who tries a backroad here and there and passes through tiny towns will enrich his or her visit.

Along the interstate highways, rest stops are interspersed. These usually include rest rooms, drinking water, a patch of green, some picnic tables, and perhaps a map and additional information about the area. It is perfectly okay to park here overnight and sleep in the car, and it's usually safe, especially if several large trailer trucks are parked nearby. People sometimes flop their sleeping bags down on the grass. Usually they are not disturbed, but officially it is not allowed.

Some Driving Tips

In both San Francisco and Los Angeles, parking can be a problem. Parking is not allowed alongside red or white curbs, green curbs mean limited-time parking only and even at unpainted curbs parking may not be allowed during rush hours, street-cleaning hours, etc.

Right turns are allowed at red lights, unless otherwise indicated. Drive here as you would at a stop sign. At a marked crosswalk, drivers must yield to pedestrians. This can sometimes be annoying and some pedestrians exercise their power by giving a driver little time to stop. As a pedestrian, however, you will appreciate the law.

The maximum speed limit on highways and freeways is 55 miles per hour (88 kph), though there has been much grumbling about that, and on the L.A. freeways many drivers ignore the speed limit. In residential areas the speed limit is 25mph (40 kph). On main thoroughfares the speed limit may vary.

California has one of the strictest drunk-driving laws in the country, requiring the immediate arrest of anyone found to be driving under the influence of alcohol.

*I*NTRODUCTION

Auto Clubs

The *American Automobile Association* is the best known of the auto clubs. Membership fees vary from state to state, ranging from about $20-$50. Services include trip planning, maps, travelers' checks (American Express) and — especially important — 24-hour emergency road service anywhere. Also worthwhile is the club's auto insurance.

In northern California, the AAA is listed as the California State Automobile Association. In southern California it is listed as the Automobile Club of Southern California (ACSC).

Accidents

Call the police immediately in the event of any accident. On municipal streets, call the local police. On freeways, even within cities, and on highways and roads between cities, call the California Highway Patrol (CHP). On city freeways, the phones in the emergency callboxes link automatically to a CHP office. Otherwise, ask the operator for Zenith 1-2000, the CHP emergency number.

Rides and Hitchhiking

Someone seeking a passenger to share expenses and company, or someone seeking a ride, would do well to check the nearest college or university. Most such centers have some sort of "ride board". Alternative radio stations and newspapers also provide this service.

Hitchhiking has declined a bit in California. A few gruesome incidents, with both drivers and passengers as the victims, have occurred, one's decision is a personal matter. Obviously, the vast majority of hitchhikers and helpful drivers are not hurt.

As either the driver or the rider, ask a few questions first before entering the situation, all the while trying to size up the person the best you can. In a region of a national park, a hitchhiker with a backpack standing in the middle of nowhere has probably just emerged from a trail and is trying to reach the nearest bank, shower and burger stand.

Hitchhiking within the city is generally less successful than between cities. It is generally easier to find the nearest bus.

Sometimes, if waiting by a restaurant or gas staion, approaching a driver will more likely get a positive response, but not always.

Backpacking

California offers a whole world to explore for the packpacker. Information about backpacking is easily accessible, and trails in parks around the state are well-maintained.

*I*NTRODUCTION

Numerous guide books on hiking and backpacking are available. Likewise, many stores sell camping equipment. Sometimes the big department stores and discount houses sell good equipment at cut-rate prices. Always check, though, that the equipment is of good quality.

Army-navy surplus stores, often found in the downtown sections of larger cities, can supply many of the smaller items. Today, camping has become a gigantic business, and new and improved equipment is produced anually. Everything but a jet-propelled backpack is on the market!

The *Sierra Club* is an excellent source of information for camping in California. Although a national conservation organization, the club originated in California. In addition to organizing hiking trips for members, the various branches will be able to provide printed guides and maps on specific regions in the state.

Accommodations

The range of accommodation in California is almost unlimited. Luxurious hotels which look like old Roman villas, quaint lodges perched above the beach, sleazy downtown rattraps, sterile stucco motels, homey inns, and trailer campgrounds resembling suburbs on wheels — they are all here.

Lodging is not particularly cheap, and real bargains in overnight accommodation are hard to find. Most decent and reliable facilities, even in a standard motel, begin around $25.

Many local Chambers of Commerce distribute lists of local accommodation, as do visitors centers. Policies vary at these agencies about listing prices or making recommendations. Those who list accommodation are all members of the local chamber.

A list of suggested accommodation is available from the *California Hotel and Motel Association*, 414 29th st., Sacramento, CA 95816. Tel.916-444-5780.

Remember when considering price, that hotels in California tag on a hotel tax. This rate differs from area to area, ranging usually from 6% to as high as 10%.

The major hotel chains are well represented in both the major cities and outlying areas of California. In resorts, prices tend to rise on weekends. In major cities, hotels which cater to a business population and host conventions, often change things around: they offer discounts on weekends, which are sometimes very sizeable ones. This may be done on a haphazard basis by the individual hotel depending on the booking situation that weekend, or it may be part of a regular weekend special program followed in many branches of a hotel chain. This is worth checking out, for the reductions are substantial and allow for a luxurious weekend at very reasonable prices. Often these rates will only be mentioned upon request, so be sure to inquire about any weekend discount or special package. Below is a sampling of some of the available specials. The toll-free numbers listed are generally reservations and information numbers that give details about weekend specials or refer you to particular hotels. Even within a single hotel chain, the discount may vary from hotel to hotel, city to city or season to season.

Best Western International: tel. 800-528-1234. Discounts of 20-50% off regular rates.

Hilton Hotels: Various areas have their own 800 numbers. Ask specifically about the "Rainbow Weekend".

Hyatt Hotels: tel. 800-288-9000. Various weekend programs may include reductions of up to 50% on deluxe rooms.

Marriott Hotels: tel. 800-2888-9290. Ask about "Super Saver" and "Escape" packages for weekenders.

Ramada Hotel Group: tel. 800-272-6232. "R and R" weekend specials.

Sheraton Hotels: tel. 800-325-3535. Ask about "Time of your Life" weekends.

Westin Hotels: tel.800-228-300. Most have lower weekend rates.

Motel 6 is a safe, standard, reliable and inexpensive motel-chain. Most have pools but television is extra. There is nothing surprising here, either pleasant or unpleasant. The price, about $21, is relatively inexpensive. There are about 400 motels in the chain nation-wide, and almost 100 in California alone. For a directory, write: *Motel 6*, Inc., 51 Hitchcock Way, Santa Barbara, CA 93105.

The Quest International hotel marketing organization for a $99 annual membership fee, arranges a 50% discount off regular rates at more than 500 hotels in the United States, British Columbia and San Juan. The half-price reduction is offered no matter how seasonal prices may fluctuate. Quest International, Chinook Tower, Box 4041, Yakima, WA 98901, tel. 509-248-7512.

Bed-Breakfast (B&B) Inns have increased in number and popularity in recent years. There are several hundred scattered throughout California, but they are found predominantly in the north. They tend to be rustic and old. Some may be refurbished farmhouses, others old family-run hotels or Victorian houses. Each one is individual, expressing its own personality and that of its owners. Many are small, family-run operations, perhaps even in a wing of a private home. The rooms vary in style and furnishings and often there is an emphasis on old-time decor. Such inns may be located in the center of town, in completely residential areas, or in the country side. They can offer an inside glimpse of country life that hotel guests may not otherwise see. Staying at a B&B is a little more adventurous than staying in a conventional hotel. The atmosphere is often warm and casual, it is easy to meet the other guests or the owners. The breakfasts may include such touches as freshly-squeezed juice

*I*NTRODUCTION

and home-baked muffins, as opposed to the standard coffee-shop fare. Often there are complimentary afternoon beverages, or use of the library or a bicycle, or other touches that make the experience more home-like.

There was a time when B&Bs were generally less expensive than hotels. Now the prices are on a par, and sometimes they are over-priced, not to mention outrageous. Nevertheless, there are plenty around which, while costing no more than the average motel, offer an individual experience to which a motel cannot compare. Because each inn is run at the fancy of its owner, features you would expect at a motel must be double-checked in a B&B: How big is the bed? Is the room furnished? Is the bathroom private? Is there a bath or only a shower? Are there any extras? Is breakfast full or continental (beverage, juice and rolls)? Are there weekday or off-season rates?

Various organizations who represent B&Bs in different regions have appeared, making it easier for the visitor to find a special one. These organizations know the characteristics of the different inns, and can also make suggestions and sometimes handle bookings.

Besides the B&Bs, there is also the "homestay", in which guests actually rent a room in a private residence. This can be less expensive and more homey than a B&B. Information is often available through the B&B associations.

In addition to the associations noted below, smalller organizations represent the inns of specific regions.

Bed and Breakfast Innkeepers of Southern California: P.O.Box 15385, Los Angeles 90015. tel. 805-966-0589.

Bed and Breakfast Innkeepers of Northern California: 2030 Union st., Suite 310, San Francisco 74123. tel. 415-563-4667.

Association of Bed and Breakfast Innkeepers of San Francisco: 737 Buena Vista W., San Francisco 94117. tel. 415-861-3008.

A brochure listing B&Bs throughout the state is published by the California Office of Tourism in Sacramento.

Youth Hostels provide another lodging alternative. A national network of Youth Hostels is operated by *American Youth Hostels* (AYH). The AYH is part of the *International Youth Hostel Federation*. Its membership card is valid for International Youth Hostel facilities. Conversely, a card from abroad is valid in the United States.

Hostel facilities are often found in schools, old hotels, and YMCAs, but sometimes they have their own buildings. Some hostels have smaller private rooms as well as dorm-like rooms, and most have kitchen facilities.

Youth hostels are by no means only for youth. Many others, such as professionals and seniors, use hostels in order to spice up their vacation. Hostels are ideal places for the lone traveler to strike up acquaintances and pick up travel tips.

Overnight fees are usually around $5-$6 for members, and a dollar or two more for non-members. AYH offices can be found in most major cities in the country.

In California there are over 30 hostels. Information can be obtained on them from your local AYH office. Some of the California hostels in which membership is sold include:

In San Francisco: 240 Fort Mason, S.F. 94123, tel. 415-771-7727.

In Los Angeles: 1502 Palos Verdes dr., N Harbor City 90710, tel. 213-831-8109.

In San Diego: Armed Services YMCA, 500 W. Broadway, SD 92101. tel. 619-232-1133.

The AYH operates other youth hostels as well in these metropolitan areas.

YMCAs have traditionally provided wayfarers with decent and simple lodgings, often in dormitories. Today they may range from the very inexpensive to the price of an average motel room. Usually, the price includes use of some or all of the sports facilities. The lodgings may range from shabby to sleek. Reservations are often recommended. For a listing of YMCAs and general information, contact: *The Y's Way*, 356 W. 34th st., New York, NY 10001. Tel. 212-760-5856. If you want a catalogue, send a self-addressed stamped envelope.

The Young Women's Christian Association (YWCA) offers the same type of lodging and facilities, but generally for women only. Contact: *The Young Women's Christian Association*, 726 Broadway, New York, N.Y. 10003. tel. 212-614-2700.

Food

As with almost everything else in California, the world of food is rich, colorful and diverse. Eating out is a common pastime. Restaurants range from the elegant, elite and outrageously expensive to the incredibly cheap. In addition to American steak restaurants, Chinese and Mexican restaurants are extremely popular, widespread and accessible on any budget. More varieties of both Asian and Latin American food are becoming available. Italian restaurants are very common as well.

The grilling of fish and meats on mesquite coal is common in many California restaurants, especially in the north. There is an emphasis on fresh produce of excellent quality, mixed together in myriad ways. In recent years, with an increased emphasis on health, vegetarian cooking has developed into an art. Vegetarian

*I*NTRODUCTION

restaurants are common, and serve a surprising variety of dishes, some tremendously imaginative. In conjunction with this is the increasingly common appearance of the salad bar, available as part of a larger meal or by itself. These salad bars are creations in themselves; the old days of tomatoes and shredded lettuce are gone. An average salad bar may include an array of cheeses and dressings, several kinds of nuts, potatoes, bread, fish, noodles and fruit — in other words, a salad can be a delicious and filling meal in itself. One of the best and most reliable salad bars can be found in the *Sizzler* chain of restaurants. The emphasis in this buffet type restaurant is on steak, but the salad bar, at about $4.25, is a welcome sight to those who prefer not to eat red meats.

Fast-food stands line the highways of California. They have branched out from the old simple burger stands and now include pizza, tacos, roast beef, chicken and ice cream. Prices at different branches of the same company are generally uniform. Occasionally, a chain will run some sort of special and proclaim it in the media, but sometimes a typical burger-fries-milkshake meal at a fast-food stand, besides containing dubious nutritional value, can cost as much as a sit-down meal at, for example, a small Chinese lunch counter.

The 24-hour coffee-shop chains form another characteristic California institution. They are far from the down-home diners of yesteryear. In each chain there are standardized designs, prices, menus, quality and employee uniforms. One can imagine that the same innocuous soft music plays simultaneously at hundreds of different coffee-shops.

However, there can be something comfortable about these places, especially when it is 2am and, up ahead at the next highway exit, the bright sign of a *Denny's*, *Sambo's*, *Norm's* or *Bob's* shines invitingly in the darkness. The soft lights, familiar booths, smiling waitresses, never-ending coffee and precisely sliced pie is somehow reliable and reassuring, even if rather bland.

Instead of tasting California's superb produce in a restaurant, it is possible to get it yourself direct from the farm. As mentioned throughout this book, many regions publish maps showing which local farms accept visitors, what the farm produces, etc. This is a good way not only to obtain fresh produce, but to break out of the tourist mold and meet the locals in an unusual setting. The produce you can sample ranges from vegetables and fruits to nuts, wines and cheeses. The regional directories can be obtained through local chamber of commerce offices, or through one central office: The Dept. of Food and Agriculture, 1220 N st., room 427, Sacramento 95814.

INTRODUCTION

Parks and Reserves

National Park Service (NPS)

An extraordinary diversity of preserved land is under the juristriction of the *National Park Service* including Yosemite, Death Valley, the Channel Islands and Redwood.

The park service enforces strict rules about the protection of natural areas. Entrance fees are charged and camping fees are extra, starting at $4. Fees for primitive campsites are nominal, and for backcountry free, but permits are required.

The *Golden Eagle Passport* allows unlimited entry into national parks for the holder and accompanying passengers in a single car. The pass costs $10 and can be purchased at a national park or NPS regional office.

The *Golden Age Passport* is free to seniors from age 62. It provides free life-time entry to all park lands, and 50% discounts on various fees, such as camping. Available at most national parks, it must be obtained in person. A similar pass, the *Golden Access Passport*, is available for blind and disabled individuals. This too must be obtained in person.

National Forest Service

National Forest Service lands differ from National Parks in that they are multi-purpose. Logging and grazing, for example may be permitted under carefully controlled conditions. Few specific sites or regions are preserved for public visits, and there is not the same system of guided tours and activities as in National Parks. National forest land can, however, be stunning and certain areas have been designated as protected wilderness. There may be extensive trail networks throughout national forests. Camping is usually less expensive than in national or state parks, and in many areas it is free.

A new system allows campers to buy *camp stamps* at designated retail outlets or forest service offices, equal to the necessary camping fee. The user pays only 85% of the amount listed, thereby saving 15%. For further information contact *National Forest Service* headquarters in San Francisco.

State Parks

California runs a huge state park system, with some land as stunningly beautiful as that protected in the state's national parks. There are extensive camping and hiking possibilities within the park system. With its mobile and recreation-oriented population, California's state parks can often be crowded. Campsites can cost $6 or more per vehicle, 50 cents for walk-ins and bicycles. Backcountry sites are generally free but permits may be required. At most parks reservations are accepted. They may be made through any *Ticketron* outlet (with an extra fee tagged on) or by a new reservation system called MISTIX. Call toll-free tel. 1-1800-I-GO-PARK.

Practical tips for getting around

Mail

Mail can be received at hotels. It can also be sent to the General Delivery of the post office of any city or town. In a large city, this is usually found in the main post office downtown. Users of *American Express* travelers' checks can use that company's offices to receive mail, but only if they previously request to do so.

Telephones

Telephone numbers are preceded by a 3-digit area code. There are 9 area codes within California. In some areas the boundary for area codes may fall within a populated area. Dialing from one area code to another, the prefix "1" must sometimes be added. By no means is it assured that within one area code all calls are local calls. In the Los Angeles area, with the recent splitting up of ATT, additional charges may be added to calls within the same area code. At public phones, local calls in some areas cost 20 cents. The phones take nickels (5 cents), dimes (10 cents), and quarters (25 cents). The operator is not needed to make a long-distance call from a pay phone. Just dial "1", the area code and the number, and an operator or a recording will tell you how much money is needed, so keep a pile of change handy. If an additional charge is owed at the end of the call, the phone will ring when you hang up.

Long-distance rates are substantially lower between 6pm and 8am, and on weekends from 11pm Friday to 5pm Sunday. For international calls, the lowest rates are between 3pm and 9pm.

Many companies now use toll-free numbers, recognizable by the 800 prefix to the number. No area code is necessary to call this number, but sometimes a "1" must precede the 800. An 800 number which is good for in-state calls may not be operable for calls from outside the state, and some companies have both in-state and out-of-state toll-free numbers. Local Yellow Pages list a company's toll-free numbers.

Currency and Exchange

Foreign currency can be exchanged in international airports and certain banks. If possible buy travelers'checks in American dollars, at the appropriate exchange rate. Foreign currency will not be honored in the United States.

To send money to the United States it is best to give the name and address of an American bank correspondent to your bank at home. Money can be cabled, usually within 48 hours, for a charge of up to $25. A draft check, sent by mail, is a little cheaper but much slower.

Banking
Banking hours in California are from Mon.-Thurs. 10am-3pm, and 10am-5pm on Fridays. Electronic tellers are now common and widespread among all major banks.

Travelers' Checks
Travelers' checks are a must. They are available at banks or through organizations such as *American Automobile Association*, at a reduced price or at no charge.

American Express Travelers' Checks are the most widely recognized, and the company provides a measure of assistance and reassurance to those whose checks have been lost or stolen. *American Express Travel Service* offices will help arrange temporary identification, cash personal checks, arrange for new travelers' checks immediately, report and cancel credit card numbers and, in general, provide assistance. In addition, if arranged by mail beforehand, check holders may use the local *American Express* office as a mailing address.

Credit Cards
A credit card is worth taking as an emergency source of cash or to pay for large items. Recognized credit cards will allow the holder to withdraw in cash the sum remaining in his credit. Make sure you know where to report a lost or stolen credit card, and do so immediately. Major credit cards such as *Visa*, *Mastercharge* and *American Express* are recognized throughout California. If coming from another country, check whether your credit card is affiliated with an American company. When using a credit card, always check the amount before signing, and be sure to get the receipt. In addition, ask for the black carbon and destroy it immediately. Occasionally, a business will want to keep the carbon. Refuse stubbornly and on all counts. Carbons have been used to produce counterfeit credit cards and should never leave the owner's possession. Likewise, never give your credit card number for identification purposes; use a passport or driver's license instead. Credit cards can also be used for long-distance calls in specially equipped public telephones.

*I*NTRODUCTION

Smoking, Alcohol, Drugs

Smoking is no longer "cool" in health-conscious California. It is prohibited by law in elevators, city buses and many public rooms, and is permitted only in restricted areas in restaurants and inter-city buses. Californians have become increasingly bold and insistent in requesting others in their proximity not to smoke.

The drinking age in California is 21. It is against the law to drive with an open container of alcohol in the car. Drunk-driving laws in California are strict and strictly enforced.

California is viewed by many as the land with a free-and-easy attitude towards drugs, especially marijuana. Possession of marijuana is no longer a felony, though one sometimes has to pay a fine. Marijuana is, frankly, very common and accepted, but it is not something to be brazen about and foreigners should be especially careful.

Photography

If you are a photography buff, you will find ample material in California, among the stunning and diverse natural scenery and among the tremendous mixture of people and lifestyles.

If wanting to buy a camera, you might wait until you reach California, where competition is fierce, and many discount houses and department stores have camera departments which undercut the prices of regular camera shops. The camera shops, however, can give expert advice, which a clerk in a discount house is unlikely to have.

In the urban areas, one-hour and one-day developing services can easily be found. The large chain drugstores will often handle developing, and periodically run specials, such as two rolls for the price of one.

Disabled Travelers

New hotels and other public buildings must, according to California law, be accessible by wheelchairs. Businesses and communities are becoming more aware of the needs of the disabled. Car rental companies can supply special cars for the disabled. *Greyhound*, *Trailways*, *Amtrak* and the airlines are now equipped to accommodate the disabled. Some companies give special rates to the disabled as well as to the elderly. Special parking spaces are reserved for the disabled.

For information on travel for the disabled, contact: The Society for the Advancement of Travel for the Handicapped, 26 Court st., Brooklyn, N.Y. 11242, tel. 212-858-5483.

Senior Citizens

Many seniors are taking advantage of travel discounts and

programs oriented towards them. Discounts are available in theaters, museums, on public and private buses and in many other places. The American Association of Retired Persons (*AARP*) offers information on traveling for seniors, as well as considerable discounts on lodging and other travel expenses. For information, contact: AARP Membership Communications, 1909 K st. NW, Washington, DC 20049. tel. 202-872-4700.

Important addresses and phone numbers

California is a very tourist-oriented state. Material written to assist vistors is voluminous and accessible, from public and commercial sources. The **California Office of Tourism** in Sacramento, will, for the price of postage, send its booklets to those interested. This office can provide a directory of Chambers of Commerce and Visitors' Bureaus throughout the state, a map and small pocket guide, a calendar of events, and a listing of Bed & Breakfast Inns. Write to: California Office of Tourism, Publications, 1121 L st., Suite 103, Sacramento, CA 95814. tel. 1-180-TO CALIF for toll-free information.

Some other useful addresses and numbers:
Department of Parks and Recreation: Distribution Center, P.O.Box 2390, Sacramento 95811. A guide to California's state parks is available for $2.00.
State Park Campground Reservations: tel. 1-1800-IGO-PARK.
National Park Service Information: 450 Golden Gate ave., San Francisco, CA 94102.
California Region, U.S. Forest Service: 630 Sansome st. San Francisco, CA 94111. For national forest information. A wide range of brochures available.
Ticketron Information: Northern California, tel. 414-393-4089 or 393-6914. Southern California, tel. 213-642-5870.
Department of Fish and Game: 1416 9th st. Sacramento, CA 95814. For fishing and hunting information and regulations.
U.S. Bureau of Land Management: 2800 Cottage Way, Sacramento, CA 95825. For a list of BLM campgrounds.
The Sierra Club: 530 Bush st., San Francisco, CA 94108. For information on California's ecological resources, as well as the clubs organized trips.
The Nature Conservancy: Western Regional Office, 425 Bush st., San Francisco CA 94108. Information on educational trips designed to teach about the environment.
The Wine Institute: 165 Post st., San Francisco, Ca 94108: A free booklet, *The Pleasure of Wine with Food* is available.
The local **Chamber of Commerce** of any city or small town is a resource worth exploring throughout your travels in California. These offices can tell you about small, obscure attractions that you might otherwise miss. The people in these offices are proud of their hometowns — sometimes inordinately so — and can share

unusual stories. In the popular resort areas, many Chambers of Commerce carry fliers with various discount coupons for sites in the area. Most interesting of all is the opportunity to meet people. If you express curiosity and interest in someone's hometown, you may be surprised at the open response.

Electricity, Measurements, Time

Electric current is 110-115 a.c. 60Hz. For those planning to buy U.S. appliances, note that the U.S. plugs are two flat pins which will require adapters. Foreign appliances brought to the United States, generally require a transformer as well as an adapter.

Measurements: The U.S. measurement system is not a decimal one. Following are several conversion tables and "instant" tricks.

Weight
28.349 grams — 1 ounce
0.453 kilograms — 1 pound

Volume
0.473 liters — 1 pint
3.785 liters — 1 gallon

Distance
2.540 cm — 1 inch
30.480 cm — 1 foot
0.914 meter — 1 yard
1.609 km — 1 mile

Temperature
To convert Fahrenheit degrees to Centigrade (Celsius) subtract 32 from the Fahrenheit temperature, multiply by 5 and divide the total by 9.

Time
All of California is within the Pacific Time Zone, which is GMT-8. This is one hour behind the Denver region, two hours behind Chicago and the Midwest, and three hours behind the East Coast. Daylight Saving Time begins on the last Sunday in April, and ends the last Saturday in October.

CALIFORNIA

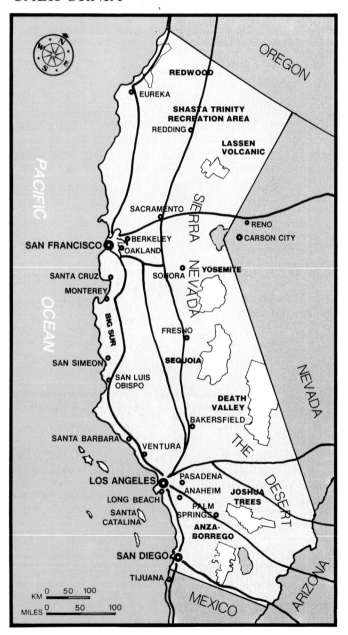

C ALIFORNIA

Monterey Peninsula

North of Big Sur, the Monterey Peninsula juts forth into the ocean. From the northern end of the peninsula Monterey Bay curves inland towards Santa Cruz and the mountains. The bay is studded with small fishing towns and state beaches, and inland toward the coastal mountains there are small farm towns. The towns of Carmel, Monterey and Pacific Grove are located on the peninsula. The weather is fair, sunny and breezy, with rain in winter and beautiful coastal fog which drifts in and condenses on trees and shrubbery.

The beauty and charm of this area attract over six million visitors each year. There are old hotels, quaint countryside inns, excellent seafood restaurants, numerous golf courses and tennis courts, as well as places to walk, wade and watch crabs and seals. Those interested in history, art or science can find plenty to see, and one can always sit drinking a cup of coffee and watching the crashing surf.

How to get there

By air: Monterey Airport is served by *United Airlines*, as well as by regional and in-state carriers.

By land: The Monterey Peninsula is located just off the Pacific Coastal Highway. Just north of Monterey, this highway is connected to Route 101, which is the fast route to Monterey. Route 1 is more scenic. *Greyhound* also serves Monterey, with a depot at 351 Del Monte ave. Buses available to and from L.A., San Francisco and more. The coastal *Amtrak* route stops in Salinas, with free bus links to Monterey. For those traveling to or from Santa Cruz, the transfer point between the Santa Cruz and Monterey bus systems is at the Watsonvillle terminal. Hopping from one local system to the next is generally a cheap but time-consuming way to travel. *Greyhound* is more expensive but much faster.

The *Monterey-Salinas Transit* (MST) system is convenient, and the schedule, available at the Visitors Center, clearly shows the layout of the routes. There are three main terminals; at Monterey, Salinas, and Watsonville. The terminal in Monterey is really just a small plaza right in the middle of downtown, where Munras, Pearl, Folk, Alvarado and Tyler converge. From here the bus lines radiate, including those to Carmel. Buses 4 and 5 run to the center of Carmel, and 1 and 2 to Pacific Grove. The main loading point in Carmel is near Ocean and Mission. During the summer, two buses a day serve the Pt. Lobos State Reserve and Big Sur, reaching as far as

Nepenthe (Bus no. 22). If you plan to have more than 2-3 rides a day get the Day Pass ($3.00). After Labor Day this service is rescheduled.

Accommodations

Lodgings on the Monterey Peninsula fill up very quickly and reservations are recommended year-round. During the summer, especially around the time of the Monterey Jazz Festival, reservations are essential. Fremont ave., towards the fairgrounds, is Monterey's approximation of a motel and hotel row. Here a wide range of accommodation can be found, mostly along conventional lines.

It is important to remember that during the tourist season, the hotels in the Monterey area fill up to capacity, and if you do not have a reservation by 4pm, then you must take a break from sight-seeing and find a place for the night. Otherwise, you might find that you have no choice but to spend the night in your car. At the weekends, the problem worsens and you must ensure a place in advance.

The Chamber of Commerce will supply a list of local lodgings. For last-minute help in finding a room, call tel. 800-822-822 for Monterey and Pacific Grove; tel. 624-1711 for Carmel.

Luxury Hotels ($125 and up)
Carmel Highlands Inn: tel. (408) 624-3801. Condominium-style units at a superb site, offering a view of the Pacific Ocean. Plenty of facilities, as well as privacy. On Highway 1, south of Carmel.

Moderate Hotels ($50-$80)
Carmel Mission Inn: Highway 1 and Rio rd., tel. (408)624-1841. Modern hotel with Jacuzzi and pool etc. Close to fashionable shopping centers. Big but convenient.

Valley Lodge: Carmel Valley rd., tel. (408)659-2261. If you wish to stay more than 2 days in the area, this might be the right place. Good cottages and very nice patio in the garden.

Ardor Inn: 1058 Munras ave., Monterey, tel. (408)372-3381. An interesting mixture of a motel and a home-stylw inn. Jacuzzi. Freindly management.

Inexpensive Hotels (less than $50)
Asilomar Conference Center: Asilomar State Beach, Pacific Grove, tel. 372-8016. A unique place to stay. Rooms are offered to travelers when not filled by pre-arranged groups. Pine lodges are scattered in a forest. Reservations can be made up to two months in advance. Lodges range from $30-$50, depending on the room and number of people.

Motel 6: 2124 Fremont st., Tel (408) 646-8585. Very popular, so reserve well in advance.

Monterey Peninsula Youth Hostel: Summer hostel in one of the public schools around town. Location changed yearly, so call AYH for information (tel. 408-298-0670).

Monterey Peninsula Bed & Breakfast Association: 598 Laine st., Monterey 93940, tel. 375-8284. Can make suggestions for local inns. Free brochures available.

Food

Along Cannery Row are a number of seafood restaurants, each with early bird specials and good seafood.

Bullwacker's: 653 Cannery Row, tel. 373-1353. Here the specials are only $3.50, with a choice of several house specialities that include red snapper and calamari.

Captain's Cove: 643 Cannery Row, tel. 372-4000. The early bird specials include salad or soup, pasta or fries, fresh vegetables, beverage and a seafood entree, with sparkling wine for 50 cents extra. $6.95.

Steinbeck Lobster Grotto: 720 Cannery Row, tel. 373-1884. A fine location over the water, and a wide variety of seafood entrees. $6.95 for early bird specials.

Rosine's: 80 Bonifacio on Alvarado st. near Old Monterey, tel. 375-1400. An elegant but relaxed setting and a wide range of entrees, with trimmings, starting at about $7.

Sancho Panza Restaurant: 590 Calle Principal, tel. 375-0095. Set in the Casa Gutierrez, an adobe which dates back to 1841 and is part of old Monterey. The interior is dark and cosy, and the patio is beautiful. The Mexican food is good, the prices reasonable and the service friendly.

Adobe Inn: Dolores and 8th st., Carmel, tel. 625-1750. Excellent early bird dinner specials which include prime ribs, the day's fish catch, freshly baked bread and salad bar, for $6.95, between 5-6pm.

Hogs Breath Inn: San Carlos st. and 5th ave. A local hang-out, with a delightful courtyard and Clint Eastwood as owner.

The Whole Enchilada: At Route 1 near the turnoff for Moss Landing. An unbeatable combination of fine Mexican food and fine jazz every Saturday and Sunday night.

Restaurant Hotline: tel. 372-DINE. A free service which makes recommendations and reservations for restaurants in the Monterey area.

The Covey at Quail Lodge — 8205 Valley Greens dr. Carmel, tel. (408)624-1581. One of the best restaurants in the area. Continental cuisine. Elegant and expensive. Reservation needed.

Carmel — the town center

Carmel

Carmel is a combination of a quaint country village, an artists' colony and a well guarded enclave of wealth. There are strict controls on everything including street signs, billboards, cutting trees (it's forbidden), house numbers (there aren't any), and the selling of ice cream cones. Yet, with all these stringent controls aimed at keeping the gingerbread facade from crumbling, the villagers gladly accept tourist money. The restaurants and lodgings tend to be more expensive than in Monterey, although some good eating deals can be found. Numerous galleries sell the usual luminous crashing waves, but there are many good artists in the area too, as well as further down the coast toward Big Sur.

Since the late 1920s, Carmel has been a center for the art of photography. Edward Weston, who experimented with the limits of photography and influenced a whole generation of photographers, lived in Carmel for about 30 years, and got to know the area intimately. Some of his last photographs were of the Pt. Lobos coast. Carmel has many fine photographers carrying on the Weston tradition. Examples of local photographic art can be seen at the Photography West Gallery Ocean ave. and Dolores. Open daily 11am-5pm, tel. 625-1587, and at the **Weston Gallery**, 6th and Dolores, Tues.-Fri. 11am-5pm, Sat. 10am-5pm.

Just south of the town's center, off Route 1, is the Mission San Carlos Borromeo del Rio Carmelo — the **Carmel Mission** for short.

Along the Seventeen Mile Drive

Green and blue at Point Lobos

The mission and its three museums are worth a visit. 3080 Rio rd. Self-guided tours Mon.-Sat. 9:30am-4:30pm, Sun. 10:30am-4:30pm. Donation requested, tel. 624-3600.

Built in 1771, this mission succeeded the one built in Monterey a year earlier. The graceful structure is one of the finest surviving examples of California mission architecture. Father Junipero Serra, the founder of the chain of California missions, is buried inside. In the cemetery some 2,000 local Indians are buried, and some of the graves are marked by abalone shells.

The Carmel Mission is also the site for the highlight concert in the **Carmel Bach Festival**. This renowned and popular festival is held in July. For tickets and details contact: The Carmel Bach Restival, P.O. Box 575, Carmel, 93921, tel. 624-1521.

Ocean ave. heads to the ocean at Carmel City Beach. From here the gorgeous beaches of central California stretch southwards. Parking can be a problem on weekends, but heading south just a few blocks on Scenic will bring you to easier parking and a beach with fewer people. Still further south, reachable by foot or by car along Scenic drive, is River Beach. Around Carmel Point is the **Carmel River State Park**, a great place (and legal) for a driftwood fire.

At the corner of Ocean View and Scenic drives stands **Tor House**, which the poet Robinson Jeffers built himself using boulders from the beach. Tours Fri.-Sat. from 10am-3pm. Reservations required, admission required. No children under 12, tel. 624-1813.

The shopping centers of Carmel have become very popular with tourists. Particularly attractive are **Carmel Plaza** in the eastern part of the village, and **The Crossroad**, which has over 100 shops and is situated south-east of route 1, at the entrance to the town.

About three miles (5 km) south of Carmel, the smaller peninsula of **Pt. Lobos State Reserve** juts out into the Pacific. This mosaic of rugged headlands, coves, meadows, tidepools and rocky promontories is strictly protected and has retained its pristine character. Here you can find natural stands of Monterey pine and gnarled Monterey cypresses. The reserve has a network of easy trails heading from several parking lots, making the stunning views available to virtually anyone. Here at close view one can observe sea lions, sea otters, seals, elephant seals, grey whales and an occasional killer whale off the coast during the migration season. Deer graze in the meadows.

The adjoining tide area and the submerged rocks of Carmel Bay, just to the north of the Pt. Lobos headlands, comprise the **Carmel Bay Ecological Reserve**, and include the underwater canyon 1,000 ft. (340 m) deep just beyond Monterey Beach. The surf here is dangerous; children must be carefully watched, and the water approached with caution.

Even though it is not large in size, the **Point Lobus Nature Reserve** is a beautiful spot in which lovely trekking routes have been forged for the convenience of visitors. It is particularly recommended to leave the car and proceed on foot for a short spell. A good time for a visit is before sunset, when the reserve is quieter and its fauna more alert. It is important to remember that the speed limit within the reserve is 15 mph (24 kph).

Pt. Lobos can be crowded on weekends, even during the winter. The main ranger station is off route 1. No camping is allowed. Open from 7am-11pm in summer, but the parking lot closes at sunset. During the rest of the year, open 7am-5pm. On a crowded weekend, the parking lot can be full by noon. Divers interested in exploring the underwater reserve must show proof of certification and must register at the ranger station. Guided walks are led by rangers or docents, as staffing permits, usually every day in the summer, and on weekends during the off-season, tel. 624-4909.

Monterey and Carmel are separated by the **Del Monte Forest**, a 5,600 acre chunk of beauty turned into a barony. Entry to the famous **Seventeen Mile Drive** is $5. There are numerous turnoffs with each stunning view surpassing the previous one. If you stop to photograph the lone cypress, you won't be the only one. The forest includes a game preserve, where deer are allowed to nibble at the gardens. Behind the walls stand some modest mansions built between the world wars. There are four famous golf courses, including the one at Pebble Beach. The beautiful Lodge at Pebble Beach has sea views, several restaurants and free hors d'oeuvres at happy hour. Nevertheless, it seems unnecessary to pay good money to visit a rich man's estate when incomparable Pt. Lobos and Big Sur are just down the road. There is no charge for cyclists between 8-11am, and no charge for pedestrians at any time.

Pacific Grove is a small quiet town which is virtually contiguous with Monterey, and separated from Carmel by the Del Monte Forest. Tide pools are scooped out of its rocky shore. Old Victorian buildings and small cottages are common. John Steinbeck did much of his early writing in a cottage here. Waves of monarch butterflies arrive here every October and the town welcomes them with a festival. The monarchs migrate thousands of miles, on their delicate wings, from the autumn chills of the north. They literally hang around for months on foliage, except when warm weather allows them to seek food. When spring comes they fly north again.

The **Pacific Grove Museum of Natural History** houses displays on the monarch butterflies as well as on sea birds and sea mammals. A relief map depicts the deep oceanic canyon off the peninsula and explains how the nutrient-rich cold water allows such great diversity of marine life. Forest ave. and Central ave. Open Tues.-Sat. 10am-5pm. Admission free. tel. 372-4212.

At **Lovers Point** there is a small rocky beach, and glass-bottomed boats are available in summer. Further on, the **Point Pinos Lighthouse**, built in 1855 and the oldest on the west coast, overlooks both ocean and golf course. There is a small U.S. Coast Guard Maritime Museum upstairs. Seventeen-Mile Drive. tel. 373-3304. Open on summer weekends, 1-4pm. Admission free.

Monterey

Monterey played an important role in early Californian history. Discovered by Juan Rodriguez Cabrillo in 1542, it was only in the 1770s that Spanish settlers, soldiers and priests began to settle in the area. Eventually, it became the capital of Spanish, and later Mexican, California. From the 1820s onward, a trickle of American sailors, whalers, trappers and traders based themselves in Monterey. A sea trading line was established between Monterey and Boston. After the Mexican War in 1846, with California in American hands, Monterey became the capital of the new American territory, and when California became a state, the constitution was drawn up in Monterey. However, with the discovery of gold in the Sierra foothills in 1849, the focus of business and trade shifted to the new port of San Francisco and the inland nodal center of Sacramento. The graceful capital of the Old California became something of a backwater.

The center of Monterey and its fisherman's wharf has undergone a great deal of tourist development, so that little remains of the charm and innocence of yesteryear. During the hectic tourist seasons, the restaurants and boutiques are full of tourists, and it is difficult to find parking space. Those in search of quieter spots should go on to the beach towns north of Monterey.

Monterey today has the greatest concentration of tourist attractions on the peninsula, the main ones being **Fisherman's Wharf**, **Cannery Row** and historic **Old Monterey**. It has some excellent seafood restaurants — many with great early bird specials — and a wide variety of others as well. Monterey also sustains an extremely active and lively cultural life. Literature from the visitors center or free papers found around town can keep the visitor informed of what's happening. The **Monterey Jazz Festival** in September is perhaps the biggest event in Monterey, and is also one of the biggest in jazz. Centered at the fairgrounds, it features some of the greatest names in jazz. Tickets should be purchased months in advance, and by the time the festival begins, the hotels and motels are packed.

Old Monterey

Over 40 original adobe buildings in Old Monterey survive from the pre-1850 era, and about 13 are open to the public, today housing museums, restaurants and a theater. Monterey's "Path of History", a self-guided tour of about two miles (3 km) through Old Monterey, is available at the visitors' center. A fee of $1 per adult provides entry to all the state historical buildings for one day. Some of these

Old Monterey — architecture of yesterday

are more interesting than others, and some are not interesting at all, but the stroll through the area is easy and pleasant. The transit plaza provides a convenient place to begin. Nearby Alvarado st. has plenty of reasonable eating spots. Some of the buildings on the tour are:

The Custom House: 1 Custom House Plaza, 115 Alvarado st. The first U.S. government building on the Pacific Coast, restored and filled with piles of cargo from the era: casks of liquor, cases of coffee, and an old harpoon gun.

Pacific House: 8 Custom House Plaza. Used as a tavern, newspaper office, court, church and ballroom over the years, and now a museum featuring the life and artifacts of the local Indians, the Spanish explorers and the early American settlers.

Colton Hall: Pacific and Jefferson streets. The first constitutional Congress of the new State of California convened here in 1849. A "Path of History" map is obtainable here.

The **Monterey Peninsula Museum of Art** focuses on Western and local art, and the Charlie Russel bronze statues will make the West alive for you. 559 Pacific ave. across from Colton House, Tues.-Sat. 10am-4pm, Sun. 1-4pm. Admission free, tel. 372-7591.

Larkin House: 35-minute tours from 10am-4pm. Jefferson st. and Calle Principal. Built by Thomas Larkin, the first, last and only U.S. consul to Mexico in California. The grand house could have been transferred from New England. The little house in the garden housed

William Tecumseh Sherman years before he marched through Georgia. A small museum portrays the roles of the two men in local history. Admission required. Closed Tues. and noon to 1pm.

Stevenson House: 530 Houston st. Robert Louis Stevenson lived in a rooming-house here in 1879, having come to visit the woman he later married. Much of *Treasure Island*'s vivid Pacific scenery was inspired by the Monterey landscape. There is lots of Stevenson memorabilia here. Admission required. Closed Wed. and noon to 1pm. Hourly tours, 10am-4pm.

Fisherman's Wharf

You know you're near Fisherman's Wharf when you hear the hoarse yelping of sea lions begging food from tourists. The wharf is crowded and touristy. It is lined with tourist seaside restaurants and stands selling little seafood cocktails. Some of the restaurants offer early bird specials of fresh seafood. The general atmosphere of the wharf, however, is gaudy and circus like. Sport fishing and sightseeing cruises are available from the wharf, as are whale-watching tours during the winter months. Check out several offices to compare prices. A free shuttle bus runs every 15 minutes from 9am-10pm daily, from Memorial Day to Labor Day, and on weekends only after Labor Day. There is all-day parking at the East Customs House garage for a small fee. Between the wharf and Cannery Row is a small stretch of beach and a breakwater where the more sedate sea lions bask on rocks. The adjacent strand of beach is popular for snorkeling and scuba diving.

Cannery Row

The canneries rumble and rattle and squeak until the last fish is cleaned and cut and cooked and canned and then the whistles scream again and the dripping, smelly, tired Wops and Chinamen and Polaks, men and women, straggle out and droop their ways up the hill into the town and Cannery Row becomes itself again - quiet and magical.

John Steinbeck, *Cannery Row*

Cannery Row began about the turn of the century with the building of one packing plant for the local sardines, used then as bait by salmon fishermen. With the introduction of larger, more efficient nets and seines, and modern packing systems, new canneries opened. Cannery Row became a center for the sardine industry. Small businesses sprang up to serve fishermen and cannery workers, and cheap rooming houses opened up on the blocks behind the canneries. In the middle of all this industry, a biologist, Ed "Doc" Ricketts opened a laboratory at the ocean's edge. He supplied sea specimens for larger research facilities and conducted his own experiments. His study of marine life along this central coast was innovative, for he identified plants, animals, invertebrates and micro-organisms according to the habitat in which they lived rather than by genus or species. He noted that several distinct habitats existed along the coastline, each dependent on the others. Into this teeming, smelly, rough and tumble row wandered a local writer, John Steinbeck, who was raised just over the hills in the farm country of the Salinas Valley, and who was developing, in his own way, a penchant for writing about the little guy, the lowlife, the down-and-outers.

What was there, really, that made this row of canneries, redolent with the smell of fish, so romantic? Everywhere, neighborhoods centered around a central plant or industry, each with its own raw drama, but this one, perched on the edge of a beautiful natural realm managed to find its poet laureate, and Steinbeck vividly captured the rhythm and atmosphere of this jumble of canneries, warehouses, whorehouses, flophouses and tiny stores.

Over 250,000 tons of sardines were hauled in each year and processed through the two dozen plants along this row. Ricketts, Steinbeck's close friend, was one of the naysayers who warned that overfishing might destroy the industry. The yearly haul did indeed shrink, and disappeared completely by 1951. Workers and fishermen left, stores closed, and Cannery Row became a corrugated ghost town. In the 1960s and 70s, a few seafood restaurants opened, and suddenly developers and various commissions have become aware of the tourist potential of the area. The row of rusted canneries and rotted flophouses has become prime real estate for tourist oriented development. There are proposals for hotels to accompany the cute stores, the malls and the wax museum. The row has its protectors too, fighting to keep its historical ambience.

Walk a block behind the strip of tourist traps to catch a taste of the old world. A few tiny clapboard and shingled houses, and old flophouses and dormitories still stand. The railroad tracks are neglected and overgrown with weeds. A few of the stores on the row date back to earlier days. *Kasila's*, at 851 Cannery Row, is a funky old bar and sandwich shop. The *Old General Store* at 835 Cannery Row was once a Chinese grocery store — on which Steinbeck modeled Lee Chong's store in his book. In the back is a room of Steinbeck memorabilia. Across the street, Doc Rickett's old laboratory has been converted into a dance club, bordered by restaurants with great views, serving fresh seafood, at early bird prices of $6-8.

To complete the meal, visit the **Paul Masson Museum** on 700 Cannery Row. Touring the museum and listening to the explanations on the process of painting, is not as interesting as tasting the wide selection of wines produced by the famous vineyard. In addition to the tasting (free of charge), the visitor can enjoy the view of the bay, seen from the windows of the local bar. Open daily between 10am and 6pm, tel. 646-5446.

Monterey — Fisherman's Wharf

Opened in 1984, the **Monterey Aquarium** in the old Hovden Cannery at the end of Cannery Row, displays some of the marine life from the teeming oceanic environment in the North Bay area. 886 Cannery Row. Open daily 10am-6pm. Admission fee, tel. 375-3333.

The deep reefs, the sandy sea floor, the shale reefs, the open sea and the wharf each support their own community of plants and animals. The kelp forest exhibit towers over the viewers' heads and shows how big these plants, which usually we see only on the surface, are. During the summer, the aquarium conducts a number of half-day field trips and field courses on the marine environment and the marine biology of the Monterey Bay area.

Further east, on El Estero dr. is the **Dennis the Menace Playground**, a collection of imaginative playground equipment on which the parent may want to join the child.

Around Monterey

Due east of Monterey, at the junction of Route 68 and the 101 highway, lies the farm country of the Salinas Valley, a world away from the smells and sights of Monterey. This area, and the town of **Salinas** itself, was immortalized in the works of John Steinbeck. The Nobel Prize-winning writer was born in Salinas in 1902, in a house that still stands at 132 Central ave. (now a restaurant). He lived most of his life elsewhere, but he is buried here, and his modest grave can be seen at the Garden of Memories at the outskirts of town, 768 Abbott st. The **Steinbeck Festival** is held in August in Salinas. The **John Steinbeck Library** has various displays on the writer's life, including original manuscripts. 110 West San Luis st., Salinas, tel. 408-758-7311.

Salinas is also the place to catch the **California Rodeo** in July. It's the closest this farm town comes to the Mardi Gras, kicked off by a big western dance on Saturday night. The competition draws the country's top cowboys and about 50,000 spectators. It's hot and dusty, so wear your ten-gallon hat, tel. 757-2951.

Salinas doesn't attract many tourists, and most of its inhabitants today are farmers and Mexican immigrants who toil the fields.

South of Salinas on Route 101 and just east of Soledad, the spires and jagged teeth of **Pinnacles National Monument** jut out from the surrounding gentle hills. The pinnacles are the partial remains of a volcano, the other part of which lies far to the southeast. It was the San Andreas Fault, which runs right past this area, that split up the formation and left these jagged shapes. The terrain offers rugged hiking trails and the sheer walls challenge rock climbers. Although the roads approach the monument from both east and west, they do not connect.

This site, on the west side of the San Andreas fault, has shifted 195 miles (321 km) north over the last 23 million years or so. The volcanic remains have been polished and eroded by the elements to form sharp spires thrusting up from the surrounding rounded hills. There are caves and canyons in the area. Spring is the best time to visit the park, when the trees are green and the slopes are covered by a multi-colored carpet of wildflowers. There is one campground in the monument, at Chaparral, and one private campground outside the eastern boundary. The western Ranger Station at Chaparral and the Bear Gulch Visitor Center at the eastern entrance provide information and exhibits. There are evening programs at both the east and west campgrounds. For information contact Park Headquarters, Pinnacles National Monument, Paicines, 95043, tel. 408-389-4578.

Located in the Salinas Valley just west of Soledad, the **Paraiso hot springs** bubble up with hot, healing mineral waters. It is about an hour's drive from Monterey. The setting is tranquil and strict rules help keep the area in its natural state. There are outdoor and indoor pools in which to relax, and a library, recreation room, and free cookies and coffee. Take the 101 to Soledad, then follow the Arroyo Seco road west to Paraiso Springs road, and take that all the way to the springs. There are hook ups for trailers, and simple accommodation, tel. 408-678-2882.

Just north of Monterey on Route 1 is Castroville, a small farmtown at the mouth of the Salinas Valley which would be indistinguishable from similar towns, but for its claim to be the artichoke capital of the world, and home of the annual Artichoke Festival in September. At the end of the main street of town is the **Giant Artichoke**, housing a gift shop and restaurant. The speciality of the house is french-fried artichoke. Incidentally, in the campaign to promote artichokes in 1947 the first California Artichoke Queen was crowned, an aspiring young actress named Marilyn Monroe.

If you are driving yourself, the place to stop is beside the fresh fruit and vegetable stalls on the road-side. The abundance of excellent products at low prices will serve you for the rest of the way.

To the north of Castroville, on Route 1, is the tiny fishing village of **Moss Landing**. It's just opposite the gigantic power station. Cross the tiny bridge that spans the tiny estuary to the town itself. This is a real fishing village. Near the fishing boats is a row of small dilapidated bait shops, garages and bars. Here the fishermen haul in catches of salmon, albacore and other fish, getting down to business without catering to tourists.

Important addresses and phone numbers

Monterey Peninsula Chamber of Commerce and Visitor and Convention Bureau: 350 Alvarado st., Monterey, tel. 649-3200. Mailing address: P.O. Box 1770, Monterey, 93940.

Pacific Grove Chamber of Commerce: Box 157, Pacific Grove, 93950, tel. 373-3304.

Carmel Business Association: P.O. Box 444, Carmel, 93921, tel. 624-2522.

Amtrak: 40 Railroad ave., Salinas, tel. 422-7458.

Greyhound: 351 Del Monte ave., near Fisherman's Wharf, tel. 373-4735. (They run a tour to Hearst Castle that includes entry fee.)

Gray Line: Tel. 373-4989. Tours of area, including Hearst Castle.

Monterey-Salinas Transit (MST), tel. 899-2555. Main stop is Transit Plaza in downtown Monterey.

Sierra Club, Ventana Chapter: Box 5667, Carmel 93921, tel. 624-8032. An ongoing schedule of trips available, to members and non-members. Brochures on trips available.

Santa Cruz

Santa Cruz is situated at the northern end of Monterey Bay, where ocean, forested mountains and fields combine to create absolutely gorgeous scenery. The sandy beaches are sheltered by the northern promontory of land, and the water is fairly warm and the surf comparatively gentle. The northern promontory also protects Santa Cruz from the fog that saturates most of the central coast.

Like many Californian coastal towns, Santa Cruz began as a Spanish mission. Later it developed because of the availability of local resources: lumber, fishing and agriculture. Today it is a commercial center for farmers, flower growers and the region's many wineries. By the turn of the century, resort hotels had opened along the beach, and with the completion of a narrow gauge railroad link with Los Gatos, Santa Cruz became a fully fledged vacation town, which it has remained.

Perhaps because of the influence of the highly innovative University of California at Santa Cruz (UCSC), and because of its semi-isolated location, Santa Cruz is a trendy rural center. Here artisans live in the hills, smoke marijuana and eat vegetarian food. There is a vibrant cultural life, a strong environmental movement and a variety of cults.

In contrast, the beach, boardwalk and old ornate amusement park are crowded with cruisers — everybody from punks to gays to staid well-dressed couples sharing a sentimental cotton-candy cone.

How to get there

From the San Francisco Bay area, the Route 17 freeway crosses over the Santa Cruz mountains from the suburban Santa Clara Valley. On a busy weekend, the traffic can crawl along bumper to bumper. Route 9 is even slower, winding through deeply shaded redwood canopies and small towns that seem a thousand miles away from an urban area. Highway 1, the Pacific Coast Highway, extends from the spreading suburbs to a peaceful coastline of state parks, beaches and small towns. From Monterey in the south, Route 1 is alternately freeway and small road. Even if traveling along the faster Route 101, you must cut over Route 1 from either Marina or Gilroy.

Although it is possible to travel by local transit systems to Santa Cruz, this is very time consuming. *Greyhound* is much faster, and serves both Santa Cruz and Watsonville. Santa Cruz's public bus system is efficient and extensive. It reaches all corners of this relatively spread out county. The new transit terminal, off the Pacific Garden Mall at Walnut and Pacific, presents schedules clearly, and also shows art from local schools. There are two other transit centers at Capitola and Watsonville. The rider's guide, called *Headways*, details the routes and schedules. Basic fare is 50 cents, $1 for an unlimited day pass, and $20 for one month's unlimited use. There is a half-price reduction on fares and passes for seniors and the handicapped. From Memorial Day to Labor Day, a summer shuttle runs every 15-20 minutes, connecting the **County Government Center**, the metropolitan center and the wharf area.

Santa Cruz has been a paradise for both recreational and racing cyclists for many years, and it hosts many races. Extensive cycling lanes on roads and separate bike paths criss-cross the city and reach the rural hills and flatlands. The Bikecentennial Pacific Coastal Route from Oregon to Baja runs through Santa Cruz. The **Santa Cruz Cycling Club** offers weekly rides that visitors can join, tel. 425-8688. The club also distributes an excellent map of local routes, available in local cycling shops. Another map of local routes is supplied by the **Santa Cruz Transportation Commission**, 701 Ocean st., Santa Cruz, 95060, tel. 425-2951.

Accommodations

Bed & Breakfast Inns abound in Santa Cruz County. Some are in old Victorian buildings a few blocks from the boardwalk, others are in country farmhouses.

A Place to Stay: tel. 662-3400, or tel. 800-621-0854, ext. 622. Free referrals.

Innkeepers of Santa Cruz: P.O. Box 464, Santa Cruz, 95061, tel. 425-8212. Free referrals.

The Tyrolean Inn: 9600 Highway 9, Ben Lomond 95005, tel. 336-5188. A little bit of the Austrian Alps in the midst of redwood country. Cozy cabins and friendly atmosphere. Accessible by bus from downtown Santa Cruz. $34-$40.

St. George Hotel: 1520 Pacific Garden Mall, tel. 423-8181. An old, safe, cheap residential type of hotel. Starts at about $15 without bath..

UCSC: tel. 429-2611. Rooms available in summer.

Youth Hostels

The **AYH** operates a hostel in Santa Cruz each summer at a varying temporary location. Call the hostel office, tel. 423-8304.

Two interesting hostels run by AYH are located on the coast north of Santa Cruz: *Pigeon Point Lighthouse*, tel. 879-0633; *Montara Lighthouse Hostel*, tel. 728-7177. (These are described under San Francisco lodging.)

Camping

Camping options are plentiful, and there are many state parks in the immediate Santa Cruz area so it is generally possible to find camping spots even on crowded weekends. Camping facilities range from trailer lots to walk-in primitive and isolated sites for hikers and cyclists. It is best to make reservations. For information call the State Parks Dept, tel. 688-3241 or tel. 335-5858.

Some stunning camping areas for vehicles and hikers can be found in Big Basin State Park, tel. 338-6132.

Food

El Palomar: 1344 Pacific Garden Mall, tel. 425-7575. In the old *Paloma Inn*. Very unusual and delicious Mexican food, from Michoacan in the south. Reasonable prices, but you might get a stiff neck while gazing at the beautifully decorated high ceiling. Live music on Friday and Saturday nights.

Sweet William's: 538 Seabright ave, tel. 429-1077. Soup, corn bread and live jazz.

Common Ground Coffee House: 2015 N. Pacific ave., tel. 425-8469. A popular place to sip coffee and ponder existence.

Cafe De Palma: 415 Seabright ave., tel. 426-5558. For solid and inexpensive breakfasts.

Saturn Cafe: 1230 Mission st., tel. 429-8505. A good way to ease into organic Santa Cruz.

Zoccoli's Delicatessen: 1534 Pacific Garden Mall, tel. 423-2267. When you have tired of sprouts on crackers, taste the lasagna lunch special here.

What to see

One can get much information on the Santa Cruz area at the local Convention and Visitors Center and the Chamber of Commerce. The local free weekly paper, *Good Times*, has full listings of Santa Cruz's lively nightlife. A dozen or so local bars and clubs showcase music. Santa Cruz is close enough to the currents wafting downtown from San Francisco to foster a rich and varied music scene. The university hosts various exhibits, films, concerts, lectures and drama. For cultural events at the university call: The **UCSC Barn Theater**, tel. 423-4734 and the **Performing Arts Theatre**, tel. 429-4168.

The **Pacific Garden Mall**, lined with flowers, trees and benches, has a relaxing small-town atmosphere, yet is also distinctly Santa Cruzian with its would-be singers crooning stoned-out versions of Dylan songs and a store sponsored by Greenpeace, the activist environmental group whose boats have hurled themselves before whalers and nuclear ships. In the past years, it seems that here too, as in all of California, the smart, expensive yuppified shops are taking over the quaint stores. Much of the old western architecture is preserved. The shops are unusual, the restaurants varied and surprisingly reasonable, the book stores eclectic, and the cafes hip and intellectual. The mall's stores have a special atmosphere. They extend along the side streets to Front st. Both Pacific and Front extend beyond the commercial section to the beach area.

The **Octagon**, set in a beautiful old building, is a small historical museum featuring local exhibits, 118 Cooper, Mon.-Sat. noon-5pm, tel. 425-2540. The **Art Museum of Santa Cruz County** presents nationally circulated exhibits, 224 Church, Tues.-Sun. noon-5pm, Thurs. 6-9pm. Admission charge except on Sunday. tel. 429-3420.

The **Artisans Cooperative**, on the mall, is a multi-media cooperative gallery with some pleasant surprises. 1364 Pacific Garden Mall, Mon.-Sat. 10am-4pm. tel. 423-8183.

The Santa Cruz **Boardwalk**, built in 1907, is the last of the elegant old amusement parks extant on the West Coast. 400 Beach st. Admission free. Individual rides cost 75 cents for adults, 50 cents for kids, with various ticket plans available. Open daily from Memorial Day to Labor Day, and weekends the remainder of the year, tel. 426-RIDE.

Shooting galleries, organ music, teenage boys trying to win kewpie dolls for their girls — all the grand old amusement park scenes are here. The people parading along the boardwalk range from the sedate to the ultra-hip, while the architecture and props belong to another era. The oldest ride is the 1911 **carousel**, with a pipe organ and seventy hand-carved horses, some of which are more valuable today than live ones. The Giant Dipper roller coaster is wild, rated as one of the world's top ten. Yet even at an old time amusement park time marches on, and the vintage arcade games are being elbowed out by Pac-Man and Dragon-Slayer. The **Coconut Grove Ballroom**, built in 1907, hosted most of the major big bands during the 1940's swing era, and still showcases that same sound in regular concerts today.

Beachfront Santa Cruz throbs with action. Across from the Boardwalk are the cheap beach joints with big gaudy signs that you would expect to find at Coney Island. Young kids zoom up and down in revved up wheels. It is only appropriate that this is the spot for the annual vintage 1950s and 60s car contest, when all those gleaming '56 Chevys roll out. The **Clam Chowder Cook-off and Festival** in February draws thousands of contestants and even more volunteer tasters, but it is hard to imagine anything surpassing the **Brussel Sprouts Festival**, held every October. These festivals are held at the beach area.

At the adjacent **municipal wharf**, commercial fishermen operate and there are a number of small restaurants, bait shops and small bars. It is usually possible to see sea lions, happily frolicking on the lower scaffolding of the wharf. During August, skydivers land on the boardwalk every Friday at 11am, 4pm and 9pm.

It's a nice bike ride and an exhilarating walk to **Lighthouse Point** from the wharf area. Seals and surfers hang out here. The **Santa Cruz Surf Museum**, which recently opened in the lighthouse, depicts Santa Cruz as a long-time surfing center, and surfing as a consuming passion. Open daily. Hours vary. Admission free, tel. 429-3429.

Take West Cliff drive to the abuttment of land that marks the end of Monterey Bay until you reach the **Natural Bridges State Park**. Here the surf has pounded holes through the jutting walls of cliff. Located just west of the park, on Delaware st., is the **Long Marine Laboratory**, maintained by UCSC. Open Tues.-Sun. 1-4pm, tel. 429-4087. East of the Boardwalk across the San Lorenzo River is the **Santa Cruz City Museum**. Just look for the stone whale. 1305 E. Cliff dr. Tues.-Sat. 10am-5pm, Sun. noon-5pm. tel. 429-3773. Inside, the displays focus on local tidepools, mammals, geological history and Indian culture.

At **UCSC**, hills covered in redwoods slope gently down to the ocean. Besides having a beautiful campus, UCSC is unique in the UC system and one of the most innovative schools in the country. It is really a cluster of interdependent small colleges. Each college is a small, self-contained, architecturally distinct community. Each has its own classrooms, resident halls, library, etc., but there are various connections between the colleges through courses and various activities. The emphasis here is on theses, not on letter grades. The visitors center in Kresge Hall provides information and guided tours, tel. 429-0111.

Along the coast and in the valleys to the east, apples, figs, corn, berries and other seasonal fruits and vegetables are grown, and this is also a wine region. A visit to these farms gives one a glimpse of the countryside and also a chance to purchase fresh produce, sometimes at bargain prices, and a chance to meet the local people. Many farms encourage and welcome visitors, but it is best to call ahead. A self-guiding tour map is available, with a detailed listing of local farms, ranches and their produce. The Chamber of Commerce and Convention and Visitor Bureau distribute these maps. Also available is a list of regional wineries which dot the countryside.

The coast, the hills and the canyons around Santa Cruz encompass many state parks. **Henry Cowell Redwoods State Park**, along Route 9, is a short ride north of Santa Cruz and includes, 4,000 acres of magnificent redwood forest. There are 15 miles (24 km) of hiking and riding trails, as well as camping. The popular trail looping through Redwood Grove begins and ends at an exhibit shelter. The largest part of the park is accessible only by foot or on horseback. **Fall Creek State Park**, a part of Henry Cowell State Park, is a hikers' park, with no roads. It is heavily forested, with deep canyons. Campfire programs and guided hikes are conducted in the summer. Park headquarters, tel. 335-4598.

Adjacent to the Henry Cowell State Park is **Roaring Camp and Big Trees**, where old-fashioned steam-powered trains chug along

Santa Cruz — the beach

a winding narrow gauge rail line. This is a faithful recreation of the lines that carried giant redwood logs from forest to sawmill. Every Memorial Day weekend there is a three-day re-enactment of the Civil War period, including battles staged with infantry, cavalry and artillery battle tactics. Take Route 9 to Felton, turn southeast on to Graham Hill rd., and continue half a mile. Admission fee. Open daily in summer, and weekends and holidays year round. Trains start in summer at 11am or noon, on a varying schedule, tel. 335-4484. The covered wooden bridge in Felton is not the awesome sight lauded by the local brochures, but it is a quaint photo spot.

Further to the north is the 16,000 acre **Big Basin State Park**, an immense primeval redwood forest preserve on the ocean-facing slopes of the Santa Cruz Mountains. There are 60 miles (95 km) of trail in this park. From the park headquarters just opposite the campground is the popular Skyline-to-Sea trail. A short route (20-25 minutes walk) is the Redwood route next to parking lot at the entrance to the reserve. This will take the visitor to see interesting trees, such as the "Chimney Tree" through whose trunk you can see the sky. There is also "Mother of the Forest" which, though it is the tallest in the forest (329 ft/112 m) is less impressive than "Father of the Forest" which is a wonderful example of the dimensions which these trees can reach. This is a much visited park, but since most visitors come for a picnic or short stroll through the most accessible redwood groves, it is easy to find uncrowded trails and pockets of solitude in shaded canyons or beside misty waterfalls. Guided hikes and evening campfire programs are held from mid-June to Labor Day. Pick up a trail map at the Visitor Center for 75 cents. The park has four major campgrounds and backcountry camping is allowed. Permits are required. To reach Big Basin, drive north on Route 9 to Boulder Creek and turn northwest on Route 236 to the park, tel. 338-6132. Admission fee.

Important addresses and phone numbers

Area Code: tel. 408.

Emergency: tel. 911.

Santa Cruz County Convention & Visitors Bureau: PO Box 1476, Santa Cruz 95061, tel. 423-6927. Office is upstairs in the small mall at Center and Church, but call for exact directions. Much material available.

Public Transit Information: tel. 425-8600, or tel. 688-8600.

Greyhound Peerless Stages: tel. 423-1800 or tel. 722-4457.

Green Tortoise: tel. 462-6437.

Amtrak: tel. 800-872-7245.

Santa Cruz Airporter: tel. 423-1234. To San Jose Airport and San Francisco Airport.

California State Parks Dept.: tel. 688-3241 or tel. 335-5858.

San Francisco

Every year, San Francisco unleashes a "City Fair" in September, the urban equivalent of a good 'ole country fair, held until now at the old brick Fort Mason near the Marina. Contests for the best apple pie are replaced by contests for the best quiche. Garbage can painting replaces quilting, and instead of bronco-riding and cattle-punching, street-wise kids laden down with earrings and medallions perform amazing stunts on skateboards and small bicycles to breakdance rhythms. In addition to the usual burgers and fries, there are booths selling chow mein and egg roll, sushi, enchiladas, felafel, curry, souvlaki, piroshkis, Thai broiled fish, Salvadoran rice, Ethiopian injira, and New York kosher pastrami-on-rye with a pickle on the side. At the entrance to the fair, various municipal and civic organizations dispense literature and urge support for various projects, from recycling bottles and newspapers to supporting mobile libraries for the elderly. Among the displays there is a heavy emphasis on spiritual readings.

San Francisco has the richness, diversity and the crowded neighborhoods of a major urban center, but without the hectic pressure of a big city, although it is among the largest cities in the state. The financial district with its glass and concrete towers, its crowds in dark business suits, and its leather-padded hide-aways could be Wall Street, yet one bus ride away there are neighborhoods of small houses and fenced-in yards, that might be found in any small town. Toward the east end of the city, the streets and alleys of Chinatown are packed with crowds, noise and delicious smells, but nearby at the tree-covered slopes at the western edge of the city, soothed by the rhythm of surf and foghorn, you can hardly believe there's a city behind you at all.

San Francisco is a city that conjures many different images. It is the bastion of old-world, cosmopolitan urbanity, with a rich ethnic fabric. It is the epitome of wealthy, cultured and self-absorbed hedonism, a place where the leisure-loving, young and upwardly mobile love to make their money and spend it on expensive toys. Here homosexuality is open, widespread and almost fashionable, and there are enough self-liberating, consciousness-raising, spiritually awakened groups, cults and movements to form their own yellow pages. Here experimental art and theater proliferate. New ideas spring from the cultural soil and every second clerk or waitress claims to be an artist, writer or musician.

There is, obviously, a more serious side to the city as well. San Francisco is a rapidly changing city. It was at one time the end of the American West, but now the west is extending so far west that it becomes the Far East. The strong ties between San Francisco and the Far East come from several sources. Chinese and other Asian groups have median incomes exceeding those of Whites. They are hard-working, persistent and family-oriented. A higher percentage of their children attend college, often in the most technical and advanced sciences. Chinatown and the surrounding area, one of the most densely populated areas in the country, burst its seams a while ago and spilled over not only into the neighboring Italian neighborhood, but into suburban neighborhoods far away. The decrepit Tenderloin area suddenly had an influx of Cambodians and Indonesians. There is a steady influx of immigrants from Asian countries in political turmoil — Laos, Vietnam, Cambodia, Thailand and especially the Philippines. Moreover, trade with Asia has soared. Cities in the Pacific are growing rapidly. With one exception, the eight largest banks in the world are from the Pacific nations, and Pacific investors are buying San Francisco property.

Added to this ethnic mix there is a great influx of people from unstable Latin American countries — El Salvador, Nicaragua and Peru — and an increasing Mexican population. Numbers are elusive and misleading because many of the immigrants are not legally registered.

A casual survey of Latino neighborhoods reveals a great increase in numbers and national diversity. What the influence of these groups will be in the future is anybody's guess. The Latinos have not integrated into society as rapidly as the Asians, but they bring rich cultures and often a powerful sense of political radicalism. The San Francisco images of career-conscious single yuppies, prosperous gay entrepreneurs, Victorian houses and bohemian poets are partial at best. The city is changing, from its foundations upwards.

The term "Pacific Rim" is making the rounds in California, and will in the next decade be as commonly and widely understood as "Third World", "Middle East" or "Old World". It hints at a new global orientation, towards the Pacific and the coasts lining its huge expanse. San Francisco, in the city's finest tradition, is on the cutting edge of great change.

But, back in the present, San Francisco is a traveler's city, food-lover's city, a walker's city, a music-lover's city. Eat in a burnished, padded grillroom, or survive on burritos. Have the valet park your car or hop through the city by bus, subway and cable car. Hear the biggest names in classical or rock music, or catch a violinist in a doorway on a windy night.

Orientation

San Francisco is located at the tip of a peninsula extending north from the San Mateo hills. The peninsula separates the San Francisco Bay from the Pacific Ocean. The Golden Gate, the sole

SAN FRANCISCO

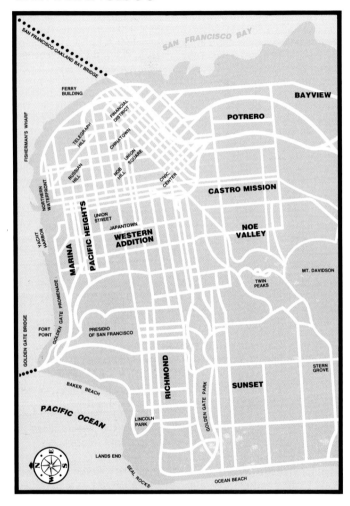

entrance from the Pacific to the bay, is narrow enough to have been overlooked for over two hundred years after the first explorations of the coast.

Across this narrow strait to the north lies the peninsula of Marin. To the east, across the bay, lie Oakland and Berkeley and a series of suburban communities.

CALIFORNIA

The first European settlement, built by the Spanish in 1776, included a presidio at the western tip of the peninsula, and a mission. The settlement that grew up around these two points remained small for years. At the time of the discovery of gold, the settlement had only several hundred inhabitants, and was of secondary importance to Monterey and other towns.

The sparks of the gold rush ignited an explosion of growth. The port developed at the northeast bend of the peninsula. Early photographs show a veritable forest of masts. The city expanded in a ragged progression of tents, shacks and muddy streets up the hills. From the very beginning, San Francisco was an ethnic patchwork. Gold-hungry immigrants streamed in from all over the world. Europeans, Americans, Mexicans, Central Americans and Chinese were thrown together into the maelstrom that was young San Francisco.

The core of old San Francisco was in the hilly northeast corner, and the city fanned out from there. The original area included the wharves of the Embarcadero, the Barbary Coast (whose dance halls and brothels were eventually replaced by the towers of the Financial District), Union Square vicinity, Chinatown, North Beach and Fisherman's Wharf.

Telegraph Hill, between the Embarcadero and North Beach, eventually became a neighborhood for Italian workers and fishermen, and is easily recognized today by Coit Tower at its peak. West of downtown rise Nob Hill and Russian Hill. On Nob Hill the industrial and financial overlords of the rapidly growing city built their mansions.

From the Embarcadero, the main thoroughfare, Market street, slants to the southwest. The area south of Market st., SOMA, was, until recently, a rundown collection of warehouses and lots, but artists, dance clubs and trendy restaurants are now moving in. Further along the axis of Market st. is the expansive layout of public buildings around the Civic Center. Neither of the neighborhoods bordering the Civic Center — the Tenderloin area to the northeast, and the Western Addition to the west — is especially attractive or safe. A small Japantown clings to the northern edge of the Western Addition. Further along Market st., and just to its south, is the predominantly Mexican and Latino Mission District. Market street leads up to the gay Castro st. neighborhood, and to Twin Peaks Park.

Twin Peaks and the adjacent Mt. Davidson, the highest point in the city at some 1,000 ft. (340 m), provide breathtaking panoramas of the entire city spreading below in every direction. From here it is easy to see how the southern reaches of the city blend into the suburbs of Daly City (reputedly the inspiration for Malvina Reynolds' famous song about suburbia, *Little Boxes*).

West of the restaurants and malls of Fisherman's Wharf, along the city's northern shore, rises the promontory of Fort Mason, which houses the National Park Service, and a youth hostel. The old red-brick military buildings on the docks have been converted into studios, museums and workspace for various grassroots organizations. Beyond Fort Mason lies the Marina, used for pleasure crafts. To the south of the Marina rises Pacific Heights, a pretty neighborhood of old houses squeezed side by side. On the way up is Union street with its refurbished Victorian buildings and its renowned singles scene.

Further west lie the residential Richmond neighborhood, with its excellent restaurants along Clement st. To the south stretches the green belt of Golden Gate Park, with Haight-Ashbury at its eastern end and the ocean at the west. Public beaches stretch in both directions from here. To the north they rise into high and rugged bluffs fringed by forest and hiking trails. Situated on Fort Point is part of a large army base, the Presidio. Most of the shoreline includes a recreational strip. At the northernmost point, above Fort Point, the Golden Gate Bridge stretches north toward Marin. Grass and walking paths follow the rocky shore east back to the Marina.

San Francisco's famous cold and heavy fogs can obscure the Golden Gate Bridge and block the sun from the western neighborhoods, while the sun still shines on the inland districts buffered by the hills. Sometimes the fog rolls over the whole city, bringing with it dampness and chill. Mark Twain said that the coldest winter he ever experienced was a summer in San Francisco. A heavy sweater can be necessary even in summer. The weather can change sharply not only between neighborhoods but within the day. Summer temperatures are generally moderate and comfortable. Cold days of damp fog or heavy rain may be interspersed with warm clear days.

Such a variety of neighborhoods, each with its own centers and identity, packed so tightly together, makes exploring this city a joy. Most popular sites are concentrated in the old northeastern section of the city. These neighborhoods can easily be explored on foot (though the hills undoubtedly pose a challenge).

The public transportation grid is extensive but takes a little time to understand. It is fairly easy to get from one area to another and tour each area on foot, and this can be a lot more convenient than going by car.

How to get there

By air: San Francisco International Airport (SFO), serves airlines and flights from around the world, but it does not have the overwhelming bustle and chaos of a major airport. It is located 14 miles (22 km) south of the city on a small peninsula stretching into the bay.

There are three terminals: North, Central and South, with various airlines divided between them. The upper tier is for departures, the lower one is for arrivals. Traffic moves smoothly at the arrival level and Airport Information can handle all enquiries about transportation, hotels, etc.

San Francisco proves that it is an individual city even at the airport. Instead of passing the time with a cheap novel, you can visit the airport's museum, with its art exhibits, or take a tour and get a glimpse of airport operation.

The airport is easily and quickly reached by car via the Route 101 freeway. During rush hours the highway may be congested in the city itself, but once outside the downtown tangle of freeways, the traffic generally flows fairly fast. Barring a major traffic jam, it takes about half an hour to reach the airport from the central city.

Public and private transportation from the airport to downtown San Francisco is convenient and inexpensive, compared to Los Angeles. If you require public transportation, make sure to ask about it specifically when seeking information, otherwise you may only receive information about private *Airporter* buses. *San Mateo County Transit (Samtrans)* runs buses between downtown and SFO about every half hour, from early morning to about 1:30am. These include the 7 and 7B, tel. 761-7000. From the airport these buses arrive at the Transbay terminal a few blocks south of Market. From there, local public transportation pulls right up to the entrance. The neighborhood itself is not the greatest, nor are there many facilities in the immediate vicinity, something you should consider if arriving at a late hour.

If traveling to the east bay area — Oakland, Berkeley — the ride downtown is unnecessary because *Samtrans* also runs a bus to the Daly City terminal of the *Bay Area Rapid Transit (BART)* system. The sleek futuristic train will whoosh you under the city and bay.

The *Airporter* bus runs a shuttle between airport terminals, and also to its downtown terminal in Union Square. Buses run every 20 minutes, from 5am-midnight. Fare is approximately $5, tel. 495-8404.

Smaller shuttle and van services go from door to door for a few extra dollars. Inquire from information services at the airport. Direct private transportation can also be obtained for outlying destinations, such as Napa. Inquire at the airport. Representatives of the major car rental firms are located in the terminals. Taxis will charge about $25 for the 25-minute ride from the airport to downtown area.

Major airports in Oakland and San Jose also provide full flight schedules for major national as well as regional carriers. The airport at Oakland has been extended and renovated. It now services many San Francisco-bound travelers. The best connection between the airport and the center of San Francisco is with the *BART* train, which stops regularly at the airport.

San Francisco's skyline

San Francisco International Airport (SFO) Information: tel. 761-0800.

By land: The two major bus companies, *Greyhound* and *Trailways*, both serve San Francisco. The stations of both companies are open 24 hours and located on the south side of Market st. — the wrong side if it happens to be late at night. *Trailways*, tel. 982-6400, is located in the Transbay Terminal on First and Mission st. several blocks south of Market st. *Greyhound*, tel. 558-6789, is located on 50, 7th st. just south of Market, and is a little more accessible to more transportation lines and decent, safe lodgings.

Behind the Transbay terminal is *Green Tortoise*, tel. 821-0803, the bus line with bunks in the buses, which offers trips which are somewhat adventurous and unconventional to destinations around the state and country. There are frequent and cheap ($30) trips to Los Angeles, up the coast, to Yosemite, or across the country.

Amtrak stops (or starts) in Oakland. A free shuttle bus connects the *Amtrak* station and the Transbay Terminal in San Francisco. The shuttle trip takes about half an hour.

*C*ALIFORNIA

By Train: There is train service to Oakland from Reno and to the east from Los Angeles and Seattle.

By car: The fastest way to get from Los Angeles to San Francisco by car is to take the I-5 along the western edge of the San Joaquin Valley, and then to go west along I-580 to the bay area. Route 101 is not as spectacular as the Pacific Coast Highway or as fast as I-5, but it's more interesting than the valley route. The coastal route along Route 1 through Big Sur is a breathtaking drive. From the Monterey and Santa Cruz areas, several routes approach the bay area. Route 101 swings east into the Santa Clara Valley, enters San Jose, and approaches the east bay. Route 1 becomes a freeway south of Santa Cruz, and connects with Highway 17, which crosses over the Santa Cruz mountains to the network of freeways running on both sides the bay. Route 1 continues up the coast as a small road, passing state beaches, gentle hills and several small towns before it reaching the lower edges of suburbia. Another alternative route runs along Route 9 from Santa Cruz, and passes under a canopy of towering redwoods.

From the north, whether driving along Route 1 or Route 101, the two roads merge and Route 101 takes over, as the highway crosses the Golden Gate Bridge. From Sacramento, Tahoe, Reno and the east, the transcontinental I-80 leads directly to the Oakland Bay Bridge.

Local transportation

In 1873, the cable car was invented in San Francisco, to replace horse-drawn carriages which had difficulty in climbing the steep hills. In 1912, the city launched a municipal railway street car system, the first publicly owned municipal transportation system in the country. With a tradition like that, and with its physical compactness, it is no wonder that San Francisco has a superb public transportation system today, both within the city limits and connecting its satellite communities. There is such an array of overlapping and interconnecting systems — cable cars and trolleys, buses and municipal subway, *BART, AC Transit, Samtran, Caltrain* and *Golden Gate Transport*, plus shuttles between the various systems — that it can be baffling to a visitor, especially if he must travel out of the city itself. There is also a variety of tickets, designed to save money for the regular traveler and encourage the use of public transportation.

MUNI is the principal municipal transportation system, with several components: trolley cars, cable cars, buses and the fairly new metro (subway) system. Trolleys are the cars attached to overhead wires (that spark occasionally), and cable cars are the squat multi-colored open cars that run up and down the hills near the central city. The fare is 75 cents for all systems except the cable cars, which cost $1.50 (seniors 15 cents). Free transfers are good in any direction for 90 minutes. Exact change is required. A *MUNI* Fast Pass costing $23 allows unlimited travel for one calendar month on *MUNI* (including the cable cars) and *BART* (*Bay Area Rapid Transit* — see below) within the city limits. They are available at *MUNI* ticket oulets, and if you are planning an extended stay in the city they are well worth considering. In addition, an all-day pass, good for the entire *MUNI* system, is available at automatic ticket machines located along the cable car lines.

The **cable cars** have no motors: a big motor at the cable car station pulls a steel cable, guided by an intricate network of pulleys, through a trench beneath the tracks. The cable is held and released by a grip on the car that works like a pair of pliers. The brakes are mechanical. This system was widespread in other cities as well as San Francisco, until it was supplanted by the trolley on all but the steepest routes. After the 1906 earthquake, the trolley replaced the cable cars on most routes. The cable car system, overhauled in 1984, is an official National Historic Landmark that is still operational.

The cable cars operate along three routes today. The *Powell-Hyde* line begins at Powell and Market streets and ends at Victorian Park near the Maritime Museum and Aquatic Park. The *Powell-Mason* line also begins at Powell and Market but terminates at Bay street, just three blocks from Fisherman's Wharf. The *California street* line runs from the foot of Market street to Van Ness avenue. Cable car riders should, if possible, purchase tickets before boarding from the self-service ticket machines at all terminals and major stops. There is usually a lengthy line waiting to board the cable-cars, and you must expect to wait as long as an hour during the summer season. The station with the shortest line is the one on Van Ness ave.

Hop off any Powell st. line, at Washington and Mason, for a visit to the **Cable Car Museum**, the humming center of the cable car operation. Open 10am-6pm daily, admission free, tel. 474-1887. The building was restored on the original foundation in 1984 and presents a wide display of historical exhibits and memorabilia on the cable car, including the original prototype car. A 16-minute film is shown continuously.

The five-line **metro** train system, operating both above and below ground, is the newest addition to the general *MUNI* system. Downtown, between the Embarcadero and the Civic Center, it follows the *BART* route. It then branches off to the west and southwest, reaching Castro st., the Twin Peaks area, and the San Francisco Zoo near the beach. Another line heads for the beach, just south of Golden Gate Park. It operates from 5am-12:30am weekdays.

BART is the sleek futuristic system that shoots from Daly City in the south, through downtown, and beneath the floor of the bay

Cable cars in San Francisco

to Oakland, Berkeley and other East Bay cities and suburbs. The tube under the Bay, over three-and-a+half miles (5.5 km) long, is one of the longest underwater crossings in the world. Within the San Francisco area (from Balboa Park to the Embarcadero stations) a *MUNI* pass is also valid for *BART*. Take time to study the charts and the system before you use it. Everything, from the ticket purchase to entry through the gate, is automatic. Fares start at 80 cents and are pro-rated according to distance, up to $3.00. There are various longer-term, regular-use tickets available as well as arrangements between companies on ticket use. Should the automatic ticket system baffle you, there is an attendant at every station. If you walk out from a *BART* station into San Francisco, a two-part transfer at the station for 75 cents, will allow you to ride on *MUNI* (not the cable car) to your destination and back to the *BART* station. One can also take a bicycle aboard *BART* lines. If traveling all day through a pneumatic tube thrills you, you can buy the *BART* excursion ticket for $2.60, which allows you to tour all the *BART* stations; but the catch is that you can only leave from the station you entered, and an exit anywhere else into the sunlight will nullify the excursion ticket.

The *Trans-Bay Transit Terminal*, at 1st and Market, is the San Francisco center for three bay area bus lines. *AC Transit*, tel. 839-2882, operates between San Francisco and the East Bay, and between the East Bay communities themselves. The terminal also houses *Samtrans* tel. 761-7000, connecting to the airport and to peninsula cities as far south as Palo Alto.

Golden Gate Transit connects Marin County to the city via the Golden Gate Bridge, as well as serving the cities within Marin County. The connections within Marin can sometimes be sporadic, but the 76 can bring you from downtown San Francisco right to the wild edge of the Pacific in the Marin Headlands Reserve.

Caltrain, with a terminal at 4th st. and Townsend, operates commuter trains between San Francisco and San Jose, and links with the *Santa Clara County Transit System*. Weekday shuttle buses run between the terminal and the Financial District at the peak commuting hours. Also located here is the San Francisco station for *Amtrak*, with shuttle buses stopping along 4th st. for connections with *Amtrak* trains at the Oakland train station.

Accommodations

As might be expected, San Francisco offers a wide range of accommodation, something to suit the taste, needs and budget of almost any traveler.

There are, of course, the classic old San Francisco hotels, which include the *St. Francis*, the *Sir Francis Drake*, the *Fairmont* and the *Mark Hopkins*. All these are in the area of Powell st. or the adjacent

Nob Hill. Some afford fantastic views, as well as tasteful luxury. They are, as one might guess, quite expensive.

There are other, newer luxury hotels that have sprouted in the central areas of the city. There is the *Hyatt*, at the Embarcadero, and there are several in the area of Fisherman's Wharf.

On Geary st., near the Marina neighborhood, there are more standard motels at various prices. At the lower end of the spectrum, there is a concentration of cheap, but still decent and safe hotels and hostels in the Tenderloin area and the area south of Mission st. The neighborhood may be questionable at a late hour, but the facilities themselves are generally secure. The best bet, in this price range, is one of the youth hostels in and around the city.

In recent years, the number of Bed & Breakfast Inns in the city has increased. Some of these are located in beautifully restored Victorian buildings.

For information, referrals, and brochures on local B&Bs, contact the Association of Bed & Breakfast Innkeepers of San Francisco: 737 Buena Vista West, San Francisco, 94117, tel. 861-3008.

Luxury Hotels ($125 and up)
Each of these is opulent in its own way. Rooms are distinctive, often individually designed. Services border on pampering. Most have a turn-of-the-century atmosphere, and most start at well over $100 per night for a single.

The Fairmont: 950 Mason, tel. 772-5000, or tel. 800-527-4727.
Four Seasons Clift: 495 Geary st., Downtown, tel. 775-4700, or tel. 800-332-3442. Perhaps the best hotel in town. Great location, spacious rooms and excellent service, make it one of the most desirable hotels in the whole of California.
Mark Hopkins Inter-Continental: 999 California, tel. 392-3434, or tel. 800-327-0200.
St. Francis: 335 Powell st., tel. 397-7000, or tel. 800-228-3000. Still housed in the original stone building. A beautiful lobby and attached bar.
Sir Francis Drake Hotel: 450 Powell st., tel. 392-7755.
Hyatt Regency: 5 Embarcadero Center, tel. 788-1234. Different from the traditional hotels, this modern luxury hotel has a lobby like an immense greenhouse and a famous revolving bar high above the streets.
Sherman House: 2160 Green st., Lombard, tel 563-3600. Only 15 rooms in this first-rate hotel. Advisable to reserve rooms well in advance. European style decor and service create an old-world atmosphere not easily forgotten.

Moderate Hotels ($50-80 per night)
Cartwright Hotel: 524 Sutter st., tel. 421-2865, or tel. 800-227-3844. Cozy and central, with individually designed rooms.

Hotel Beresford: 635 Sutter st., near Mason: tel. 800-533-6533. A very warm, friendly Victorian-style hotel, with gaslight lamps. Attached is the *White Horse Tavern*, a replica of the 18th-century original pub in Edinburgh.

Hotel Cecil: 545 Post st., tel. 673-3733, or tel. 800-227-3818. Rooms are bright and large, with tiled baths. Sun-deck and cabanas.

Lombard Hotel: 1015 Geary st., tel. 673 5232, or tel. 800-227-3608. Pleasant hotel with different rooms in terms of quality and price. Better ask to see room before checking in. Close to many tourist centers.

Inexpensive Hotels (less than $50 per night)

Temple Hotel: 469 Pine st., tel. 781-2565. situated in the Financial District, clean, quiet and inexpensive. Rooms available with or without bath. Excellent weekly rates.

Adelaide Inn: 5 Adelaide Place., tel. 441-2261. Clean, no private baths. Small, *pension*-like establishment, with kitchenette for guests. Continental breakfast. Singles $20, doubles $24.

Obrero Hotel: 1208 Stockton ave., tel. 986-9850. A small, simple hotel in Chinatown, serving huge breakfasts that will keep you satisfied all day. Singles about $30, doubles $35.

Olmpic Hotel: 140 Mason st., tel. 982-5010. A modest hotel near Union sq., not far from local *Hilton*. Rooms vary in size and price. Situated in a relatively safe location, though it is not advisable to walk down Eddy st. after dark, where there are bound to be many drunks and homeless people.

The Red Victorian Bed and Breakfast Inn: 1665 Haight st. tel. 864-1978. In the heart of the Haight right next to the funky movie house of the same name. If there was ever such a thing as a hip B&B, this is it. Beautiful Victorian decor, individually decorated rooms. A little expensive, but definitely unique. Singles with shared bath $45, doubles with shared bath $50.

YMCAs, YWCAs

YMCA: 166 Embarcadero, tel. 392-2191. $18-$30. Use of athletic facilities included.

YMCA Chinatown: 855 Sacramento st., tel. 982-4412. $14-$20. Some rooms with bath, some without. Athletic facilities included.

YWCA: 620 Sutter st., tel. 775-6500. For women, and men accompanying women.

Youth Hostels

There are five youth hostels in the Bay area which are located right on the bay or the ocean:

San Francisco International Hostel: Building 240, Fort Mason, tel. 771-7277. Located in a Civil-War era building, with easy bus or walking access to all major areas of the city. Recommended.

Golden Gate Hostel: Building 941, Fort Barry, Sausalito, tel. 331-27777. The building is a historical landmark, set within miles of hiking trails in the gorgeous Marin Headlands, accessible to hills, lagoons, beaches and Muir Redwoods, as well as to Sausalito itself.

Point Reyes Hostel: Point Reyes Station, tel. 663-8811. An old ranch house set near the quiet beaches, estuaries and sand dunes of beautiful Point Reyes National Seashore. Reservations recommended, especially on weekends.

Montara Lighthouse Hostel: 16th., Cabrillo Highway 1, Montara, tel. 728-7177. Set in the old light station itself, 25 miles (80 km) south of San Francisco, near trails, boating facilities and tide pools of the marine reserve.

Pigeon Point Lighthouse Hostel: Pigeon Pt. rd., Highway 1, Pescadero, tel. 879-0633. 50 miles (80 km) south of San Francisco, in a series of old Coast Guard bungalows, near tidepools, trails and redwoods.

All these hostels are easily accessible by public bus, *BART* or commuter train. Call the hostel itself for exact transportation.

Food

Just walking through a crowded San Francisco street will whet your appetite. Everywhere you turn you see restaurants. Good intentions to diet will crumble. You will be a slave to your taste buds, and a sweeter slavery there never was.

The classic old San Francisco restaurants combine sparse decor with an emphasis on grilling. Fresh fish grilled on intensely hot mesquite charcoal is a local favorite. It is, however, extremely difficult to pinpoint a local cuisine, because there is so much of everything here. There are excellent Chinese, Mexican and Italian restaurants throughout the city.

Chinese restaurants often have an informal lunch-counter atmosphere which in other places you'd find only in greasy diners. The plethora of Chinese restaurants has been supplemented in recent years by other Asian restaurants: Cambodian, Laotian, Thai, Filipino and, of course, Japanese. One need only sample a few of the Asian ethnic restaurants in San Francisco to realize that each has its distinctive native cuisine. Similarly, Latin American restaurants are springing up, exposing the city to foods from El Salvador, Nicaragua and Peru. There are also the French, Russian, Persian, Basque and Greek restaurants.

Not surprisingly, San Francisco has been in the forefront of developing vegetarian restaurants beyond the sprout sandwich stage into gourmet restaurants featuring vegetables you've probably never heard of.

But for those with basic cravings, diners and fast-food stands can also be found here, as can lots of great ice cream stands — although in San Francisco you don't eat ordinary ice cream; you head for

North Beach for the famous Italian gelato. Some restaurants are described below grouped according to area.

Financial District/Downtown

The downtown and Montgomery st. environs have no shortage of old, polished San Francisco bars and restaurants. Some of the best seafood, especially grilled fish, can be found here.

Tadich Grill: 240 California, in the Financial District, tel. 391-2373. The lines can be long here, and most people are waiting for the superb seafood.

Jack's Grill: 615 Sacramento st. The bare, simple surroundings belie the quality that have made this a San Francisco by-word. Rumor is that the 3rd floor was once a brothel (seems like everyplace in the city was).

Scott's Seafood: 3 Embarcadero. A branch of the original on Lombard st., serving the same menu of seafood that is reputedly among the best in the city.

Sam's Grill: 374 Bush st., tel. 421-0594. Yet another classic standby, with curtained booths for a special rendezvous. Delicious grilled fish and sourdough bread. Reasonably priced.

John's Grill, 63 Ellis st., tel. 986-0069. Dashiell Hammet brought Sam Spade into this dark bar. Lunches about $6.

Chinatown

Many of Chinatown's restaurants serve lunch specials from $2.50 and up, consisting of rice, a noodle dish, and vegetable-meat topping. They are tasty, filling, and reliable. Many restaurants in the area also have their own specialties. Everyone seems to have a different favorite place in Chinatown. This is the place to try something completely new. Filling and delicious dinners can easily be found here for $5 or less.

Dim Sum is very popular. Waiters wheel wagons of various dishes between tables and customers choose what they want. The bill is tabulated by the number of plates, usually at about $1.50 per plate.

Sam Wo's: 813 Washington, up from Grant. Walk upstairs past the kitchen (in which you can snoop if you want). Excellent lunches.

Hunan Restaurant: 853 Kearny. A remarkable little hole-in-the wall. One of the first to popularize the hot, spicy, northern Chinese cooking. Don't come here for atmosphere. Often there's a line, but there's usually space at the counter, from which you can watch the performance of the cooks.

Ocean Garden: 735 Jackson. Excellent seafood, from about $5.

Caledon: 881 Clay. A few notches above the cheap chow mein joints. Dinners start from $9.

Fong Hang: 761 Jackson. A tiny bakery selling delicious fresh pastries.

Chuck's: Powell and Clay: The lunch counter in the back is as uninspiring as the name. However, in this strange combination of an American diner and Chinese restaurant, you can find your basic Chinese soups and chow mein dishes. It is extremely inexpensive, and you can finish off the meal with a thick-shake for $1.30.

Louie's: 1014 Grant ave. Large and always busy. Delicious and fresh food, *dim sum* specialties pushed up and down the aisles. Very reasonably priced.

North Beach

Eating out and hanging out in North Beach is a local sport which is extremely easy and inviting to take up. Many restaurants run lunch specials, which often consist of a heavy meat-and-pasta meal and start at about $6.

Washington Square Bar & Grill: 1707 Powell st., tel. 982-8123. This is a known hangout for local newspaper writers and other literati. The food leans toward the Italian, the atmosphere towards well-dressed informal, and the piano player is fantastic.

The US Restaurant: 431 Columbus, tel. 362-6251. Another veritable local institution. In the old days, customers would cram into the little wedge-shaped restaurant (immediately next to the open kitchen) wherever a free space could be found. Now, the restaurant has expanded next door, and customers still cram in wherever space can be found. Large portions of meat and pasta. The crowded tables and friendliness of the local regulars make it easy to strike up a conversation. Dinners start at about $6.

Little Joe's: 525 Broadway. The sign says "Rain or shine, there's always a line" and it's true. Noisy, bustling, smoke-filled, with a happy atmosphere which will help you digest the hefty Italian meals that start at about $6.50.

Il Pollaio: 555 Columbus, tel. 362-7727. Compared to the surrounding establishments it looks like a small fast-food joint, and the name, which means chicken coop, doesn't add to the character, but the chickens, marinated and grilled until they glisten, make delicious meals starting at about $4.25.

Des Alpes: 732 Broadway. This Basque restaurant is tucked away from the bustle of Broadway. There are specials every night. The set meal, which will take you all the way to coffee and dessert, costs about $8.50.

Maykadeh: 470 Green st, tel. 362-8286. The Persian haute cuisine served here is exotic to the American palate. Even the Middle Eastern Basmati rice stands out. The *ghorme sabzee*, roughly translated as braised and spiced lamb, is worth trying. Then again, just about everything is. Portions are large, and most main courses cost about $6.

Capp's Corner: Powell and Green. A small and very well-known North Beach joint, with celebrity pics all over the walls, and the large Italian lunch specials scribbled daily on the board. $6.95.

Dixie Cafe: 532 Columbus. Seafood from Creole-Cajun New Orleans country. Come here for your Gumbo Smoky Shrimp and Redfish My-O-My.

Moderate

Iacopi Deli: Union and Grant. One of the last of the small local delis, with plentiful offerings for a picnic in Washington Square inculding home-made cheeses. Diagonally across the corner is a bakery.

The Bohemian Cigar Store: At Union and Columbus, shaped like the prow of a ship, it is located at the point where the two streets meet across from Washington Square. This tiny, homey place draws a regular crowd of young locals. At peak hours you might have to stand at the counter.

Cafe Trieste: Vallejo and Grant. An old North Beach standby with pictures of patrons singing Italian opera all over the walls. Bring your leather jacket, leather bag, and your sketchbook so you can sketch as you are sketched by others. At the large central table eavesdrop on discussions on art education and some great dirty jokes.

Vesuvio's: 255 Columbus. Stained glass, poetry on the outer wall and poets in the dark interior. A beat survivor.

The Mission District

Taqueria San Jose: 2830 and 2282 Mission. There are those who claim that these are the state-of-the-art burritos.

La Olla: 2417 Mission. Latin American spicy meat dishes in surroundings of beautiful crafts. $4.50 up.

La Boheme Cafe: 3318 24th st. Old tables, books, a community bulletin board and good coffee are found here.

El Faro: 2813 Mission. Very popular for its stuffed burritos.

Tenderloin/Civic Center

Kimball's: 300 Grove st., tel. 861-5555. A light and airy decor. Opposite the Performing Arts Center, it is crowded and popular after performances.

Hayes Street Grill: 320 Hayes. The grilled fish and sourdough bread have made this place a big hit. Fish starts at about $12.

The Billboard: 678 Post. Reasonable and delicious Indonesian food.

Padang: Post and Jones. Another excellent Indonesian surprise deep in the Tenderloin area.

Athens Greek Restaurant: 51 Mason. Looks almost like a small lunch counter. Authentic and filling, heavy on meats, $5 and up.

The Hippopotamus: Van Ness and Pacific. North of the Civic Center area on Van Ness, this is a famous local burger place.

SOMA

The latest in trendiness includes restored old 1950s diners. The decor looks authentic, but misses the unpretentiousness that made the old places what they were. Several are found around Church and Market. Try *Sparky's Diner*, 242 Church st., for one that strikes true with its decor, food and prices.

Union Street

Perry's: 1944 Union st. A popular and busy place. The grilled food is excellent, but a bit overpriced.

Cheshire Cheese and Mad Hatter Tea: 2213 Fillmore. Cheese, muffins and coffee served in a cozy setting.

Clement Street

Just a stroll down this aisle of restaurants, cafes, diners and pubs will make you hungry even if you have just eaten a prime steak and eggs.

Taiwan Restaurant: 445 Clement. A diverse menu, and a $3.25 lunch special. Often very crowded.

The New Ocean: 239 Clement. Often hailed as the top Cantonese restaurant in the city. Starts at $4.50. Open until 3am on weekends.

Hong Kong Cafe: 651 Clement. By selecting from the small stuffed dishes in the counter window, you can build yourself a sizeable and inexpensive meal to be enjoyed while strolling along.

The Mandalay: 4348 California st., one block off Clement near 6th ave. This is something rare even in San Francisco: a Burmese restaurant, though most of the menu is Chinese. The distinctive cuisine includes dried shrimp and a salad made from green tea.

Churchill's: Clement and 6th ave. A comfortable, relaxing neighborhood bar.

Haig's Delicacies: 642 Clement. The place for chutneys, nuts, exotic canned fruit, olives and coffee served in the long-handled coffee pots of the Mideast.

Hamburger Haven: 9th and Clement. A simple unpretentious diner with $1.79 breakfast specials.

Japantown

Isobune: 1737 Ost st., Japan Center, tel. 563-1030. A sushi restaurant, in which platters of sushi come around by boat on a small stream. Besides the novelty, the morsels are so delicious you'll be tempted to reach for more and more (the bill is figured by the plate).

San Wan Restaurant: 1682 Post st., tel. 921-1453. A fantastic Chinese restaurant, located in Japantown, across from the Japan Center. Enormous portions, many Chinese customers, endlessly running waiters who somehow manage to get you everything you need, and scorching hot-and-sour combinations.

Mifune: 1737 Post st., tel. 922-0337. Delicious and reasonably priced Japanese noodles.

Haight-Ashbury

La Pyramide: Corner of Haight and Cole. A delicious giant burrito costs $2.00.

Seventh Heaven: 1448 Haight. A French-Russian bakery. Try the piroshkies.

Chabela: 1803 Haight. A great take-out Mexican place for a hot picnic in the park. The long lines for lunch serve as ample testimony.

Cha Cha Cha: Next door to Chabela. Very small, tastefully done,

The gigantic Golden Gate Bridge

serving Spanish food that is several cuts above the standard burrito-and-bean fare.

Haight Victorian Spirits: 1621 Haight. Gourmet deli, cheeses and wines, whatever one needs for a park picnic. There are also tables near the window.

Blue Front Deli: 1430 Haight. They serve a great felafel.

Crescent City Cafe: 1418 Haight. Cosy, simple and reasonably priced for breakfast.

The Ganges: 775 Frederick. This small and friendly Indian restaurant is not in the core of the Haight itself, but around the southeast corner of Golden Gate Park. A delight, with delicious vegetarian dinners costing about $5.

Clubs

The music scene in San Francisco changes constantly. The city is rooted in traditions of jazz, but picks up and helps shape the latest trends as well. New wave and punk rock have reached raucous prominence in recent years and many new clubs have opened in SOMA. Stand-up comedy has gained popularity in small clubs and cabarets. The listings here are, of course, only partial. Check the local newspapers and entertainment weeklies to catch the latest in music.

Full Moon Saloon: 1725 Haight, tel. 668-6190. Hanging in with good old rock, blues and reggae.

I-Beam: 1748 Haight, tel. 668-6006. Started out predominantly gay, and still is on Sunday afternoon, but patronage is mixed during the rest of the week. One of the early new wave and rock discos.

The Mabuhay Lounge: 433 Broadway in North Beach, tel. 956-3315. The Filipino restaurant has been transformed into punk paradise. The action warms up toward midnight. One-drink minimum.

The Oasis: 11th st. and Folsom. A clear dance floor over the pool.

The Stud: 11th and Folsom.

Bajone's: 1062 Valencia, tel. 282-2522. Part of the Mission's Latino music scene, filled with locals, featuring jazz, blues and world beat.

The Great American Music Hall: 859 O'Farrel st, tel. 885-0750. The best of the best in everything from jazz to folk.

Keystone Korner: 750 Vallejo st., tel. 781-0697. Played by local and visiting artists, great jazz bursts the seams of this club. $3 minimum.

Milestones: 5th and Harrison. A fine club for jazz.

Finocchio's: 506 Broadway, tel. 982-9388. The granddaddy/mama of drag shows, what was once outrageous and shocking is now a tourist attraction.

The Holy City Zoo: 408 Clement st., tel. 752-2846. A small club featuring aspiring comics.

The Boarding House: 901 Columbus, tel. 441-4333. Folk, country-rock and some comedy. Often features big names.

Pier 23: At the Embarcadero, two blocks north of the Ferry building, tel. 362-5125. It's Dixieland jazz in an old longshoreman's bar.

Getting to Know the City

On first entering the city, a tourist is likely to be confused by the abundance of attractions available to him, since this beautiful city is packed with wonderful things that should not be missed. The city of San Francisco came to the aid of visitors when, in 1938, it initiated an all-encompassing route that includes most of the its treasures. This route, more commonly known as the 49-mile drive, takes approximately half a day to complete, and is clearly sign-posted throughout town in blue and white signs carrying the emblem of a sea-gull. This is the best way to familiarize yourself with San Francisco. The route includes China Town, Telegraph Hill, Golden Gate Park, the Civic Center and more. This route can be undertaken in your own car or with one of the tourist companies, such as *Grayline*, that begins the four-hour tour (known as Tour 1) a few times a day. ($21.50 per adult, $10.50 for children between the ages of 5 and 11, tel 558-9400).

The Financial District

The theme of this area is, predictably, money, money, money. Down here in this glass-and-steel grotto, you can see how it is made, where it goes and how it is spent.

At the **Federal Reserve Bank of San Francisco**, 101 Market st., tel. 974-3252, you can see "The World of Economics", a large, fascinating display that fills the lobby with computer games, video tapes and murals. A computer game gives you the opportunity to become chairman of the Federal Reserve Board for 48 months. You can fire everybody or turn the country into a kibbutz, but in the end the computer will can you, and you'll be back at your old routine.

The **Museum of Money of the American West**, in the Bank of California, 400 California st., tel. 765-2188 will give you an idea of the fever and explosion that the discovery of gold in California really caused. Continue your tour at the **Old Mint Museum** for still more dreams of gold. 5th and Mission. Open Mon.-Fri.10am-4pm. Admission free, tel. 974-0788.

The **Wells Fargo History Room** at the Wells Fargo Bank, 420 Montgomery st., tel. 396-2619, gives a history of the bank. An interesting stop. Open during banks working hours.

The **Pacific Heritage Museum**, 608 Commercial st,. at Montgomery. Daily 10am-4pm, admission free, tel. 362-4100, in the Bank of Canton Building. Exhibits displays about the history of artistic, cultural, economic and other interchanges between people on both sides of the Pacific Basin. The museum emphasizes the role of various groups from the Asia-Pacific region in the development of California.

Enter the old **Monadnock Building**, at Third st. and Market to glimpse the new wall and ceiling murals that look as if they might have come from a Renaissance Piazza.

The tall sleek **Transamerican Pyramid** at Montgomery between Clay and Washington stands out among the other towers and has become a San Francisco landmark. This is the tallest building in town at 853 ft. (290 m). There is a good viewing area on the 27th floor. which is open to the public Mon.-Fri. 9am-4pm. Next to the pyramid is Redwood Park, a small peaceful haven of green, where lunch time concerts are performed throughout the summer. On the éastern edge of the Financial District, the Embarcadero is currently being renovated, but the best facelift of all would be to remove the ugly freeway that cuts off the entire view of the east bay. More than one renegade town planner has suggested that. At the foot of Sacramento street stands the three-level **Embarcadero Center**, tel. 772-0585. Attached to this complex of expensive stores is the *Hyatt Regency*, which has a high, translucent atrium and a famous revolving bar, the *Equinox Lounge*, at the top. Dress well here. You can nurse your drink for the 45-minute spin. The interior of this hotel is very impressive and turns the place into a popular attraction even for those who cannot afford its prices.

Union Square

Also at the Embarcadero Center, the **Levi Strauss History Room** relates how an immigrant tailor and his company transformed workpants into international fashion. Mon.-Fri. 10am-4pm. Admission free.

Downtown

Downtown and the Financial District can be spoken of separately or together. Market st. is their common southern boundary. The plaza where **Powell and Mason** meet Market coming in from the seedy Tenderloin district to the west, is a small downtown hub of sorts. This is where the Powell st. cable car turntable, heading to Ghiradelli Square, is situated. During the summer there is always a line of tourists here, waiting for the cable car.

Downstairs, to the side of the plaza is the main Visitor Center for the city. The *BART* and *MUNI* metro station here can supply information on all the municipal systems — rail, trolley, bus, and cable.

A few blocks up Powell street is **Union Square**, a popular spot with office workers and street performers during weekday lunch hours. The street has a lively atmosphere and flower stalls on the street corners do a brisk business with the executives. Around Union Square are the big department stores, *Macy's* and *Magnin's*. On the east end of Union Square is a *Bass* ticket office and booking service selling tickets for a wide variety of theater events throughout the city.

On the west side of Powell st., opposite the square, is the dignified,

DOWNTOWN SAN FRANCISCO

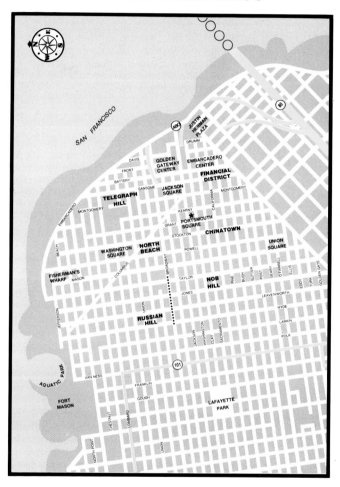

St. Francis Hotel. Up the hill, west of Union Square is the wealthy neighborhood of **Nob Hill**, known locally as Snob Hill. In addition to the *St. Francis*, there are other classic, established and opulent San Francisco hotels on Powell st. and on the slopes of Nob Hill. These include the *Fairmont Hotel*, 950 Mason, the *Sir Francis Drake*, Sutter and Powell and the *Mark Hopkins*, California and Mason. All these hotels have elegant bars, cocktail lounges, or restaurants on their higher floors, offering fine views of the city.

The **Tenderloin** district, just west of the downtown area around Powell and Market, is a decrepit area of drunks, pushers, addicts, peep shows, porno movies, depressing residential hotels and boarded up shops. Yet something new is stirring here. Immigrants from Vietnam and Cambodia are moving in, and there are a number of very good, reasonably priced restaurants springing up. As threatening as it may appear, it is safe (relatively) to walk around during the day. So, if you feel a bit adventurous about discovering interesting eateries, this is the place to go.

Chinatown

The old Chinatown, squeezed in roughly between Powell and Kearney, Bush and Broadway, is crammed with crowds, shops, colorful Chinese signs, and the delectable smells of Chinese food. Two cable car lines skirt Chinatown. Two blocks up the hill to the west run the two Powell st. lines. The California st. line, running between the Embarcadero and Van Ness, crosses Grant st. just where it turns into the crowded, brightly-lit and touristy main boulevard of Chinatown. Grant, lined with innumerable shops, runs north into Broadway and the Italian section of North Beach. This stretch and the surrounding streets are easily walkable. On Stockton, a block up from Grant, and on some of the sidestreets, the signs and restaurant menus may be only in Chinese. The main activity in Chinatown is simply to stroll around, browse in the Chinese spice shops, examine all the strange little gadgets and trinkets being sold, stare at the meats hanging in the butcher shop windows, photograph the old men playing various games in Portsmouth Square, watch the rush of people, and breathe in the enticing aromas which beckon you from one restaurant to the next.

It is amazing how many good restaurants there are along the Chinatown streets. Each seems to have its clientele, and many have newspaper clippings taped to the window proclaiming that particular place as positively the best Chinese restaurant in the city. Avoid the ones with gaudy, contrived settings and a primarily tourist clientele. You may make some fine discoveries of your own if you seek out that special hole-in-the-wall with bare walls, chipped linoleum tables, Chinese menus and crowds of Chinese customers.

The number of specific sites to see in Chinatown is limited. There is the large, ornate Chinese gate at Grant and Bush, which was given to the city as a gift from the Rep. of China in 1969. The **Chinese Culture Center**, in addition to serving as a community center, houses a museum for the appreciation of Chinese arts and culture, with regularly changing exhibits. 750 Kearny st., 3rd floor of *Holiday Inn*. Tues.-Sat. 10am-4pm. Admission free. Tel. 986-1822.

The museum of the **Chinese Historical Society of America** is concerned mainly with the role of the Chinese in the California gold rush, and the subsequent rapid development of the West coast. 17

Adler Place, off 1140 Grant ave., near Pacific. Tues.-Sat. 1-5pm. Donation requested. tel. 391-1188.

You can also visit a Chinese shrine, such as the **Tien Hou** Temple in 125 Waverly Place which is one of the first Chinese buildings in the city, or the less interesting **Jeng Sen** Temple, 146 Waverly Place or **Norras** 109 Waverly Place.

North Beach

North Beach abuts Chinatown at Broadway, and extends north along Columbus ave. toward Fisherman's Wharf, and east up the steep slope of Telegraph Hill. An old Italian neighborhood, lined with small delis, bakeries, restaurants and cafes, it became a magnet for the emerging "Beat" movement in the early 50s.

"I saw the best minds of my generation destroyed by madness, starving hysterical naked..." — with that line from the poem *Howl*, delivered in a semi-chant in a small North Beach forum, Allen Ginsberg helped to bring to the public the new Beat poetry and literature scene that had been developing in San Francisco in the post-war years, spearheaded by Ginsberg and Jack Kerouac, Lawrence Ferlinghetti and others. They headed to San Francisco for a freer atmosphere and congregated in North Beach because of the cheap rents and the village-type surroundings.

Ferlinghetti's *City Lights Bookstore* at Columbus and Broadway showcased the works of the Beat poets even when they were banned, and became a focal point for a new era of artistic, intellectual and social rebels.

In the clubs on **Broadway**, post-war free-form jazz bloomed, and comedians such as Lenny Bruce and Mort Sahl honed a comedy edged with piercing political and social criticism. A few years later the clubs presented the folk and protest music which emerged as a powerful influence in the early 60s.

The glitter from those lively scenes began to fade. All the old clubs became strip joints and new ones opened. Their flashing signs lined the street and dazzled the eyes. Glib "barkers" at the entrances lured in tourists with "free peeks". Finally, however, the glamour of that world dimmed too. The big signs were turned off and they still hang above boarded-up doors. Only strip joints remain. Often the girls themselves try to lure in patrons.

Broadway deteriorated and became the center of San Francisco's sleazy side, bastion of punk music, the cruising hang-out for kids from the suburbs hunting down a little big-city action. The street witnessed a rise in crime, and although it is safe to walk the brightly lit street, it is not rcommended to veer into one of the small side-streets at a late hour. Grassroots groups and city planners are considering the problem of the Broadway strip, and may try to transform it into a district of small theaters.

Chinatown

Concurrently, there is a very marked increase in the numbers of Chinese signs which have crossed the old border of Broadway. Many of the old, reliable, family-owned Italian stores have closed. On the sidestreets of old and new cafes people park themselves at tables with notebooks and sketchpads. A few survivors from the old days hang out at *Vesuvio's*, near *City Lights*. *City Lights* itself is still

Climbing a hill by cable car

open; its basement provides a peaceful respite from the bright rush on Broadway. On Columbus, just north of Broadway, are clusters of cafes and restaurants from which one can watch the passing parade. All kinds of people pass by: old Chinese, punks, open-eyed tourists and hip young professionals.

Washington Square, near Columbus, is a nice place to enjoy a bit of greenery. All sorts of characters float by here. It is the perfect place for a picnic, with several good delis and bakeries bordering it. The slope of **Telegraph Hill** begins to the east of Washington Square. It is a steep walk, through some beautiful staired streets that are quiet even though they are right in the heart of the city. Bus 39 reaches the famous **Coit Tower** at the top of Telegraph.

The tower was erected in 1933 during the Depression by famous philanthropist Lillie Coit. Admission required for the climb or elevator ride to the top. Open daily 10am-6pm. The view from the base, a smidgeon lower, is just as spectacular and is free. The murals in the circular hall surrounding the lobby are impressive. They are wonderful examples of the populist frescoes which emerged from the school of modern industrial realism in American art. At the time they caused such a stir, because of their clear political implications, about the role and destiny of workers, that they had to be touched up a bit.

For a visual feast continue down the east side of the hill, towards **Filbert Street**. Along with a few old wooden houses, pre-dating the 1906 earthquake, a pocket-sized paradise clings to the slope. The lovely overflowing garden was the creation of Grace Marchant who moved here in 1949 at the age of 63. She began by hauling away the bedsprings, tires and other garbage. By the time of her death at the age of 96, Marchant had transformed the neglected hillside into a lush and wild corner that attracted birds, wildlife and people.

Bus 39 runs between Coit Tower and Fisherman's Wharf. A popular route for a day's excursion could include the cable car ride up Powell st. to Ghiradelli Square, a stroll along the docks and colorful tourist traps of the wharf area, the bus 39 ride to Coit Tower, a ride or walk back to Washington Square and North Beach, continuing by foot across Broadway into Chinatown, and a walk, bus or cable car (Powell is two steep blocks west of Chinatown) back downtown or wherever you need to go. This route invites detours and diversions. One popular place that every tourist must experience once is "the crookedest street in the world", **Lombard Street** between Hyde and Leavenworth, in the northwest corner of North Beach.

Fisherman's Wharf

Fisherman's Wharf is an overpriced, gaudy, tourist trap, but it is worth strolling around, simply to see the bright and colorful crowds and the bay shining in the sun. The old established seafood restaurants, such as *Castagnola's* and *Alioto's* have beautiful views, with their tables set beside wide picture windows over the bay, but they are over-priced, as are the sidewalk crab stands. There are several shopping complexes here, in gutted old brick warehouses. At the foot of Polk st. is **Ghiradelli Square** named after the chocolate manufacturer. The shops are situated in several floors around an open square. The restaurants are lavish and expensive, but it is worth indulging in Ghiradelli chocolate. Although the prices are high and lines can be long, the chocolate is outstanding.

At the foot of Polk st., just beyond Ghiradelli Square, is the **National Maritime Museum**, part of the small **Aquatic Park** near Fisherman's Wharf. Open daily 10am-6pm, but shorter hours in winter, closed Monday. Tours daily, Admission free, tel. 556-8177. The museum houses a wide range of sailing ship models, old photographs and artifacts. The photographs illustrate the phenomenal growth of the San Francisco port from a collection of tents to a sprawling city. Connected to the museum are several historic sailing ships berthed at nearby **Hyde Street Pier**. They include an old car ferry, steam schooner, tugboat and the *Balclutha*, a Cape Horn sailing ship. Hyde Street Pier has convenient hours, 10am-5pm, and offers guided tours, self-guided tours, films and demonstrations. Admission fee, tel. 556-6435. Beyond them, along the Embarcadero and the ferry to Alcatraz is another historic ship: The *Pampanito* at Pier 45, a World War II submarine. Admission fee, tel. 441-5819.

On Hyde st., just opposite the cable car landing, is the *Buena Vista*, another venerable institution, claiming to be the first place to serve Irish coffee. It's still good after all these years, and this is one of the few wharfside spots patronized by a number of San Franciscans, often of the young sleek-suited variety.

At the **Cannery**, east of Ghiradelli, the shops are a shade lower in price but just as touristy. Amid the boutiques and cute card stores are a few art galleries with some high-quality art. There are often performers in the square. Further along Jefferson, are the Wax Museum, Ripley's Believe It or Not and other similar establishments which are rather mediocre.

Fisherman's Wharf itself is a real wharf with real fishermen. If you come about five in the morning you can see them unloading their haul while the seagulls hover above. At more civilized hours, you can charter a boat from here. There are signs advertising boats for charter, or cruises, starting from about $10 per head per hour.

The history and process of wine making are displayed at the **Wine Museum**, 635 Beach st. Tues.-Sat. 11am-5pm. Tours 2-4pm. Admission free, tel. 673-6990.

The wharf area attracts a wide variety of street performers. Some, having earned their stripes here, move on to play in places with roofs, while others fade into the sunset. One well-known attraction is the jukebox man, who will pop out of his little box on the insertion of a coin and play a tune on his trumpet; the fellow in the Captain Kidd get-up with the parrot on his shoulder wants money just for being photographed, even though the bird does all the work. You can sometimes see a couple who combine mime and modern dance in an intricate, fantastic act set to breakdance music. The acts change all the time here.

Lombard Street

The **Anchorage** is yet another mall. **Pier 39** is the newest, extending out over the water. *Only in San Francisco*, at the entrance of the pier, offers free information and maps, but on little else other than the pier itself. One worthwhile spot here is the old *Eagle Cafe*, which was moved from the Embarcadero and was one of the old fishermen's and longshoremen's cafes during the port's heyday.

Near **Pier 41**, just west of Pier 39, is the docking point for the *Red and White Fleet*, which operates ferries to Angel Island, Sausalito, and Tiburon. Eat at one of several restaurants in Tiburon and save $2 on the ferry ticket. *Red & White* also supplies free maps, tel. 546-2896; In-state, tel. 1-800-445-8880. Sausalito and Larkspun can be reached by *Golden Gate Ferries*, leaving from the terminal at the edge of Market st., tel. 332-6000.

The *Blue and Gold Fleet* runs loop tours between the Golden Gate and East Bay bridges. One-and-a-half-hour tours for $10, ages 5-18 $5, free under five, tel. 781-7877.

In the middle of the entrance of San Francisco Bay, with an enticing view of the sunset beyond the bridge, the silvery towers of the city and the green mountains to the north, sits **Alcatraz**, "the rock". Alcatraz, not a typical national park, is worth a visit. A complete visit lasts about two hours. Wear good walking shoes and bring some warm clothes even in summer. Boats leave every 45 minutes from Pier 41 at Fisherman's Wharf, from 8:45am to 2:45pm in winter

The Fisherman's Wharf

and to 5pm in summer. Tickets are available at the pier or through *Ticketron*. Adults $4.50, until age 12 $3, under five 75 cents, tel. 974-6391 for reservations. Advance purchase is recommended in the summer.

A tour of Alcatraz makes it easier to understand how, surrounded by tantalizing beauty, some of the hardened criminals in this maximum security federal prison must have reached the depths of hopelessness. On Alcatraz rehabilitation was an unknown word. Guards were plentiful, discipline harsh, the routine rigid, endless and boring. The most notorious gangsters — Al Capone, Machinegun Kelly and Doc Barker — were incarcerated here. It is hard not to admire the desperate determination of the 39 men who tried to escape across the expanse of freezing cold water with its strong currents. Ten died, most were recaptured and five disappeared.

Six years after it was abandoned as a prison, Alcatraz had a brief renewal of life when 85 Indians seized it and declared it an Indian cultural center, in an "occupation" that lasted one-and-a-half years.

Fort Mason

Situated on the promontory between San Francisco's Marina and Fisherman's Wharf, Fort Mason has two main functions. The upper part houses the headquarters of the National Park Service, which is the central information source for all the scattered portions of the Golden Gate National Recreation Area in San Francisco and Marin County. An AYH youth hostel is also located here.

The lower part of Fort Mason, among the old docks and brick military buildings, serves as a "regional cultural center". In more concrete terms, it is a collection of innovative, political, social, cultural and counter-cultural grassroots organizations. It is a fairground, classroom, dance studio and performance center. Its organizations and exhibits range from the Mexican Museum, to Greenpeace, to Friends of the River, to the Young Performers Theater. There are many offbeat, unusual exhibits, activities and tours for the tourist who wants to see beneath the touristy veneer of this city.

Do not miss out on a visit to the S.S. *Jeremiah O'Brian*, last of the World War II Liberty Ships, a national monument that still sails. Pier 3 East. Laguna st. and Marina blvd. Open daily 9am-3pm. Admission fee, tel. 441-3101.

The famous *Tassajara Bakery*, tel. 822-5770, run by the San Francisco Zen Center is worth visiting just for its graceful decor. For a recording of Fort Mason events, call tel. 441-5705.

Exploratorium

The Exploratorium, located in San Francisco's Palace of Fine Arts opposite the Marina, is a unique institution for the teaching of science.

The dome of the grandiose Palace of Fine Arts is easily visible. 3601 Lyon st. Open Wed. 1-9:30 pm, Thurs.-Fri. 1-5pm, Sat.-Sun. 10am-5pm. Opens earlier on summer weekdays. $4 adults (good for six months), $2 seniors, 17 and under free. Free on Wednesday after 6pm, and free the first Wednesday of each month, tel. 563-7337.

Whether creating magnetic sculptures, unleashing waves, or gazing half-hypnotized at a "sun-painting", the visitor is thrust directly into the world of science and becomes an eager, curious child facing the natural world. This scientific funhouse grew out of the experience, philosophy, values and never-ending initiative of an amazing man.

Frank Oppenheimer, brother of J. Robert Oppenheimer, the "father of the atom bomb", was an eminent scientist in his own right. Before and during World War II, Oppenheimer was deeply immersed, like his brother, in the development of atomic energy. He was involved in the early atomic tests and the application of nuclear energy toward aircraft propulsion and land research on cosmic rays. Then, like his celebrated brother, and many others, he suffered from harassment by the House of Un-American Activities Committee during the McCarthy purges of the 1950s. The eminent research scientist suddenly became an outcast, and took up cattle ranching in a small Colorado town. Even in this enterprise, he remained the creative experimenter who made his own tools and tried new solutions.

Oppenheimer began teaching science at the local high school and urged his students to explore the wonders and reality of the scientific and natural worlds with their own hands, through direct experience and experimentation, whether it meant designing their own lab experiments or examining car parts in the local dump. Students from that obscure Colorado town garnered state and national science prizes.

Oppenheimer eventually returned to the world of university teaching. He studied science museums in Europe, and in 1968 opened the Exploratorium, which, in his words, is not really a museum, but rather "the woods of natural phenomena through which to wander".

The one-time scientific pariah and his staff created a "woods" of 450 exhibits, centered around the myriad phenomena available to the human senses. Artists are much involved in planning exhibits. A harp sings in the wind. Sunbeams shoot through prisms and mirrors to create a mural. The wave organ, jutting over the water at the Marina itself, creates music from the motion of the waves.

The workshop, in which exhibits are created, is out in the open and becomes part of the exhibits itself. In this enclave of educational chaos, there are no guards, no rules, and no lists of restrictions.

Alcatraz — the rock

Civic Center

In one of those classic ironies of municipal layout, the beautiful, expansive complex that makes up the **Civic Center** is located on the western edge of the decrepit Tenderloin district and the wide, open plaza is a favorite hangout for vagrants. The plaza is also the site for large public arts exhibits. Extending for five blocks, west from McAllister and Market to Franklin, the Civic Center network includes the UN Plaza, Public Library, City Hall, Civic Auditorium, Opera House, Museum of Modern Art and various administrative buildings.

The **City Hall** has a dome higher than the national Capitol's, and a long pool reflecting the lights at night. Contrasted to this, the glass and white concrete **Davies Symphony Hall** is very modern in design. This hall is part of the **San Francisco War Memorial** and **Performing Arts Center**. Tours are offered every Monday, 10am-2:30pm on every half hour, tel. 552-8338.

The **Veteran's Building**, adjacent to the Opera House on Van Ness, houses the **Herbst Theatre**, which was the site of the signing of the United Nations Charter in 1945 and now houses large murals from the 1915 Panama-Pacific Exposition. Next door, the **San Francisco Museum of Modern Art** houses rotating collections of works by Matisse, Klee and other 20th century masters. The museum also has a café and bookstore at Van Ness and McAllister. Open Tues., Wed. and Fri. 10am-5pm, Thurs. 10am-9pm, Sat.-Sun. 11am-5pm.

Performance near Fisherman's Wharf

Admission $3.50, under 16 $1.50. Tues. free. Discount on admission on Thurs. after 5pm, tel. 863-8800. The nearby area of Hayes st., behind Davies Hall, has cafés, restaurants and some interesting galleries and bookstores.

SOMA

South-of-market (SOMA for short) was an area of run-down apartments, flophouses, greasy chili joints, parking lots, warehouses and factories, but this area has been going through a renaissance of sorts. In the last few years, artists have taken over some of the warehouses, and punk and rock clubs as well as trendy resturants are opening, as are new theaters.

A strange and interesting museum, typical of the area's spirit, is the **Tattoo Art Museum** at 30, 7th st. This museum is the private collection of the owner of the tattoo studio situated in the same building. For an adequate price, he will happily tattoo an indelible souvenir of the city on you, tel. 864-9798.

Japantown

Japantown, also known as Nihonmachi, is a new center and not very big. The Japanese population of San Francisco is about 12,000. Japantown is located on the edge of the Western Addition, a neighborhood of low-income housing units.

Japantown basically consists of a five-acre complex of modern shops and restaurants, centered around the **Peace Plaza**. The adjoining **Buchanan Street Mall**, between Post and Sutter is a small walking area lined with cherry trees. Beyond this, there is a sprinkling of Japanese restaurants and shops on the surrounding streets.

In the center of Peace Plaza is the five-tiered **Peace Pagoda**, donated by the children of Japan in memory of the victims of the atomic bombings of Hiroshima and Nagasaki.

Japantown loyalists claim that the sushi rage on the Pacific coast started right here, but then Little Tokyo in Los Angeles makes the same claim. In any case, there are numerous sushi bars, some very well-reputed, as well as several places specializing in Japanese noodles.

If you want to extend your knowledge of Japanese culture, Japantown is the place to search for books. The bookstore here carries an enormous variety of books (both in English and Japanese) on every aspect of Japanese history and culture. On the bottom floor of the shopping complex, at the east end of Peach Plaza, there is a display of amazing wooden sculptures. They are so finely and realistically detailed that the huge sea serpents seem about to breathe fire. Such sculptures sell for about $5,000.

Japantown, normally quiet and sedate, explodes with life during its several annual festivals. **The Cherry Blossom Festival**, held during two consecutive weekends towards the end of April, is an extravaganza. Some shows and exhibits charge admission, while many others are free. Thousands of people of all racial and ethnic groups gather for the parades, the performances, the incessant taiko drumming and the endless rain of cherry blossoms, a symbol in Japan of transient beauty. In August, the **summer festival** is held and shortly after that is the **Nihonmachi Street Fair**.

Union Street

Cow Hollow, once a dairyland area curving around the marina from Van Ness to the Presidio, might today be renamed Yuppie Hollow, and the only milk found here today is used in the coffeehouses along **Union Street**. The old Victorian buildings here have been refurbished and transformed into miniature shopping malls. Pedestrian malls between the buildings lead to courtyards lined with boutiques, and to barns filled with antiques. There are restaurants, bars and cafés in the nooks and crannies of the Victorian row. On Sunday the patios are filled with brunchers. In the evenings, the singles bars are patronized by trim and healthy looking pleasure seekers.

Around Union almost everything is slightly overpriced, in keeping with the atmosphere. Up Fillmore, toward California and Sacramento, are pockets of the same type of bar, but these are a little more reasonably priced.

Clement Street

Many San Franciscans who want good Chinese food prefer the area of Clement street to Chinatown. This new "restaurant row" of San Francisco is located not in one of the old, quaint, downtown established neighborhoods, but rather in the Richmond district, an everyday neighborhood set apart from the more bustling downtown area. It was once an area of Russian-Jewish immigrants, but now has a large Chinese population. The neighborhood would be basically nondescript if not for the strip of great restaurants running through it. On Geary, the main street parallel to the south, there is also an abundance of good new restaurants. A Saturday afternoon on Clement st. will find local neighborhood residents milling around the street, shopping or just window shopping at small shops, or hanging out at the local watering holes. There is hardly a tourist in sight. It has the atmosphere of a small-town main street. Clement st. is easily accessible by public transportation. Check with *MUNI* for exact routes.

The Mission

The predominantly Mexican **Mission District**, south of Market and between 16th and 24th sts., had a reputation for being run-down and dangerous. It is actually a very exciting, lively place to walk, but its best to dress casually and not carry flashy photo equipment.

There was a time when it was solidly Mexican, and filled with cheap *taqueras*. The *taqueras* are still here, the food cheap, delicious and filling, but they are being complemented now by Peruvian, Bolivian, El Salvadoran and Nicaraguan restaurants, in addition to the Arab and Asian restaurants on the fringe, and *McDonald's* and *Pioneer Chicken*. The Mission is filling with immigrants, many of them unofficial and uncounted but, illegal or not, culturally they are enriching this neighborhood. Meanwhile, there is also an influx of little expresso joints, and crowded cafes with a bohemian clientele. Walk around this area, take in some of the bright and powerful political murals that pop up in unexpected places (the public mural is a well-developed Mexican art form), and watch the people. Some of the best Latin beat music in the city can be found in little joints in the Mission.

The Mission is the place to buy a meal-in-a+burrito. It is impossible to eat a burrito elegantly as it is likely to explode on first bite. When you are finished and your temples throb from the hot sauce, cool down with a *paletta*, a fresh fruit bar which is refreshing and cheap, available in exotic flavors like mango.

On Capp and 16th, one small block east of Mission, is the old, ornate **Victoria Theater**. A little way down, at 65 Capp, is the **Capp Street Project**, a unique art program in which an artist lives on the premises for a specific time, working on a large art project which will be open to the public.

Mission Dolores, the oldest building in the city, dates back to 1782. It was originally established at another site in 1776, as the sixth in Junipero Serra's chain of missions. Dolores st. and 16th st. Open 9am-4pm. Admission $1, tel. 621-8203.

Castro Street

The strutting street-wise youths of the Mission make a sharp contrast to the men along Castro Street, the next neighborhood up the hill to the west. Castro Street is the center of a proud, strong and organized gay community. Strolling along and taking in all the color can be enjoyable, though the card stores are not for the easily embarrassed. The chic "fern bars" each seem to have their own particular type of gay clientele. The development is now extending to upper Market street as well. The neighborhhod is easily reached by *MUNI* Metro.

The gays of Castro have recently helped shape the city physically, culturally and politically. Gay entrepreneurs have transformed some of the pre-earthquake Victorian buildings into boutiques, bookstores and bars. They have elected a number of gay representatives. The **Gay Games** and **Gay Pride Day** attract spectators and participants of all ages and preferences.

The local gay community was recently shocked by the murder of gay supervisor Harvey Milk and Mayor George Moscone. More recently, the appearance of AIDS has devastated the community. With the first shock over, local gay organizations have taken assertive action in mobilizing public action to fight AIDS.

West and south of this area are **Twin Peaks** and **Mt. Davidson**, both of which offer expansive views of the city. Mt. Davidson is the highest point in the city, nearly 1,000 ft. (340 m) high. A visit to the Twin Peaks should be undertaken on a clear night, so as to enjoy the panoramic view.

Haight-Ashbury

Twenty five years ago, **Haight Street** and the surrounding Victorian neighborhood (of Haight-Ashbury) was filled with the electrifying excitement, color, vibes and drugs of the "new age" — the hippie era. Some of rock's greatest and most drug-pumped musicians lived and played in the area. When George Harrison walked down the street, it might as well have been the second coming. The Panhandle and Golden Gate park filled with youth for impromptu concerts, frisbee games and LSD sharing. The smell of pot was everywhere. The Victorian houses became crash pads, the stores took on new, garish fronts and sold the latest in drug paraphernalia. Underground newspapers heralded the new revolution. Psychedelic posters covered the walls. Streets were jammed with long-haired, blue-jeaned, beaded, broke and bloodshot youth.

Inevitably the crash came. Those who had turned on, burnt out. The pushers and exploiters moved in. Heroin made the rounds. Jimi Hendrix, Janis Joplin and Jim Morrison were only the better-known of the many who pushed and drugged themselves to death. With the start of robberies, rapes, muggings and sordid premature deaths the "new age" proved as tarnished as the old. Later the punks moved in with their dyed hair and shaved heads, their chain and leather fashions and fashionable rage.

Now the Haight is on an upswing, while still keeping its funky and alternative character and a feel for its past. The street has a strip of reasonable and tasty eateries. It's a good place to stoke up on a solid breakfast before a day of walking through Golden Gate Park, or to warm up with a cappuccino and a burrito. Along the Haight are small unusual art galleries displaying everything from primeval African masks to post-modern grotesquery.

Within a compact area are various stores which, in different ways, express some echo of the explosions of the sixties: a good old-fashioned "head shop", a radical bookstore, a fantasy bookstore, a record store of great oldies, several vintage clothing stores, a few organic veggie cafés, ethnic art and pop-art posters, and a boutique of sexual gadgetry. To keep the spirit authentic, there are still groups of bizarre-looking people floating up and down the street, some with hair below their shoulders, some with hairdos like peacock plumage. Some look incredibly young and others sadly old.

In the middle of the Haight is the *Red Victorian Moviehouse*, 1659 Haight, tel. 863-3994. Next door is the bed and breakfast inn of the same name. This theater offers great old movies, including daily matinees, in a setting as pretty and entertaining as anything on screen, and the popcorn is free.

At *Haight Books*, 1682 Haight, the books are piled high and there are places to sit. A bright arched store front with gargoyles and other creatures marks *Play With It*, 1660 Haight. Inside there is every kind of toy that your nephew, kid or you could want. There's a play table for children, and an artificial waterfall plunges from the gallery into the miniature boat pond.

The *Anarchist Collective Bookstore*, 1369 Haight, includes a library and reading area. Don't request Ayn Rand. Despite the heavy name, *Bones of Our Ancestors*, 622 Shrader, off Haight, sells fine silver work, gems and cut stones, crafted by a couple who could win mellow-of-the-year award.

Bicycle rentals are available at *Avenue Cyclery* on Haight just up from Stanyon, for $2 or $3 per hour.

Golden Gate Park

The long, narrow, green strip that is Golden Gate Park, is criss-crossed with cycling paths and foot paths, and has small secluded spots for reading, relaxing or courting. There are wide fields, ponds with ducks and swans, several museums, bright gardens, and an open-air stage for weekend concerts. One could easily spend a day in the park, especially on a weekend when it is closed to traffic and all sorts of people gather and stroll through. Some of the weekend roller-skating here is almost ballet.

The area was covered with shifting sand dunes when acquired by San Francisco in 1852. Squatters claimed it as their own and backed that claim with armed guards. When the city proposed plans for a large municipal park, the idea was ridiculed. Yet the city administration — with tremendous foresight — persisted with the plan, battling shifting sands and shifting politicians. In 1887, John McLaren, a Scottish gardener, was appointed park superintendent at the age of 40 and, until his death at 96, he dedicated himself to shaping a beautiful, variegated landscape with thousands of species of plants from all around the world.

Ironically, the park which was once ridiculed, helped shape the city. The trolley lines, that were laid down from the east to make the park accessible, defined areas for rows of houses and new neighborhoods. The park also became a refugee center after the 1906 earthquake, and was home to some families for almost a year.

The park is bordered by Stanyon st. on the east, the ocean on the west, Lincoln on the south and Fulton on the north.

Several bike and skate rental outlets can be found along Fulton. The narrow Panhandle extends east from Stanyon, skirting Haight-Ashbury.

Park headquarters, at Fell and Stanyon sts. can provide maps and information. Open daily 9am-6pm, tel. 558-3706.

The **Conservatory of Flowers** just west of headquarters, resembles an old Victorian palace which some wizard, with a sweep of his hand has turned into glass. Among the 7,000 plants are rare orchids that normally grow at elevations up to 5,000 feet in dense fog. The conservatory's mark of distinction is its ability to grow plants from high-altitude subtropical and cloud forests. Open daily, admission fee.

Centered around the music concourse, which hosts free Sunday concerts at 1pm, are the park's main museums: The California Academy of Science, with the Steinhart Aquarium and Morrison Planetarium, and on the opposite side of the concourse, the de Young Art Museum and the Asian Art Museum.

The **Academy of Science** is the oldest scientific museum in the west. Open daily from 10am-5pm, until 7pm in summer. Admission fee. The first Wednesday of every month is free, tel. 750-7145. It presents a varied array of exhibits, depicting natural history, the physical sciences, the evolution of man and the diversity of primitive cultures.

The **Morrison planetarium** offers special shows on such subjects as Halley's Comet and extraterrestials. Separate tickets. $2 for adults, $1 for youth and seniors. For recorded schedules and sky information, tel. 750-7141. The planetarium also presents the colorful, wild Laserium show. $5 regular, $4 matinee, $3 seniors and youth, tel. 750-7138 for schedules.

The **M.H. de Young Museum** has a well-rounded selection spanning the history of western art from its Egyptian and Classic origins, through to modern European art. The American Galleries span the history of America as depicted through its art. Open Wed.-Sun. 10am-5pm. $4 admission valid for the Asian Art Museum and Palace of the Legion of Honor on the same day. Saturday morning and the first Wednesday and Saturday of each month is free, tel. 750-3600. During the summer, both the de Young and the Asian Art Museum are open late each Wednesday to 8:45pm, with free entrance after 5pm, free tours, and free special events such as concerts or lectures. There is also a café in the museum, which makes a summer Wednesday evening an ideal time to absorb yourself in art.

The **Asian Art Museum** in a wing of the de Young, is internationally known for the scope of its collection of eastern art, which includes the famous Avery Brundager collection. The library is open Tues.-Fri. 1-4:45pm. Entry to this museum is free the first Wednesday of each month, tel. 668-8921.

Near the two art museums is the **Japanese Tea Garden**, constructed in 1894. Open from 8am-6pm, $1 adults, 50 cents seniors and youth, and under age six admitted free. Free to all before 9am and after 5pm. A brochure with a map and history of the garden is available at the ticket booth for 25 cents. The tea house is a pretty spot to relax. Open 10:30am-5:30pm.

The distinctive Japanese landscape was created by a wealthy Japanese gardener who had worked with nobility in Japan. He and his family lived in a house in the garden and sculptured the landscape around them, with the help of immigrant gardeners from Japan who worked on the grounds in exchange for room and board. However, ugly political reality penetrated even this delicately sculpted Japanese garden and the family was expelled and interned, along with many thousands of American Japanese during World War II. The "Japanese Tea Garden" became "The Oriental Tea Garden". Only several years after the war was the original name restored but the original gardening family never regained its position. The garden today is an exotic little island of pagodas, fish ponds, curved wooden bridges and carved Japanese gates.

Exotic plants flourish in the **Strybing Arboretum and Botanical Gardens**, which contains a huge variety of plants from Chile, Australia, Southeast Asia, the Mediterranean and California. Open weekdays, 8am-4:30pm, and 10am-5pm weekends and holidays. Admission free, tel. 661-0668. The **Garden of Fragrance**, designed for the visually impaired, displays plants chosen for their color, texture and fragrance.

Scattered throughout the park are 11 lakes, each with its own character. Rent a boat and row to Strawberry Hill in the middle of Stow Lake, where you'll find Rainbow Falls. For something completely American, there is the buffalo paddock. The park has riding stables toward the western end. For those who want to experience the Victorian atmosphere of the park, there are buggy rides, ranging from 10 to 90 minutes, and $5 to $60, accordingly.

South of Golden Gate Park, near the corner of 19th Ave. and Sloat, is the **Stern Grove**, a beautiful natural amphitheatre surrounded by fir, eucalyptus and redwood trees, where a great series of free concerts is held every Sunday during the summer. For programs, tel. 558-4728.

The City's Coast

Although San Francisco is a crowded city, the entire western edge of the city's peninsula is fringed with parks and recreational areas, from Fort Fenston in the south to the tip of the peninsula beneath the Golden Gate Bridge, and continuing east along Crissy Field and the Marina to Fort Mason. Most of these areas are joined, and together they comprise the **Golden Gate National Recreation Area** (GGNRA) administered by the National Park Service. Following the paths that link these areas together — either in their entirety or in sections — is an excellent way of getting to know this unique city. This urban-natural area extends across the bridge into Marin County up to Point Reyes. At Fort Ferston it is possible to see the concrete remains of the bunkers and gun emplacements designed to protect the Pacific Coast from Japanese invasion during World War II. It is a great place to watch or photograph hang gliders as they leap off the cliffs or soar above the beach and water. Opposite Ocean Beach, on Sloat st. near the Great Highway, is the

San Francisco Zoo, which includes a children's zoo. Open daily 10am-5pm, tel. 661-4844.

Ocean Beach extends north to the rocky headland on which the *Cliff House* is built. Since 1863 this restaurant has offered refreshment and gorgeous views. It is an extremely relaxing place to sit and sip some Irish coffee. Downstairs below the *Cliff House* is a platform affording a closer view of **Seal Rock**, covered with seals which are easily seen and heard. Located here is a National Park Service Visitor Center, tel. 556-8642, with a small exhibit on the history of the area. Information is available on the trails which lead from here to the Golden Gate Bridge and beyond. Across from the Visitor Center is the **Musee Mechanique**, displaying old arcade games which test your strength and tell your fortune. The **Camera Obscura** gallery-museum takes the visitor inside a camera and allows a close view of Seal Rock.

Above the *Cliff House* is **Sutro Heights Park**, offering a view of Seal Rock and the coast. Down the slope to the north are the ruins of the gigantic Sutro Baths which served as a quiet country resort for many years until it burned down.

Just north of Sutro Heights, a trail leads down the tree-covered slopes to **Land's End**, a small protected cove in which you might think you're in another world, especially on a foggy day. There is no vehicle access and no swimming allowed, due to rough waves. Above these slopes in **Lincoln Park**, off California st. is the **California Palace of the Legion of Honor**, modeled after a French palace, and housing an art museum. The emphasis is largely on French art. Greeting visitors is Rodin's famous sculpture *The Thinker*, and inside the museum there are more of his sculptures. Open Wed.-Sun. 10am-5pm. A single admission fee of $4 allows entrance to the **de Young Museum** and the **Asian Art Museum** as well. Free the first Wednesday of each month, tel. 750-3600.

From the museum, **El Camino Del Mar** follows the coast through shady groves, and offers beautiful views of the Golden Gate with ships sailing under the bridge. Nearby **China Beach** is one of the few swimming beaches in the city. Open 7am to dusk with changing rooms, showers, restrooms and a lifeguard. A little beyond it is **Baker's Beach**, offering nice views but no swimming. The coastal road here runs between parkland and the **Presidio**, the large military base that looks more like a country club.

Hiking trails through the western edge of the city lead to the Golden Gate Bridge. There is a parking area for cars, and buses 28, 29 and 76 stop here. The 76 continues into the national recreation area in the western part of the Marin Peninsula. One of the nicest ways to spend a free day is to take a bus to the bridge, walk across and hike on to Sausalito via the side road to the east, past Fort Baker. After refreshment and browsing in Sausalito, return by ferry to the city.

Fort Point, now a preserved historical site is situated near the water directly beneath the Golden Gate Bridge, at the narrowest point of the strait between ocean and bay. Built before the Civil War, it was modeled after the many fortresses in the east which were in use during the war. Fort Point, however, never had occasion to test its invulnerability. The view of the bridge is unique. There is a museum, and guided tours are available. Open daily from 10am-5pm. Admission free, tel. 556-1693.

To the east of Fort Point is **Crissy Field**, with a foot path and open beach. This brings a walker to the Marina, and the long green with its guided exercise path. Beyond that lies Fort Mason, which houses the GGNRA headquarters (see ''Fort Mason'').

San Francisco Bay

San Francisco Bay is not actually a bay, but an estuary, the transition zone between fresh and salty water. The 50-mile (80 km) long estuary is made up of delicate ecosystems that weave together to form a unique biological and ecological community which includes grey whales that migrate along its coast (every year one or two stray into the bay), marine organisms that are born here and migrate out to sea, and crustaceans and plankton in the inland marshes. Rivers fed by fresh water in the Sierras and the Cascades flow into the Great Central Valley, and then out into the San Francisco Bay.

Unfortunately, the bay has been somewhat spoilt by landfill and dumping of wastes. Parts of the bay were filled to create additional land for residential and industrial development. Once the bay was edged by 300 square miles of delicate, biologically rich marshland, but today three-quarters of this area has been filled. Untreated waste water was poured steadily into the bay right up to the 1960s.

While wastes increased, the natural flushing action that pushed them into the bay decreased. Most of the fresh water from the feeding rivers is diverted for Central Valley agriculture. This plays havoc with the delicately balanced ecosystems of the estuary.

In the mid-sixties, a citizen's organization spearheaded by a group of Berkeley women set out to oppose the developers and federal planners who had diverted water from and filled in the bay. The fight against many local cities and huge corporations seemed futile and quixotic at first, but a groundswell of support arose from local residents, and after tough political battles a state commission was assigned to study and control future bay development.

This fight helped to stir up environmental battles and protests across the country over projects that in an earlier era would have been implemented without forethought. The commission has even helped the bay start to reclaim a little of its lost territory, by assuring that if an area is filled, a previously filled area will be broken open to the water.

But the struggle for control of the fate of the beautiful San Francisco Bay is ongoing and endless. There are increased controls on landfill and dumping, and a vast increase in the amount of land set aside as parks and reserves, but freshwater, the lifeblood of the bay's ecosystems, is still siphoned off upriver.

There are several organizations, some educational and non-profit, others private, that provide "ecological" cruises. These examine and explain various ecological communities in the huge and variegated bay area. Some are seasonal, following the migration of the grey whales:

The Oceanic Society: Building 240, Fort Mason, tel. 441-5970. Field trips in the marine environment, trips to the Farallon Islands, guided cruises to bay islands.

Nature Expeditions International: 599 College ave., Palo Alto, 94306, tel. 328-6572. Whale-watching expeditions to Monterey Bay (January); all-day Farallon Islands trips, each weekend from mid-April through May; one-day nature cruises highlighting the natural history of the bay area.

Canoe Trips West: 217 Redwood Highway, Greenbrae, 94906, tel. 461-1750. Canoe trips, accompanied by naturalists, around the marshland, several times a year. Self-guided tours of the estuaries and lagoons, all year round.

Marine Ecological Institute: 811 Harbor blvd., Redwood City, 94063, tel. 364-2760. A four-hour "discovery voyage" in the southern bay. Also, "Bay Discovery Day".

Golden Gate Audubon Society: 2718 Telegraph ave. 206 Berkeley, 94705, tel. 843-2222. Bay shoreline field trips, bird trips throughout northern California, spring birding cruises to the Farallons. Trips from Monterey for bird-watching and whale-watching.

Important addresses and phone numbers

Area Code: 415.
Visitor Information Center: Hallidie Plaza, tel. 974-6900. At Powell and Market, below street level, near the entry to the *BART* station. 24-hour information recording: tel. 391-2000.
International Hospitality Center: 312 Sutter st. Suite 402, tel. 986-1388.
Center for International Educational Exchange (CIEE): 317 Sutter st., tel. 421-3473. Student travel information.
Teleguide: Recreation and entertainment information filed in computers that are available to the public in various *BART* stations. For details, tel. 957-2999.

Greyhound: 50 7th st., tel. 433-1500. Downtown.
Trailways: 425 Mission st., tel. 982-6400. At Transbay Terminal.
Green Tortoise: 1st and Natoma, tel. 285-2441.
Amtrak: 425 Mission st., tel. 556-8287. At Transbay Terminal.
San Francisco Municipal Railway (MUNI): 673-MUNI. Info from 9am-5pm.
AC Transit: tel. 839-2882. Buses to and within east bay area.
Samtrans: tel. 761-7000. To San Mateo County, and south along peninsula.
Golden Gate Transit: Buses to and within Marin County.
Caltrain: tel. 557-8661, or tel. 800-558-8661. Regional trains.
Bay Area Rapid Transit (BART): tel. 788-BART.
Travelers Aid Society: 38 Mason, tel. 781-6738; also 50 7th, tel. 868-1503. 24 hours.
Ambulance: tel. 431-2800.
National Park Service: Fort Mason, tel. 556-4122. General information, and specific information on places within the Golden Gate National Recreation Area.
Heritage Walks: 2007 Franklin st., tel. 441-3004, or tel. 441-3000. Guided tours on various aspects of old San Francisco architecture, and the history of the waterfront.
California Road Conditions: tel. 557-3755.
Ticketron: tel. 495-4089 for recording; tel. 393-6914 for ticket info.
Hospital: S.F. General Hospital. 1001 Portrero ave., tel. 821-8111.
Telex and Telegrams: Western Union. 201 3rd st., or by phone tel. 800-433-5520, 24-hour service.
Dental Referral Service: tel. 673-3189.
Post Office: Main Branch at 7th and Mission, tel. 556-2600.

Driving over the bridge

Around San Francisco

The Peninsula

South of San Francisco, the peninsula extends toward San Jose, the rich Santa Clara Valley and the Santa Cruz Mountains. The area is rapidly developing into one suburban mass.

Stanford University is the large and verdant centerpiece of Palo Alto. One of the finest and most prestigious universities in the country, it contrasts sharply with the active and sometimes stormy atmosphere of Berkeley. Around the university are some very good bookstores, plus some interesting shops, cafes, restaurants and cinemas. At the student center in **Tressider Union,** campus information and free maps can be obtained, tel. 497-4719.

A free shuttle runs through the huge campus. Bicycles can be rented on campus. Student-guided tours are conducted during the school year and summer. Swimming, windsurfing and boating are available on the artificial lake on campus. The two main sites to see on campus are the **Stanford Linear Accelerator** and the **Museum of Art.** The mile-long research facilities of the accelerator can be viewed by pre-arranged tour, tel. 854-3300, ext. 2004. The Museum of Art includes ancient art as well as a Rodin collection.

The city of **San Jose**, with a population of 700,000, has grown without any apparent order. Gobbling the surrounding rich farmland and small towns, it has spread and sprawled into a city larger than San Francisco. San Jose is the unchallenged center of the high-tech **Silicon Valley**.

You can visit the **Winchester Mystery House**, 525 S. Winchester blvd., by Route 17 and I-280. In summer, 9am-5:30pm. Call to check on shorter hours in fall and winter. Admission fee, tel. 408-247-2101. Firearms heiress Sarah Winchester tried to outwit the ghosts she knew were pursuing her, by making her house into a huge maze, with 160 rooms, and doors and stairways leading nowhere. The kitschy, commercial tour also leads nowhere, but the story is bizarre enough to lure in the unsuspecting.

The string of small towns, state parks and reserves along the San Mateo coast, on Highway 1, have thus far been spared the suburban expansion climbing the eastern slopes of the hills. There are coves, beaches and tidepools to explore. South of Half Moon Bay, San Gregorio Beach, with its shoreline caves, is especially beautiful. South of Pigeon Point is the **Ano Nuevo State Reserve** for the big lumbering elephant seals. This is one of the few areas where these animals can be approached closely. Five miles (8 km) inland at **Butano State Park** there are redwood forests, laced with trails.

Two pleasant youth hostels are found at Montara Lighthouse Point, and further south at Pigeon Point. There are several state park campgrounds along the coast as well, at Half Moon Bay and Butano State Park.

Berkeley

There's a time when the operation of the machine becomes so odious, makes you so sick at heart, that you can't take part, you can't even tacitly take part. And you've got to put your bodies upon the gears and upon the wheels, upon the levers, upon all the apparatus, and you've got to make it stop.

Mario Savio, Free Speech Movement leader.
Berkeley, 1964.

Berkeley, a city of 100,000, east of the bay, has traditionally been a center of political and intellectual ferment. This was intensified during the 1960s and '70s when the city became one of the main centers of the Vietnam War protests. Citizen groups tackled rent control law, the police and the power utilities, as well as international issues. In the early 1970s, a radical coalition was elected to the city council, but somehow it never accomplished much and lost much of its momentum and original support.

It's to Berkeley's credit that it is very probably the only urban community that has retained its original charm and colorfulness — the kind that flourished in the turbulent sixties — unlike the commercialized Santa Cruz or the crime-ridden Haight-Ashbury in nearby San Francisco. On arriving in town, drive to Telegraph rd. (outside the campus entrance) with its colorful stalls, quaint shops and cafés, and absorb that special local liberal atmosphere that has disappeared totally from many urban centers on the West Coast.

How to get there

Berkeley is located off I-80 north of the Oakland Bay Bridge. The University ave. exit is the main one and leads right to the university, but finding parking in the campus area is extremely difficult.

Berkeley is easily accessible from San Francisco by *BART*. A shuttle, named *Humphrey Go-BART*, runs from the main *BART* station at Shattuck to the university campus and university properties in the hills. The local bus system, *AC Transit*, also runs to San Francisco but is generally slower than *BART*. However it covers the Berkeley-Oakland region extensively. Bicycles are allowed on certain *BART* trains, and a bicycle affords an easy and excellent way to tour the campus. They are available for rental around the campus area.

One central number serves as a transportation clearing house. No further calls should be necessary, as this number can refer you to any other transportation office you might need, tel. 644-POOL.

Accommodations

Berkeley is not the ideal place to seek lodgings. There is very little middle ground here. Lodgings are either in the very high bracket of the hotel/motel chains, or dingy old hotels along Telegraph. Along University ave. there are a few standard motels, none of them especially scintillating. On the bayshore near Route 80 there are some motor inns, and near the marina is the modern _Marina Mariott_, tel. 548-7920.

Food

There is considerably more choice in restaurants than there is in lodging in Berkeley. On Telegraph, restaurants rise and fall quickly, but there are a few standbys that have developed excellent reputations, for good reason, through many student generations. Shattuck ave., more staid as a shopping area, has seen a number of new restaurants open in the last few years. With competition tight for the student market, there are many good eating deals around.

Mario's La Fiesta: On Telegraph and Haste, tel. 540-9213. Mosaics around the entrance, tiles on the tables, large and delicious servings, and sometimes lines out the door. Very reasonable.

The Soup Kitchen: Telegraph and Dwight Way: Serves healthy food in a rustic atmosphere.

Edy's: 2201 Shattuck ave., in the heart of downtown. Carved wooden booths, old-time feeling. You almost expect to see ponytails and bobby socks. Good old-fashioned ice cream concoctions.

The Blue Nile: 2525 Telegraph. Excelllent Ethopian food. If you really want to show your worldliness, scoop up some entree with injira bread and feed your companion.

Chez Panisse: 1517 Shattuck ave, tel. 548-5525. A restaurant in a different class to most of the local places. Known for mesquite-grilled entrees. Expensive.

Spengers Fish Grotto: 1919 4th st., tel. 845-7771. Near the highway. A grotto it is, and an established, popular seafood place.

What to see

Although much of the culture of Berkeley emanates from the university, the city has a vibrant life of its own, with lots of music clubs and coffee houses, and with innumerable political, spiritual, alternative and therapeutic groups announcing themselves from every pole and billboard. In the hills to the east are the beautiful, ornate homes of the wealthy, the professionals and the prestigious professors. The campus area is dominated by thousands of students. In the flatlands toward the bay, live minority groups, as well as artists and old-time radicals who stayed in Berkeley after finishing school years ago.

The **Berkeley Campus** is the oldest of the nine University of California campuses. It started with a class of 191 students in 1873, and now has 31,000 students. Berkeley is one of the most honored and prestigious universities in the world. Its graduate school has been rated the best in the country, even better than Harvard's, and it is a public institution in which students do not pay very high fees. Relations between the huge institution and its students and the surrounding community have, however, periodically been tense.

In the fall of 1964 the Free Speech Movement split the campus wide open when the university attempted to restrict political activity on campus, especially the dissemination of political information by former students and outsiders.

An escalating game of nerves was played out in Sproul Plaza. A former student was apprehended by the police for distributing pamphlets in the plaza, and by the time a police car was called the police were astounded to find themselves blocked in by thousands of students. For 36 hours the trapped police car, with the detainee inside, became a convenient soapbox for endless political speeches. As one confrontation sparked another, 3,000 students finally engaged in a passive sit-in in Sproul Hall, the administration building, and were dragged out one by one by the police.

By the next summer, the growing discontent on campus focused on the Vietnam War. The tactics of civil disobedience used by students the previous fall were applied to military objectives in the bay area. Throughout the sixties, the Berkeley campus sustained the strongest local anti-war movement in the nation. With political activity once more flourishing on campus and various groups exchanging ideas at Sproul Plaza, a whole flurry of causes spinning off from the anti-war movement also appeared.

In 1969, the campus again exploded over a university-linked issue, centering around a tiny plot of land to be used for a new sports facility. The move would have entailed removing some homeless "street people" who had adopted the lot as their own. Suddenly "Peoples' Park" became a symbol of a basic clash of values, and the university was viewed as the personification of an impassive and dangerous power structure. There were mass rallies on campus and in the park, followed by a police sweep of the park. The days of passive sit-ins had gone. Violent clashes occurred on Telegraph avenue and, finally, one spectator was killed and another was blinded by police gunfire.

By the spring of the following year, Berkeley was one of the leaders in the nation-wide anti-war movement that disrupted the nation's colleges, as American forces bombed Cambodia. Governor Ronald Reagan called out the National Guard, and residents faced the incredible spectacle of tanks rumbling down Berkeley's streets. In Sproul Plaza, thousands of demonstrators were hemmed in by Guardsmen wearing gas masks, while tear gas was dropped on the helpless victims.

Campus protests lost momentum after that but occasionally flared up over specific campus-oriented issues. In 1974 student Patty Hearst, of the Hearst newpaper dynasty, was kidnapped by a radical group called the Symbionese Liberation Army. In a bizarre twist of events, the abducted heiress became a gun-toting, bank-robbing gang member spouting revolutionary rhetoric, and it appeared that something had gone askew with the idealistic protests of a decade earlier.

The late 1970s saw a resurgence of fraternities, sports, and a concern with practical majors leading to immediate careers. Today, issues such as Nicaragua and South Africa still stir a certain portion of the students. In the summer of 1986, a long campaign by campus and local activists resulted in the university divesting itself of financial interests in South Africa.

The student political information tables still stand in Sproul Plaza, where they caused turmoil 20 years ago, but they do not attract the same crowds. Students rush past, pause to listen to a guitarist, buy a donut or felafel or laugh at the evangelist on the corner of Bancroft and Telegraph.

At the **Student Union**, at Bancroft and Telegraph, you will find the Visitor Center. Open Mon.-Fri. 8am-5pm, Saturday 10am-6pm. Self-guiding tour maps are available and guided tours are held on weekdays at 1pm. Upstairs, watch the chess games in the lounge, or mingle with the students downstairs in the *Bear's Lair Pub.* A bookstore, student art gallery, and box office, with a schedule of all campus events, are located here. The free paper, the *Daily Californian,* lists all events, concerts, etc., on and off campus.

Walk through Sproul Plaza to **Sather Gate**, which once marked the southern end of the campus, under which many protest marches flowed in the 1960s. The bas relief sculptures of nude figures, controversial and kept in storage for over 60 years, were finally installed in 1981.

The campus, while serving a huge urban university, has a quiet, verdant almost rural beauty to it. Near the northwest corner of campus is a peaceful eucalyptus grove. Toward the other end of campus is the quaint and shady **Faculty Glen**, with an old log cabin at the top and a stream running at the bottom.

The structure in the center of the campus, resembling a set of gaping concrete jaws, is the **Moffitt Undergraduate Library**, and nearby, on the east is **Doe Library**, the main library, with its long, cathedral-like reference room. On entering Doe from the north side, to your immediate right is one of those gems little known even to Berkeley students: a plush and polished reading room, in which you half expect to see Ralph Waldo Emerson puffing on a pipe by the fire.

Rather Tower, the **Campanile**, offers a panoramic view of the bay. Take the elevator to view the 61-bell carillon. The bells chime out a variety of melodies every weekday, in concerts at 8am, noon and 6pm.

At Euclid and Hearst, on the north side of campus, away from the hubbub of Telegraph, is a block of stores, restaurants, and cafés.

The university houses a number of museums on or adjacent to campus. A list of them with phone numbers is available at the Visitor Center.

Bancroft Library is located in North Hall, one of the two original structures of the university. The library contains the university's collection of rare books and Western Americana, in addition to temporary rotating exhibitions. The library holds the first gold nugget found in the California gold rush, and the collected papers of Mark Twain.

The **Earth Sciences Building** houses the Museum of Paleontology, the **Museum of Geology**, and the **Seismographic Station**. The **Museum of Paleontology** has an extensive collection of artifacts made by Ishi, the last known survivor of the Yana Indians of California. Ishi was found near Oroville and brought to San Francisco in 1911 by Berkeley anthropologists. The displays of his handiwork are sad reminders of the Indian cultures which disappeared during the 19th century. Open Mon., Tues., Thurs. and Fri. 10am-4:30pm. Weekends noon-4:30pm. $1.50 adults, 25 cents for children under 16 and seniors. Free on Thursday.

Across Bancroft avenue, from Krober Hall, the **University Art Museum** includes 11 exhibition galleries, a sculpture garden, and permanent collections of Asian and Western art, video and film collections, and a collection of the paintings of Hans Hoffman. There is a bookstore and café-restaurant. ($2 adults, $1 non-U.C. students, seniors and children 6-17. Free admission Thursday 11-noon.)

Also housed in the museum is the **Pacific Film Archives**, entrance from Durant ave., with continuous programs ranging from the classic to the obscure.

Up in the hills behind the campus are the **Botanical Gardens**, and the Lawrence Hall of Science, accessible by *Humphrey Go-BART*. The **Lawrence Hall of Science** is a great place to experience the sense of wonder that science is all about. Viewers participate in many activities covering a wide range of the sciences. There are planetarium programs, films and lectures. Open weekdays 10am-4:30pm, till 9pm on Thursday. Weekends, 10am-5pm. $2.50 adults, $1.50 seniors, non-U.C. students, youth 7-18. Free on Thursday after 4pm.

Up the hill from the Science Hall lies green and rolling **Tilden Park**. The 30-acre Botanical Garden in **Strawberry Canyon** holds a tremendous variety of plants from several terrains. Open 9am-4:45pm daily. Admission free. In a compact area you can walk from desert to lush rain forest, and then enter a jungle created in a greenhouse.

The **Berkeley Rose Garden**, at Euclid ave. and Eunice, shows unusual roses and has a beautiful view of the bay. The **Judas Magnes Museum** exhibits an extensive collection of Judaica. 2911 Russel st. Open Sun.-Fri., 10am-4pm, tel. 849-2710.

On **Telegraph Avenue** there has been a distinct rise in the level of style and fashion of the stores, with the appearance of little expresso places, new boutiques, and chain bookstores.

However, some things along this perennial Berkeley strip remain unchanged; the street vendors selling crafts, the panhandlers, the cult missionaries, the great used bookstores and a few old hippies.

There is an interesting selection of bookstores on the stretch of **Bancroft ave.**, bordering Telegraph and facing the campus. There is the *University Press Bookstore*, the huge *Campus Textbook Exchange*, a combination bookstore-café, a map center, and the *Wilderness Press*, an excellent source for books on the outdoors.

People are still gathering at **People's Park**, east of Telegraph between Haste and Dwight Way. Young people sleep under the trees or lounge on old discarded furniture with the stuffing popping out. Backpacks, sleeping bags and ragged bundles are piled up. Mohawk haircuts and dyed hair, are blended with long hippie hair and beads, worn by kids who could be the children of those who created the style.

On the block of Telegraph between Haste and Dwight Way, some of the classic Berkeley hangouts still exist. On Dwight and Telegraph is *Shakespeare's Used Books*, next to the veritable *Café Mediterranean* (the *Med*) where customers have been discussing Kafka and announcing God for decades. Three other bookstores on the block are institutions: *Shambala Books*, where you can sit on wooden benches and browse through every kind of spiritual text you could hope to find in this incarnation; multi-leveled *Moe's Books*, and *Cody's*, a huge store with a wide selection in every major field and a café.

Shattuck avenue is the main shopping area of Berkeley. It adjoins with University to form the main corner. There are a sprinkling of good restaurants, but far more variety is packed into the lively area off Telegraph avenue.

Important addresses and phone numbers

Chamber of Commerce: 1834 University ave., tel. 845-1212.
University of California Visitors Information Center: Student Union, in Sproul Plaza, tel. 642-5215.
Council on International Educational Exchange (CIEE) Travel Center: 2511 Channing Way, tel. 848-8604. A goldmine of information for member and student travelers.
Greyhound: tel. 834-3070.
Amtrak: tel. 982-2278. Station in Oakland.
AC Transit: tel. 653-3535.
Bay Area Rapid Transit (BART): tel. 465-2278.
Berkeley Switchboard: 1901 8th st., tel.848-0800.
Ticketron: Tower Posters, 2350 Telegraph ave., tel. 548-5638.

Marin County

Marin County is located on the peninsula north of San Francisco, connected by the Golden Gate Bridge. It is a combination of small towns, affluent suburbs, beautiful hills, shady glens and rugged coast. The peninsula is served by both _MUNI_ and _Golden Gate Transit_. The latter provides the only local transportation.

The Marin sector of the GGNRA is wild, rugged cliffside country that gives a totally different perspective to the city skyline.

You can sit at isolated **Point Bonita**, thrust out into the Pacific far beyond the bridge, in the midst of a cold ocean wind and churning waves, feeling totally alone in the world, and still have time after an exhilarating hike, to sip beer or coffee in a hip, fern-filled, polished and cozy Sausalito café.

How to get there

MUNI bus 76 starts from downtown San Francisco, crosses the Golden Gate Bridge and heads west to **Rodeo Beach** on the edge of the Pacific and out of the city. From here you can choose from a network of trails that will take you in any direction, including north, to the extensive trail system of Mt. Tamalpais State Park, tel. 388-2070.

What to see

For a beautiful, not too difficult hike, follow the **Bobcat Trail** up into the ridges, to the **Morning Sun Trail**, and then across the freeway to Sausalito and a ferry ride home. There is no better place in the bay area to watch the sunset than from a ferry, as the sun sinks behind the span and spires of the Golden Gate Bridge.

Tennessee Valley, accessible only by foot from the end of Tennessee Valley Road, is worth the hike of about two miles (3 km). It is a lush narrow valley ending in a small beach, completely isolated from the urbanized world.

The Marine Headlands Visitor Center, open 8:30am-5pm, tel. 331-1540, sponsors a wide range of guided hikes, history programs, and workshops. Included in these are guided hikes to the isolated lighthouse at Point Bonito. Open 8:30am-5pm, tel. 331-1540. The *Golden Gate Hostel* is situated near the southern cliffs of the headlands (see San Francisco, "Accommodations").

Located in Fort Cronkite on the Marin headlands is the **California Marine Mammal Center**, a non-profit organization dedicated to rescuing and rehabilitating injured and ailing marine mammals, mainly seals and sea lions, but occasionally dolphins and whales as well. Open to visitors, but usually only to groups, so call first. Open 10am-5pm, tel. 331-0161.

Sausalito, on the Bay side of the Marin peninsula, was once a small, isolated fishing village, connected to the city by ferry prior to the building of the Golden Gate Bridge. Backed by the Marin headlands and fronted by the wharves and bay, its rustic houses were dug into the steep hillsides. Jack London once lived and worked here.

Now it has been elaborately decked out for tourists, its old buildings filled with quaint and pricey tourist shops. Nevertheless, it is a pleasant place to stroll through, especially after a bracing walk across the Golden Gate Bridge or through the wild headlands. There are bars, restaurants and cafés, and visitor information is available at the Sausalito Chamber of Commerce, 333 Caledonia st., tel. 332-0505.

The **San Francisco Bay and Delta Model**, built and operated by the U.S. Army Corps of Engineers, is a hydraulic scale model which reproduces the tides, flow, currents and other forces at work in the bay region. 2100 Bridgeway. Open Tues.-Sat. 9am-4pm, tel. 332-3870.

Beyond the main Sausalito docks floats a separate world of houseboats. The imagination — not to mention the material — that go into these creations is amazing. There have periodically been quarrels between the houseboat dwellers and development authorities, but they are still afloat.

The *Golden Gate Ferry* makes the run to San Francisco's Embarcadero, and the *Red and White Fleet* ferry docks at Fisherman's Wharf.

East of Sausalito lies the peninsula of **Tiburon**, with the small port section at the southern end, across from Angel Island State Park. Less crowded than Sausalito, Tiburon is also a nice place to stroll and has what is reputedly the best selection of waterfront restaurants on the bay, with a wide range of cuisine and prices.

They are lined up, literally, side by side, some with open decks. Tiny **Main Street** has the usual art shops, and you can enjoy some wine-tasting around the corner at Tiburon Vintners. Further on is **Ark Row**, consisting of turn-of-the-century boats which were beached and turned into a row of small shops.

The *Red and White Fleet* ferry from San Francisco serves both Angel Island and Tiburon, and nearby is the *Angel Island Ferry*, traveling between the port and the island park. A fine day's excursion would be to explore Angel Island by foot or bike, then continue to Tiburon for a meal, and return to the city. From time to time, the ferry company makes a special arrangement whereby, if you eat at one of several specific Tiburon restaurants, you can receive $2 back on the price of the ferry ticket.

Angel Island is a natural and historic preserve in the mouth of the bay, just south of Tiburon. Serving at various times as an Indian hunting ground for sea otters and seals, a whaling supply station and a cattle ranch and military base, it finally became the arrival point for immigration from the west. A flood of European immigrants was expected after the opening of the Panama Canal. They never came, but waves of Asian immigrants arrived, and encountered the vagaries of American prejudice. Filipinos and Japanese were admitted, while Chinese were held in barracks, where their inscriptions of frustration can still be read today.

The island is closed to cars, but bicycles are allowed. There are paths for cycling, a beautiful five-mile (8 km) loop trail, and a history and ecology museum. Campsites are available by reservation. Regular ferry service is available from both Tiburon and Fisherman's Wharf.

For ferry information from Tiburon, tel. 435-2131; from Fisherman's Wharf, tel. 546-2815; for campsite reservations, tel. 800-952-5580, and for general information, tel. 435-1915.

Mt. Tamalpais State Park is a favorite with local hikers. It has dense forests and magnificient views, as well as access by foot and car to the popular Stinson Beach Park. Its summit is accessible only on foot. "Mount Tam" is also where the newest outdoor rage was born. People who formerly spent hundreds of dollars on fancy racing and touring bicycles can now spend hundreds of dollars on "mountain bikers": lower, sturdier, wider, knobby-wheeled bicycles that can zoom up and down dirt paths, slopes and trails. A map of trails is available at the Pantoll Ranger Station on Panoramic Way, tel. 388-2070. The map indicates bike-in camping spots ($1 per night, first-come, first-serve). A trail following mountain ridges, creeks and redwood stands leads to the rustic *West Point Inn*, where coffee and granola bars await. Rooms and cabins available from Tues.-Fri. $12 per person, tel. 388-9955.

Mountain bike rentals:
Ken's Bike and Sport: 94 Main st., Tiburon, tel. 435-1683.

San Francisco skyline — from Sausalito

Point Reyes Bikes: 11431 State Highway 1, tel. 663-1768.

In a cool, moist canyon beneath the slopes of Mt. Tamalpais is the **Muir Woods National Monument**, tel. 388-2595, the natural redwood grove that is closest to the San Francisco metropolitan area. The grove, saved from felling by its inaccessibility but forever threatened, was finally placed under federal protection and named after John Muir, the inspiration behind the modern conservation movement. Reached by a loop road off Route 1, Muir Woods makes a beautiful short walk in itself or serves as a pleasant stop on a longer hike among the extensive trail network in the area. The entrance gate is open from 8am to sunset. It is hard to believe that this primeval forests, so close to the city, somehow managed to survive. On weekends parking can be a problem.

Point Reyes

The Point Reyes National Seashore is a blending and meeting of several beautiful landscapes: green rolling pasture land, scrubby chaparral ridges, lush meadows and forest, expansive sand dunes, large tidepools, sea-sculpted caves, and jutting cliffs exposed to the full force of the Pacific. All these terrains are covered by an extensive mesh of trails, suitable for both day hikes and overnight camping expeditions. Point Reyes is long enough and varied enough to give a sense of openness and space even during a crowded holiday. When you climb down to the lighthouse at Point Reyes itself or reach any of the other promontories exposed to the salty wind and smells of the tumultuous Pacific, the rest of the world just does not seem to exist.

*C*_ALIFORNIA_

At Muir Woods

Route 1, the coastal highway that reaches Point Reyes and continues north, runs right along the **San Andreas Fault** which continues into the Tomales Bay that separates Point Reyes from the mainland. Two major plates of the earth's crust meet along this fracture, causing a large rift containing large and small faults within it. Reflecting the pressures and stresses deeper in the earth's core, this fault zone is an area of comparatively rapid topographic change and motion, including the floating of the large plates, commonly referred to as "continental drift." This explains, for example, why rocks in this craggy coast match those of the Tehachapi mountains 300 miles (480 km) to the south. From fold to fold and ridge to ridge the climate and vegetation change rapidly. Even the weather changes rapidly, not only from day to day but hour to hour. These sharply contrasting ecological zones support a great variety of wildlife which feeds upon the myriad riches of this interzonal area.

Shifting winds, nutrient-rich cold water, and other climatic factors combine to create a marine ecosystem as varied and abundant as the one it meets on land. Whales and porpoises may pass south along the coast a few hundreds of yards away from grazing elk. The protected marine sanctuary, which encompasses the **Farallon**

Islands as well as the Point Reyes beach, contains the largest breeding rookery for seabirds on the American Pacific coast. Hundreds of thousands of birds live and breed here.

The strong undertows at Point Reyes make swimming too dangerous and it is forbidden. The Bear Valley Visitor Center, tel. 663-1092, posts a schedule of programs. Camping sites are spread out in the southern half of the park and are all primitive. The *Point Reyes Hostel* is on Limantour rd., off Route 1. During the summer a free shuttle bus runs from the seashore headquarters to **Limantour Beach**.

Educational boat trips sail for the Farallon Islands or follow whale migrations. The Oceanic Society Expeditions, tel. 474-3385 and the Whale Center, tel. 654-6621, both offer trips.

Marine World/Africa U.S.A.

South of the Napa Valley, the I-80 brings you to the town of Vallejo, at the very western edge of the agricultural Central Valley. The wild-animal extravaganza, Marine World/Africa USA, was moved here in 1986 from its original location in Redwood City. It is part circus, part zoo, part reserve, part research facility and part open and innovative classroom. It is bright and exciting, and has been planned with care. The theme park has an amazing variety of cats, snakes, exotic birds, elephants and primates, as well as whales, dolphins and sharks. Rare habitats have been creatively reproduced. There is always something going on, always a show, in addition to the displays that invite children and adults to learn while playing, or play while learning.

Exit off I-80 to Marine World Parkway and follow the signs. Special *Red and White Fleet* high-speed ferries now follow the San Pablo Bay to Marine World, from Pier 41 at Fisherman's Wharf in San Francisco. For details, tel. 415-546-2896. *Greyhound* also reaches Marine World.

Marine World/Africa U.S.A. is open daily in summer 9:30am-6:30pm. Only Wed.-Sun. until 5pm the rest of the year. $17.95 for adults, $12.95 for seniors and ages 4-12, age 3 and under no admission, tel. 707-643-ORCA for recording, tel. 707-644-4000 for administration.

Wine Country

Napa Valley

California produces 90% of all the wines in the United States. The Napa Valley is the finest wine-making region in California, and the lush valley produces wines of international fame. The great climatic range enables the nurturing of a surprising variety of wine grapes. The days are hot, the nights cool, and the air is filled with the smell of grapes during the harvest season.

The first grapevines were brought to the Napa Valley in the 1820s by Spanish missionaries, for sacramental purposes. By the 1850s, vineyards had spread throughout the valley, and some decades afterwards they and their reputation spread to the East Coast. Disease and prohibition, from 1919-1930, crippled the industry. When wine production revived, during the '60s and '70s, it propelled the Napa Valley into the forefront of the wine-producing regions of the world. Wine is the major theme of this valley and the main reason the highways are lined with cars on a summer weekend.

About 100 wineries grace this valley, most scattered along Route 29 between Napa in the south and Calistoga in the north. The renowned ones provide a good starting point, but there are other smaller, more obscure wineries which are also worth exploring. Poking around the small farms and wine cellars in the countryside, and meeting the vintners is part of the fun.

How to get there

It is difficult to negotiate the Napa Valley without a car, especially if you wish to visit some of the less accessible wineries. *Greyhound* service connects the towns along Route 29. Within the town of Napa itself there is a good bus system known as the *VINE*.

Those who can afford it, should see the valley by taking the *Napa Valley Wine Train*. Refurbished Pullman cars travel through the valley, stopping for tours and wine tasting at Yountville, Rutherford and St. Helena. The tour also includes a wine seminar and an excellent meal in the dining-car. Details and reservations, tel. 800-522-4141 and tel. 707-253-2111.

Cycling is an excellent way to see this valley. Bicycles can be hired in Napa or Calistoga. The flat country backroads make for easy riding. The Napa Chamber of Commerce has maps with route suggestions.

Accommodations

The emphasis in Napa Valley is on elegant country-style old hotels, or B&Bs. In Calistoga there is a concentration of spa hotels. These places are very relaxing, and some are stunning. They also tend to be a little over-priced, but have much more atmosphere than the standard motel or hotel.

Wine Country B&B Reservations: tel. 257-7757.

Hideaway Cottages: 1412 Fairway, Calistoga 94515, tel. 942-4108. Cottages ranging from small to two-roomed. Nicely furnished. Mineral pools. $35-$75. Weekly rates.

Calistoga Inn: 1250 Lincoln ave., Calistoga 94515, tel. 942-4104. Comfortable rooms in a landmark building. Shared baths. Continental breakfast, and wine in each room. $35 single, $40 double.

Silverado Motel: 500 Silverado Trail, Napa, tel. 225-9848. Simple, adequate. $26-$45.

Camping

Bothe-Napa Valley State Park: 3601 St. Helena Highway, tel. 942-4575. Located 20 miles (32 km) north of Napa, between St. Helena and Calistoga. About 50 sites, hiking trails. Can get crowded in summer. Between April and Oct., reservations through *Ticketron*.

Additional camping is available at the Fairgrounds in Calistoga, tel. 942-5111, and the Fairgrounds in Napa, tel. 226-2164. Private campgrounds by Lake Berryessa.

Some Napa Valley Wineries

Full lists of valley wineries, with their specialties, tasting and tour hours, available from the local Visitor Centers and Chambers of Commerce.

Charles Krug Winery: 2800 Main st. (Route 29), St. Helena, tel. 963-2761. The oldest in the valley, owned by Mondavi family. Frequent tours, historical displays. Open 10am-4pm daily.

Robert Mondavi Winery: 7801 St. Helena, Rte 29, tel. 963-9611. Tours and tasting.

De Moor Winery: 7481 Route 29, Oakville, tel. 944-2565. Tasting room, self-guided tours. A small but renowned winery.

V. Sattui Winery: Corner Route 29 at White ln, 2 miles (2 km) south of St. Helena east of highway, tel. 963-7774. Tasting room, gourmet deli, picnic grounds. Consistent winner in major competitions. Wines sold exclusively from here.

Beringer Vineyards: 2000 Main st. St. Helena, tel. 963-7115. Tours and tasting. A very commercial tour, but the carved caves and vaults are worth seeing.

CALIFORNIA

Wine Country — a typical wineyard

Inglenook Napa Valley: 1991 Route 29, Rutherford. Tours, tasting. Known for its Cabernet Sauvignon.

What to see

St. Helena is the center of the valley's wine making industry. Some of the best known California lables can be recognized on the visitor's map and roadside signs. Christian Bros., Beringer Bros and Charles Krug (the oldest operating valley winery) are located north of town. The architecture of these wineries can be as interesting as the wines. Some have the atmosphere of medieval castles or monasteries. The Beringer winery ages its wine in huge vats in a network of tunnels carved out of the adjacent hillside by Chinese workers. Near the town there are other smaller wineries.

The **Beaulieu Vineyards** at Rutherford have a beautiful tasting and display room. The well known **Inglenook Vineyards**, just north of Rutherford, runs a popular tour. The **Sterling Vineyard** has a beautiful view of the valley, and a tram for carrying visitors. Open 10:30am-4:30pm. Admission fee, tel. 707-942-5151.

Many events and festivals revolve around wine; the **Grape Festival** and the **Harvest Festival** are held in August, and some of the hotels sponsor weekly wine-tastings.

Driving around the valley, with stops for tasting, is one of the most pleasant things to do here. If you drive north to Calistoga along Route 29, the return drive by Route 128, skirting the slopes of the eastern hills, makes a pleasant return route to Napa. This route leads past Lake Berryessa. Public land is interspersed with private resorts. Along the western shore are restaurants, boat ramps, campsites and picnic spots.

Wine Tasting Tips

It is easy to feel overwhelmed by the volume and variety of wines in the fertile northern valleys of California. It seems that every other wine is a prize-winner. How is the novice to distinguish between them?

There are a few general guidelines for evaluating wine. Move from white, to reds, to dessert wines, because the reds leave more tannins on the tongue and dull the taste. Check the wine for clearness or cloudiness, and a pleasing color. Swirl the wine to release its "nose": a combination of aroma (from the grape) and bouquet (from the wine-making process). When tasting, check for fruitiness, tartness, smoothness or hardness.

The Davis 20-point system, based on such qualities as clarity, color, scent, sweetness, acidity, body and flavor, can give you some standards for judgement. Literature is available from the various wine organizations listed, and the winery tour guides can advise you.

There are also guidelines for proper wine-tasting behavior. It is crucial to know how to raise the glass to the light and squint critically; how to sniff delicately; how to sip, purse the lips, roll the tongue, pause meaningfully and frown. Then come the vital first words — spoken with a slow nod — such as: "A marvelous spicy rush, but a fading finish... a lovely late afternoon wine with a tickly center." After the fourth or fifth glass, more expansive poesy is allowed: "As light as a sparrow's song... as rosy as a young girl's cheeks".

It is possible to visit local farms and taste and purchase apples, peaches, strawberries, walnuts, etc. The county publishes a guide to farms that welcome and encourage visitors. Write: Napa County Farm Trails, 4075 Solano ave., Napa 94558, or inquire at the Napa visitors center. An open-air farmer's market is held on Fridays at the Dansk Square parking lot, south of downtown St. Helena.

Calistoga, at the northern end of the valley, has retained the atmosphere of an old western farmtown. The commercial section is really just one street, with old covered sidewalks. The old railroad station at the east end of town has been refurbished, as a small mall, and the old railcars are the attractions. The local Chamber of Commerce is located here. In the middle of the block across the street is the old *Calistoga Inn*, a renovated original that served travelers in the last century.

Calistoga attracted tourists with the region's mineral springs. One of California's major early figures, the flamboyant Sam Brennan, creator of San Francisco's first newspaper (which announced the gold rush to the world) first bought up the springs and pushed through a major plan to make the area a resort for city-dwellers. The springs have been tapped, channeled and sealed off by elaborate spas and inns. The luxury of wallowing in thick black mud, plus whirlpool, steam room and blanket wrap, costs from $20-$30.

Calistoga's **Old Faithful Geyser** shoots a plume of steam and water up to 60 feet (20 m) high about every 40 minutes. Located about two miles (4 km) north of Calistoga at 1299 Tubbs Lane. Open everyday, including holidays, 9am-5pm in winters, 9am-6pm in summers. Admission fee, tel. 942-6463.

Just north of town, keep an eye open for the **Treasure-House of Worldly Wares.** 1401 Tubbs Lane. Open 10am-5pm daily except Thursday, tel. 942-9976. Hopi boots, Eskimo carvings, African lyres, Persian pendants and an Egyptian mummy mask all find a place in this crammed and colorful shop. Most interesting of all is the owner, a Ponca Indian named Stevie Whitefeather.

Robert Louis Stevenson State Park is located on Mount St. Helena, five miles (8 km) north of Calistoga on Route 29. The famous Scottish writer lived there in 1880 with his new bride, in an old mining shack. Here he wrote *Silverado Squatters*, relating his experiences in the area. The forested mountain sides inspired the setting for *Treasure Island*. Open during daylight hours, the park has a hiking trail leading to the mountain summit, with vistas of the distant high peaks of the eastern ranges. The **Silverado Museum** in St. Helena features a collection of Stevenson memorabilia and manuscripts. 1490 Library Lane, St. Helena. Tues.-Sun. noon-4pm. Admission free, tel. 963-3757.

Important addresses and phone numbers

Area Code: 707.
Emergency: 911.
Napa Chamber of Commerce: 1900 Jefferson st., tel. 257-1112.
Napa Valley Visitor Information Center: 4076 Byway East, tel. 257-1102. Near a big wooden tower on the east side of Route 29.
Calistoga Chamber of Commerce: Calistoga Depot, 1458 Lincoln ave., tel. 942-6333.
General Transportation Info: tel. 252-6222.
Napa City Bus: 1130 1st st., tel. 255-7631.
Evans Airport Service: tel. 255-1559. Daily service between Napa City and SFO, $11. Reservations.
Greyhound: Napa, tel. 226-1856; Yountville, tel. 944-8377; Calistoga, tel. 942-6021.
Napa Charter Lines: tel. 224-2351.
Highway Conditions: tel. 643-8421.
Wine Country Tours: tel. 963-5760.

Highway Conditions: tel. 643-8421.
Wine Country Tours: tel. 963-5760.

Sonoma Valley

The crescent-shaped Sonoma Valley stretches north from the San Pablo Bay to Santa Rosa. The mountains to the east keep out the dry intense heat that hits the Napa Valley, and the western mountains block the heaviest fogs, and only light fogs and cool moist breezes penetrate.

In the early 19th century, Spanish, Russian and American interests collided in this fertile valley. Local expressions of larger diplomatic struggles were played out here, and Sonoma became the flashpoint for the rebellion of local American settlers against Mexican rule.

Sonoma was settled comparatively late. The **Mission San Francisco Solano**, the northernmost and last in the mission system, was founded here in 1823, and by 1830 was the dominant influence in the valley, with 1,000 local Indians under its authority, but that dominance was short-lived.

In 1833, Captain Mariano Vallejo was sent by the Mexican government to contact the Russian outposts and establish Mexican settlements, but the Franciscan mission thwarted his efforts. Returning four years later, he reduced the mission to the status of a parish church, freed the Indian workers and redistributed mission lands. Vallejo himself received a huge land grant and set up a productive agricultural empire. His far-reaching civil and military power shaped Sonoma's development. His adobe home on the plaza, La Casa Grande, drew visitors from around the world.

Amid increasing American desires for the rich lands of California, a group of 30-40 American frontiersmen captured the Sonoma settlement in June, 1846 without resistance. They arrested Vallejo and imprisoned him. They raised a home-made flag of a bear, and the famous "Bear Flag Rebellion" made California an independent republic, until the United States took over a month later. But the uprising was far from the heroic enterprise lauded in California history. The Americans had been seeking a pretext to make their move. General Vallejo returned home to find his ranch stripped of livestock and other commodities by the self-proclaimed patriots.

Vallejo had the dignity to take an active role in American politics in California even after the regime he had been part of was deposed. He was a delegate to the state's constitutional convention and was elected to the State Senate. He even offered a tract of land for the building of a permanent capitol. Although his great holdings were steadily whittled away, he never became embittered and retained his dignity. He immersed himself in composing a five-volume history of Mexican California. When he died in 1890 at age 82, hundreds of people filled the little central plaza of Sonoma, then carried the body to the small cemetery above town.

Accommodations

The greatest concentration of hotels and motels is found in the Santa Rosa area, and at various points along Highway 101. There are, however, a number of small inns scattered through the Sonoma countryside. For suggestions and information, contact: Wine Country Inns of Sonoma County, P.O. Box 51. Geyserville, 95441; tel. 433-INNS.

Food

Sonoma Cheese Factory: 2 West Spain st., tel. 996-1931. Watch how the cheese is produced by hand and sample the results. A deli as well, and a garden patio.

La Casa: Spain st. at 1st st. East, tel. 996-3406. In a historic building, Mexican food reasonably priced.

Depot Hotel 1870: 241 1st st. West, tel. 938-2980. The atmosphere is rural, the cuisine hearty.

What to see

Old Sonoma, a shady, quiet and compact area, is still centered around the original small **plaza**, and one can pass a couple of hours strolling and exploring here. The verdant plaza holds the **Visitor Center**, where you can pick up a self-guiding tour explaining the old adobe buildings that stand scattered around you. There are several good and reasonably priced restaurants and delis around the plaza.

Many of the historical landmarks, and the **Sonoma State Historical Park**, are on Spain st. just north of the plaza. Here stands Vallejo's first home, with a small Indian exhibit in the rangers' building right next to the *Toscano Hotel*. In the *Toscano* itself, built in 1858 and meticulously restored, you'd expect to find Jack London or Mark Twain lounging in the lobby with their feet up and a glass of brandy.

The park includes the **mission complex**, tel. 938-1578, near the corner of E. Spain and 1st st. The missionaries' quarters is the oldest building remaining in the complex. Exhibits depict the various stages of history in Sonoma. In the courtyard, craft demonstrations from earlier periods are held. Part of the original Bear Flag (most was destroyed by fire) is still found in the mission.

Nearby is the *Blue Wing Inn*, reportedly built by Vallejo, which may have housed John Fremont, the explorer and officer who was instrumental in consolidating American rule in California.

The **Vasquez House**, set back on 1st st. east of the plaza, was transported by ship from the east at a cost of $64,000, by Joseph Hooker, army officer who later achieved fame in the civil war. It now houses a library and tiny coffee shop where the proprieter is friendly and proud of the town, and his coffee that costs 25 cents.

The **Depot Museum**, behind Sapin st., recreates an old railroad station, with all details authentic — down to the brakeman's lantern and ticket counter. Only the "all aboard!" is missing. In Depot Park between 1st st. East and 1st st. West. Open Wed.-Sun. 1-4:30pm. Small admission fee, tel. 938-9765.

One of the most interesting spots in the plaza area is the **Stained Glass Works**, which displays and sells stained glass pieces crafted on the premises by handicapped adults. The detailed and variegated pieces, beautiful in their own right, become more interesting when the production process is seen. 115 East. Napa st., tel. 996-5180.

The Sonoma Valley witnessed the earliest experiments in the state with vine cultivation and wine production, and there are wineries throughout the valley as well as in the town.

The **Sebastiani Winery**, an easy stroll from the plaza along E. Spain st. (there is ample parking near the winery), is the largest and one of the best-known valley wineries. 389 E 4th st. Regular tours. Open 10am-5pm. Admission free, tel. 938-5532. Some of its vineyards are 100 years old. The 20-minute tour is entertaining, well organized and not full of the usual drinking jokes. The oak casks and redwood tanks here emit intoxicating smells and are decorated with beautiful wood-carvings. There is also a museum of Indian artifacts.

The **Buena Vista Winery**, about a mile east of the town center, was founded in 1857, the first in California with stone cellars. 18000 Old Winery rd. Open daily 10am-3pm, tel. 938-1266. Now a historical landmark, it is worth a visit for the limestone catacombs alone. There are picnic grounds and playground equipment made of barrels and casks. The winery also hosts performances, including Shakespearean plays.

The **Gundlach Bundschu Winery** is also one of the old-timers. The personnel are pleasant, the grounds pretty. There are regular tastings and self-guided tours. 2000 Denmark st. Open daily 11am-4:30pm, tel. 938-5277.

The foundation of the **Glen Ellen** winery can be traced back to General Vallejo's time when he owned the property, and it is one of the better-known wineries in the area. 1883 London Ranch rd, Glen Ellen. Tasting from 10am-4pm. Tours by appointment, tel. 996-1066.

Wine Seminars International offers tours, seminars and video presentations for those wishing to learn the subtleties of wine-tasting. Write or call: PO Box 1287, Sonoma, 95476; tel. 938-9060, or tel. 800-328-3029, ext. 208.

Important addresses and phone numbers

Area Code: 707.
Valley Visitors Bureau: 453 1st st., tel. 996-1090.
Sonoma County Transit: tel. 527-7665.
Sonoma Airporter: tel. 938-4246. Transportation to San Francisco Airport.

Russian River and Sonoma Coast

The Sonoma Valley connects with the **Russian River Valley** region, which leads out to the Pacific. The hillsides and valleys which are carved by the Russian River and its tributaries are exceptionally fertile, covered by deposits of loam and shady soil. The warm summers, the cool winters and the fog drifting in from the Pacific along the Russian River Valley create an environment distinct from Napa's, yet still excellent for vine-growing. In autumn, the low hills gleam an unbelievable gold and the aromas of fermenting fruit fill the air. Towering stands of redwoods grow here. The coastline is rocky, and backed by cliffs.

The Russian River Valley has attracted various populations, small-time farmers, suburban developers and commuters, vintners, fishermen, hippie back-to-the-land types, and recently an influx of urban gays who have set up resorts in some of the small towns.

How to get there

The best way to travel through this area is by car, but if limited to the bus system, it is still possible to get around Sonoma county, with a little planning. A number of municipal and regional bus companies connect all parts of the county, but it is important to check schedules and coordinate times, to avoid long waits.

Golden Gate Transit (GGT) provides a daily service between Santa Rosa, Marin County cities and towns, and San Francisco, with stops at cities and towns in Sonoma County along Highway 101. One route serves Sebastopol and Forestville. During the weekday rush hours, you can ride along with business-attired commuters on the express buses. The main transfer point between *GGT* and the other bus services in the county is at the transit mall in downtown Santa Rosa.

Sonoma County Transit reaches all areas of the county. It connects with the *City Bus* in Santa Rosa, the *GGT* system, and the local systems of the small towns along the Russian River. Transfers within the same bus system are free. A transfer to another bus system allows a reduction in fare. You can pick up the various bus schedules at city halls, libraries, Chambers of Commerce and some major businesses, throughout the towns of Sonoma County. *Greyhound* also serves Sonoma County, with direct buses from San Francisco, eliminating the need to transfer.

Accommodations

The Russian River Valley is the perfect region to indulge yourself with a stay in a cosy and rustic B&B. They are scattered throughout the valley and in the small towns, both inland and along the coast. Standard hotels and motels are found mostly along Route 101 in the Santa Rosa vicinity. For information on local B&B inns, contact Wine Country Inns of Sonoma County: P.O. Box R51, Geyserville, 95441, tel. 433-INNS.

State park camping is available at **Bodega Dunes** and **Wright's Beach**, in addition to **Anderson Creek State Park**. For reservations contact *Ticketron*, not the park. The County also operates several campgrounds. The **Doran Park** campgounds is located at the southern end of Bodega Harbor, at the very tip of the narrow jetty separating the harbor from the ocean. For information and reservations for the county campgrounds, call tel. 722-5602, toll-free in-state tel. 800-822-CAMP, toll-free out-of-state tel. 800-824-CAMP.

What to see

Guerneville is the center of the Russian River resort area. During the summer it is crowded, and the cafés and restaurants tend to be a little more expensive than in some of the other towns. From near the main junction of the town, there is an easy walk down to the sandy bank of the river itself. The houses, which are a considerable distance from the shore, were flooded and some were washed away during the great floods of 1985 which ravaged the entire valley. Guerneville has become a popular resort for the gay community of San Francisco.

Just 2.5 miles (4 km) north of Guerneville off route 116 are the cool primeval redwood forests of the **Armstrong Redwoods State Reserve**, which adjoins the **Austin Creek State Recreation Area**. About twenty miles (32 km) of hiking trails run through them, from the deep cool redwood-filled valleys to the scrubby peaks. Easy trails loop through the redwood grove which includes some of the tallest trees left in this region of California. Check local papers to see whether a play or concert is being presented at the reserve's 1,200-seat amphitheatre.

There is a drive-in campground at **Bullfrog Pond**, as well as primitive walk-in campgrounds further to the west. For information, contact the park's head office at 17000 Armstrong Woods Road, Guerneville, 95446, tel. 869-2015 or tel. 865-2391.

The **canoeing** is fantastic along the wide and gently meandering Russian River. Numerous rental companies will arrange to launch your canoe at one point and pick you up further downstream. The river is gentle most of the way and there are numerous landing beaches with road access. The information office at Guerneville will have some addresses. Rates vary from between $25 and $30

RUSSIAN RIVER

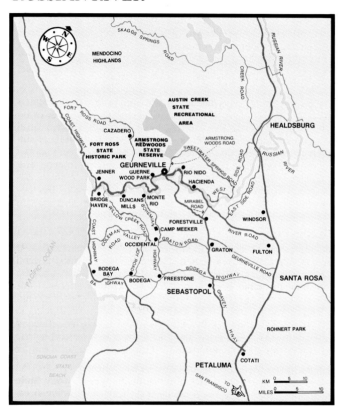

per canoe for a full day's paddling. Discount coupons are available from local Chamber of Commerce offices.

The winery of **F. Korbel and Bros**., open since 1862, is located in an old, beautifully landscaped complex, and is famous for its sparkling wines. 13250 River Road, Guerneville. Open daily, May-September. Tasting 9am-5pm, wineshop 9am-5:30pm. Call for winter hours, tel. 887-2294. In addition to its tasting room and winery tours every 45 minutes, there are free tours of its beautifully cultivated gardens.

For the annual jazz festival in August, **Russian River Jazz**, the audience gathers near the river to hear a wide variety of jazz, including some big names. For a predominantly rural county, there is a surprisingly active theater scene, with over 15 small community theaters of varying styles, approaches and degrees of professionalism. The **Odyssey Stage Company of Sonoma**, tel. 545-7708, has received good reviews for its innovative and sometimes daring productions. For general information on local and other artistic events and resources, peruse the local free weeklies, or contact the *Cultural Arts Council of Sonoma County*, tel. 579-ARTS.

A loop drive into Russian River country makes a beautiful one or two-day excursion from San Francisco. From San Francisco, take route 101 north to Santa Rosa, the main population center of the Sonoma region. Take the 116 exit for Guerneville, which passes through **Sebastopol** and other small towns up to the Russian River. The highway follows the river to the sea, at **Jenner**. North of Jenner, the winding coastal road leads through increasingly rugged land with high overlooks over the ocean. To the south, the beautiful ocean-side cliffs continue. The coastal route back to the city, passes pretty **Bodega Bay** with its small fishing town and peaceful bayside seafood restaurants. Further south is passes Point Reyes and the seaside parklands of Marin County. North of Santa Rosa on route 101 the wineries begin at **Healdsburg**.

After driving up to Healdsburg, as you head north on 101, you'll pass the town of Cloverdale, which sponsors a knee-slapping, foot-stomping fiddle festival every year. Check the date if you plan to drive through the area, by calling the Cloverdale Historical Society, tel. 894-2067. Follow the river course from Healdsburg or Cloverdale. The small roads parallel to the highway and Russian River are lined with wineries. The road follows the river which flows west past the wineries, all the way to the ocean. Some of the old wineries still age their wines in the one hundred year old stone cellars, while others are more modern.

For a map which pinpoints and describes the various wineries, as well as events and general information, contact: Russian River Wine Road, P.O. Box 127, Geyserville, 95441, tel. 433-6935.

Although route 116 is the main road leading from route 101 to the ocean, if you wander along some of the smaller roads south of the river, you'll find some incredibly green, rolling countryside. Try to direct your wandering to the town of **Occidental**. It is barely two blocks long, but firmly established on a foundation of pasta. Facing each other, like feuding castles, are two excellent Italian restaurants, the *Union Hotel* and the *Negri*. Both pile on the pasta, salads, fresh sourdough bread, sauces, meats and cheeses. The *Union Hotel* shakes up the forest on Friday and Saturday nights with foot stompin' music, and the bar has a lumberjack atmosphere like in a macho beer commercial. From route 116, take the Bohemian Highway south from Monte Rio to Occidental.

Just east of Jenner on route 116 is **Duncan Mills**, with a population officially listed at 20. An old resort, railroad depot and lumbertown, much of the original architecture has been restored, and today Duncan Mills is basically a walk-through museum of restored Victorian buildings, a railroad museum, manicured gardens and cultivated quaintness.

Route 116 meets the Pacific Coastal Highway and the ocean near the small Jenner Visitor's Center, a small semi-open shelter with self guided exhibits and explanations of the animal life along this stretch of coast. The coastal highway is like a winding roller coaster here. Bluffs and promontories divide the shoreline into a series of small, crescent-shaped disconnected beaches and coves. The climate here is much cooler than even a few miles inland. In the winter, the whales migrating south frolic just off the coast where the ocean floor drops suddenly away. North of the Jenner junction, the Russian River meets the sea, meandering around sandbars that in spring are covered with seals mating and giving birth. Sharks occasionally drift into the inlet. The largest, caught a few years back, weighed over a ton. For information, call State Park headquarters at Bodega Bay, tel. 875-3483.

North of Jenner on route 1, stands **Fort Ross State Historical Park**, the reconstruction of Russia's 19th century fort. Park and museum open daily, except holidays, 10am-4:30pm. Parking $2, tel. 847-3286. It is easy to feel the isolation the soldiers must have felt in this southernmost exposed and remote outpost.

The Russians were reaching south to hunt for sea otters and grow wheat and crops for their Alaskan settlements, and to establish a foothold for further inland expansion. The Spanish were simultaneously reaching up from the south, trying to solidify their hold on the colony which had technically already been in their possession for hundreds of years. The Americans, meanwhile, had been exploring overland as far as to the Pacific, and as far north as the mouth of the Columbia River. The local Indians had used the site seasonally to collect abalone. All this made for a clash of cultures and nationalities in microcosmic isolation. The museum depicts the story clearly and vividly. In the replicated cabins, the fur hats, leggings and embroidered leather bags are remarkably similar to the relics of an American frontier memorial. The architecture, however, has clearly Russian characteristics.

Bodega, south of Jenner, is the home of the county's fishing fleet, docked in Bodega Harbor. It is a small fishing village of less than 4,500 people. Small shacks and stands sell fresh seafood, clam chowder, smoked fish and deli items. From the restaurants at the harbor, one can watch the small fishing boats coming into dock laden with fish. The fish are hauled up in crates, swung over and dumped into the huge basins on the scales. The fishermen shovel ice over the silvery mounds of fish. No tourist props here. They gut the fish which their passengers have caught and toss the guts over the railing, while circling gulls swoop down and restaurant customers try to enjoy their seafood.

Fort Ross Park

Important addresses and phone numbers

Area Code: 707.

Sonoma County Convention & Visitors Bureau: 637 First st., Santa Rosa, tel. 545-1420.

Russian River Chamber of Commerce: P.O. Box 331, Guerneville 95446, tel. 823-3032.

Sonoma County Transit: tel. 1-800-345-RIDE (toll-free in county), or tel. 576-RIDE.

Golden Gate Transit: tel. 544-1323.

Greyhound: tel. 542-6400.

Mendocino Transit Authority: tel. 576-RIDE. *MTA* runs a van down the coast into Sonoma County.

Santa Rosa Transit: tel. 576-5306, or tel. 576-5238.

Inland Northern California

As you travel inland, away from the Pacific coast, you discover a totally new and different country. There are no rambling, industrial urban areas or sun-drenched resort centers. Their place is taken by vast green valleys, surrounded by the Sierra Nevada Mountains. This is a quieter part of the country, particularly suited to nature lovers. Among the more beautiful spots are Yosemite National Park, and of course, the Lake Tahoe gambling resort on the Nevada border.

Sacramento

The city of Sacramento boomed during the gold rush and became the state capital. It became the terminus for wagon trains, stagecoaches, steam paddlers, the *Pony Express*, the telegraph lines and, finally, the country's first transcontinental railroad. It was in Sacramento that the scheme for the railroad was born, among a group of ambitious and imaginative businessmen — Leland Standford, Mark Hopkins, Collis P. Huntington and Charles Crocker — who were destined to play a major role in the shaping of the young state's growth and economy. Sacramento became a political center and the center for the state government's bureaucracy.

Sacramento is situated on a main route connecting San Francisco to points lying east, and is also in the middle of a fertile agricultural valley, thereby making it a center for produce distribution. The city was not exactly famous, however, for its dynamism or culture.

Lately, the city has been stirring itself. The capital was renovated, the surrounding commercial area is being overhauled. A new cultural life is developing. Sacramento now has a lively music and art scene. There are numerous art galleries, featuring some excellent local artists, and there are clubs and bars scattered around the downtown area playing jazz and other music.

How to get there

Sacramento continues its role as a major intersection and distribution point. Two major interstate highways cross here. I-80 runs from San Francisco to the east coast, and I-5 runs from Mexico to Washington State. I-99, skirting the eastern edge of the San Joaquin Valley, also reaches here.

Sacramento's **Metro Airport** serves national as well as regional and state carriers. Sacramento is also a junction for major *Amtrak* lines, with trains running west to San Francisco, east over the Sierras, north to Seattle, and south through the length of the San Joaquin Valley. *Greyhound* and *Trailways* have regular and extensive service to Sacramento.

Transportation

It is easy to maneuver through the city by car thanks to the logical grid of lettered and numbered streets. Several bus lines operate locally. *Regional Transit* buses serve most of the Sacramento area and its suburban satellites. The *Yolobus* line connects downtown, Old Sacramento and West Sacramento, as well as Davis and other surrounding towns. *Commuter Bus* lines cover the city. A downtown tram line, using renovated trolley cars travels along the K Street Mall between the Convention Center and Old Sacramento. The schedule is slightly reduced on weekends. Sacramento is pleasant for cycling, with its many parks, bicycle paths and flat terrain.

Accommodations

The two major freeways that pass through Sacramento are lined with hotels and motels. Most major chains are represented.

In the heart of downtown there are some old, rather run-down and sleazy hotels. Along 16th st., in the area of the Governor's Mansion, a number of motels are clustered, ranging widely in price and facilities. In West Sacramento there are more motels, slightly lower in price, about half a mile from Old Sacramento. For a listing of West Sacramento lodgings, call the West Sacramento Hotel/Motel Association, tel. 372-5378, or toll-free in-state, tel. 1-800-962-9800.

The most basic, standard motels here start at about $22. The hotel tax is quite steep here, about 10%.

There are few camping facilities in the immediate area. On Route 50 to the east, towards Placerville, is the Folsom Lake State Park with campgrounds, as well as recreational activities centered around the lake, tel. 371-6771.

Food

Annabelle's: On J st. just east of 2nd st., in Old Sacramento. The great lunch buffet here includes all you can eat of spaghetti, lasagne and a salad bar, for $2.97, 11am-4pm.

Las Padres: J st. near Front. A bit gaudy and a bit crowded, but the decor is unusual and the portions large, and not too overpriced for a tourist haunt.

Whistle Stop: On Front st. near L st. In Old Sacramento serving reasonable breakfasts.

Zelda's Original Gourmet Pizza: 1415 21st st. Original or not, it is justifiably popular for its deep-dish pizza.

CALIFORNIA

El Charro: 2019 Q st. Delicious Mexican food.

What to see

The local **Convention and Visitors Bureau**, at 1421 K st., tel. 916-442-5542, distributes thick glossy magazines and directories listing everything you might want to do in Sacramento. A special Discover Sacramento Switchboard offers updates on art, entertainment and recreation activities. In addition, Sacramento is a fine place to dig out all sorts of unusual information, by virtue of its being the center of the state's considerable bureaucracy. The state offices offer a tremendous range of resources, libraries and public information offices.

The **California Office of Tourism** is the best one-stop information source for the visitor. Every region in the state is covered. In addition to scanning the racks of tourist-oriented brochures, ask to see the office's publication list, for pamphlets and information sheets on a wide range of subjects concerning this multi-faceted state.

Be aware that the heat and humidity in summer are often almost unbearable.

The main points of interest (with a couple of exceptions), cluster around two areas: the State Capitol, and Old Sacramento.

Old Sacramento

Old Sacramento's six blocks combine authentic historical reconstruction with predictable tourist shops. 120 years ago this booming, new city on the bank of the Sacramento River was the western hub of the telegraph, stagecoach, *Pony Express* and the railroad. Old Sacramento is situated on Front st. near the river, just west of the Capitol. The Visitor Information Center provides pamphlets for a self-guided walking tour that passes an array of old stores, warehouses, historical plaques, etc. Free walking tours are conducted on weekends, departing from the passenger depot near the California State Railroad Museum, at 10:30am and 1:30pm.

The **California State Railroad Museum** is more than just a collection of locomotives. I st. between Front and Second st. Open 10am-5pm. Admission fee, tel. 448-4466. It illustrates how the railroads broke ground across the rugged countryside and revolutionized the country. Buster Keaton's brilliant and hilarious film *The General* is shown here. Museum admission includes the Central Pacific Passenger Depot, a reconstruction of the original depot that was once a bustling, thriving center. Steam train rides are available during the summer months from the depot to Miller Park.

Next to the Railroad Museum is the **Huntington-Hopkins Hardware Store**, where the dream of a transcontinental railroad was discussed and launched. The second floor is the recreation of the Central

SACRAMENTO CITY CENTER

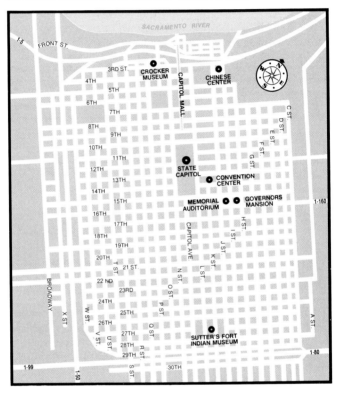

Pacific's boardroom and library. Open 10am-5pm, admission free, tel. 445-4209.

A further reconstruction of the past can be seen at the Sacramento History Center on the corner of I and Fronts sts. Here you can enter the world of the gold rush that swept the area, including an exhibition of some of the original utensils used by the gold diggers. Open from 10am-5pm. Admission fee, tel. 449-2057.

The *Old Eagle Theater*, 925 Front st., constructed as a theater in 1849, screens a 15-minute film depicting the city's past. $2 for adults, $1.25 for children, tel. 446-6761.

Old Sacramento has become the unofficial center for a variety

Old Sacramento
The State Capitol

of Sacramento celebrations, such as Admission Day festivities in September, the Dixlieland Jazz Festival on Memorial Day, and the Blues Festival in September. On these occasions, the streets and clubs spill over with crowds and music.

The Capitol Park is green and beautiful and the **Capitol** itself has been renovated. The adjacent downtown area is also in the midst of a facelift. The Capitol renovations include beautiful marble mosaic floors and crystal chandeliers, a touch of turn-of-the-century grandeur. The museum has exhibits on past governors, and a film details the restoration. Open daily at 9am, guided tours available, tel. 324-0333.

Near the Capitol is the majestic **Crocker Museum**. 216 O st. Open Tues. 1-9pm, Wed.-Sun. 10am-5pm. Small admission fee, tel. 449-5423. The first art museum in the west, the building is a beautiful work in itself. The museum was founded by the railroad tycoon Edwin Bryant Crocker. He went on an art-buying spree to Europe with his wife and picked up some 18th and 19th century masterpieces that form the basis of the museum collection. He also commissioned works by American artists. The collection today includes contemporary pieces and works by Californian artists.

An annual festival of the arts is held in May in Crocker Park, across from the museum, tel. 443-3395.

California's governors no longer hang their hats in the **Governor's Mansion**, among the oriental carpets, Italian marble fireplaces and French mirrors. The 15-room Victorian mansion is open to the public. 16th and H sts. Open daily 10am-5pm. Small admission fee, tel. 323-3047. Further north on 16th st., is the **California Almond Growers Visitor Center**. 1701 C st., tel. 446-8409. Almonds are a major California food export, and here you will learn everything you've ever wanted to know about them. Films, exhibits, and guided tours at specific times.

Sutters' Fort, the original settlement of Sacramento, was established in 1839, near the Sacramento River. Its history is presented through a self-guided audio tour. Behind the fort is the **State Indian Museum**. Open daily, 10am-5pm. Small admission required, tel. 445-4209.

As if being the state capital wasn't enough, Sacramento claims the title of **"Camellia Capital of the World"**, and salutes the flowering shrub in March with two weeks of parades, exhibits, bicycle races, a beauty queen contest and the Camellia Ball.

To conclude your visit to Sacramento, you can board the *River City Queen* and sail down the Sacramento River. Operative all year round, this is an old, refurbished steam boat, which takes tourists on a two-hour trip, twice a day from 1200 Front st. It is a pleasant sail, as well as being inexpensive ($10). The band on board plays tunes from a by-gone era. For reservations: tel. 916-448-7747. During the summer season, a further pleasure boat,

Matthew Mckinley, is operative from 1207 Front st., tel. 916-441-6481.

Important addresses and phone numbers

Sacramento Convention & Visitors Bureau: 1311 I st. Weekdays 8am-5pm, tel. 442-5542.

Old Sacramento Visitors Center: 130 J st. Mon.-Sat. 10am-5pm, tel. 443-7815.

California Office of Tourism: 1121 L st., Suite 103, tel. 322-1396.

Discover Sacramento Hotline: tel. 449-5566. 24 hours.

Sacramento Metro Airport: tel. 929-5411.

Airporter Van Lines: tel. 444-2222. Transportation between the airport and downtown.

Capitol City Coop: tel. 371-8151. Buses to San Francisco Airport.

Amtrak: 4th and I st., tel. 444-9131.

Greyhound: 1107 L st., tel. 444-6800. At Capitol Park.

Trailways: 1129 I st., tel. 443-2044.

Commuter Bus Lines: tel. 321-BUSS.

Yolo Bus-Commuter Lines: tel. 756-BUSS.

Regional Transit: tel. 444-2877.

Davis Medical Center Operator: tel. 453-2011; Emergency Dept., tel. 453-3790.

Davis

Just west of Sacramento on Route 80 is the **Davis Campus of the University of California**. Established as an agricultural school, it became a general campus in 1959, but is one of the leading agricultural research centers in the world, in such disciplines as agronomy, nutrition, plant pathology, wine-making and veterinary medicine.

The campus has about 20,000 students and it seems as if each one has at least three bicycles. The campus and adjacent student-oriented community form a separate entity, a sort of pastoral college town.

Along Putah Creek at the southern edge of campus there is a lush, shady arboretum with a bicycle path, a redwood grove and picnic grounds. A visit to the campus could include the **Gorman Museum of Native American Art** in the Tecumseh Center. The **Silo**, a "modern" dairy barn in 1914, now housing offices and a snack bar, is the student crafts center. If you're into weeds, the botany department in Robbins Hall has one of the largest weed collections in the world. If you prefer golf, the department of horticulture (near the Faculty Club) has a putting-green area for studying grass, on which visitors are welcome to try their skill. The **Memorial Union Building**, center of student life, has a coffee house, pub, bookstore and other facilities.

Across from the Union is the terminal for *UNITRANS*, a student-owned and operated bus system, featuring a fleet of authentic London double-decker buses, which runs through most of the Davis area during the school year, and connects with the *Regional Transit* system running to Sacramento.

Important addresses and phone numbers
Memorial Union Information Desk: tel. 752-2222.
Information Services: 129 Mark Hall, tel. 752-0539. For maps for self-guided tours.
Campus Events and Information Office: 4th floor, Memorial Union, tel. 752-1920.

Gold Country

Steamers and sailing-vessels came for some time as overcrowded with passengers as the passengers' brains were overcrowded with illusions.

Josiah Royce, California historian

In 1848, there were about 14,000 people in California. By 1852, the population reached about 200,000. Behind these seemingly dry numbers lay the convolutions and upheavals of the **California Gold Rush**.

When James Marshall discovered gold at Sutter's Mill, he and Sutter tried to keep the news quiet at first, but by late spring everybody in California was heading for the Sierra foothills. Other settlements were neglected, and soldiers and sailors deserted to work in the mines.

Fantastic stories spread about fist-sized nuggets in the stream beds and gold dust on the pathways. "Authentic journals" reported walking through the foothills for three weeks and picking up lumps of gold worth $50,000.

It is true that some of the first searchers had tremendous strokes of luck. The richest sources were tapped first, and fortunes were made that first wild summer of 1848. Some "enterprising" miners used Indians to work the mines while they worked the profits.

By autumn, the news of quick and easy fortunes reached the east. Dreams of a wild, free life in a faraway world lured men from their routines and families. Eager, unskilled youths made easy prey for the swindlers who sniffed fortunes in the pockets of men rather than in pockets of earth.

To reach the "golden land" was no easy venture. Travelers crossed the western frontier by foot, horse or wagon — others circled Cape Horn by steamer, or disembarked at the Isthmus of Panama, and from there went by foot or horse across to the Pacific coast and boarded steamers heading north. Travelers by sea were exposed to tropical humidity, disease and corruption. The Pacific voyage was marked by storms and the chill fogs of the California coast. Often the navigation charts used were unreliable. Beyond that, however, lay the Golden Gate. The incredible beauty of the land must have been a most welcome sight after the arduous journey: the narrow, hilly peninsula, the immense bay opening up, the city of San Francisco — a collection of tents clinging to the hillsides, and ships crowding the wharves.

The miners expected to make their fortunes and then return home. Most never made that fortune. Some left, some stayed on and found other jobs. Some wandered from camp to camp. They had no interest in sinking roots and creating a community. They were concerned only with surviving from day to day, waiting until they struck their lode. The wages they made were spent on exorbitantly priced goods. A loaf of bread could cost as much as a dollar, a blanket $100. There are many stories of farm boys dragged down into miserable lives of roaming around the drinking and gambling camps.

Enterprising newcomers made greater fortunes supplying the needs of the miners than they could have made mining. Mines required lumber and miners demanded meat. Huge areas of pine forests were felled, and vast numbers of deer, elk, bear and other game were slaughtered. Loads of jerkey and hides were exported from San Francisco. An immigrant tailor made a pair of strong canvas pants for a miner, using metal rivets for the pockets to hold heavy tools. The new style caught on, and today Levis are as universal as Coca Cola.

Foreigners, especially the Chinese, were distrusted as miners, but were exploited as cheap labor. Local Indian tribes were exposed to disease and cruel treatment at the hands of the miners, and many tribes were decimated.

The early miners sifted through stream beds with small pans resembling strainers. It was a lonely and exhausting job. With the advent of sluicing, mining became a major operation, often involving the diversion of rivers and combing of the sediments. The towns, originally ragged clusters of tents which sprang up wherever gold was found, became lines of wooden shacks and cloth houses along muddy streets. Councils were appointed to keep order. Justice for wrong-doers was swiftly decided by makeshift courts; flogging and banishment for some crimes, lynching for more serious ones.

About five hundred of these flimsy, transient mining camps sprang up between 1848 and 1860, first in the deep ravines where the first finds were made, then on the gentler slopes as the search widened. More than half the towns disappeared completely and only a handful became permanent towns. The places still seen in the gold country today give one a glimpse of a world bursting with courage, determination and greed, and which irrevocably transformed California.

Gold country runs north and south along the Sierra foothills, from Nevada City in the north to the area of Oakhurst in the south. It is beautiful countryside, with rounded hills, deep gorges and high cliffs. Route 49 is the main route through the towns and sites of the gold country. Gold country is roughly divided into three sections: From Oakhurst to the Sonora-Columbia area in the south; from Columbia to Auburn in the central region; and from Auburn north, encompassing Grass Valley, Nevada City, then Oroville to the northwest and Downieville to the northeast.

Each town is lined with the same remodeled hotels, reconstructed plank sidewalks, and old brick storefronts displaying postcards and chocolate chip cookies rather than dry goods and shovels. Despite the similarity of the towns, the region invites diversion. Following the backroads and small highways of the gold country affords one an interesting and beautiful, if time consuming, approach to the parks of the Sierras.

Traveling through the gold country is difficult without a car. Travel by *Greyhound* is possible, but may be time-consuming. Some towns have local bus systems.

I-80 slices through the hills towards Lake Tahoe and Reno, and passes Auburn close to the center of gold country. Route 50, heading east from Sacramento, reaches Placerville, the main center of gold country during the region's heyday. The road climbs east toward the southern end of Lake Tahoe.

Auburn

Auburn, on I-80, is the most easily accessible gold town. The town has an upper and lower part. The lower part has been historically preserved as **Old Town**, with restaurants and antique shops. The whole town can be walked in 10 minutes, but a mini-bus, with stops along **Lincoln Avenue**, the main street, connects the two sections. Buses leave every 45 minutes. The Chamber of Commerce provides a free guide to historic buildings.

In Old Town there is a square surrounded by sandwich bars, shops, bars and pizzerias under the gaze of a statue of a giant "forty niner". The smell of Mexican food wafts from two restaurants. *Tio Pepe*, at the end of the square behind the red fire station, is spacious, with Mexican decor, and is moderately priced. A few doors down from the fire station is the *Cafe Delicais*, which is smaller, simpler, cheaper, and usually packed. The *Hong Kong Restaurant*, 958 Lincoln Way, up the hill from Old Town, is the best deal in town and maybe in all the hills; Chinese lunch buffet at a bargain price.

Important addresses and phone numbers
Chamber of Commerce: 1101 High st., tel. 885-5616.
Placer County Transit: tel. 885-BUSS.

Nevada City

Nevada City has preserved its Victorian architecture and the atmosphere of a real town, with more than one street to stroll through. Somehow, Nevada City has established itself as the hip center of the Mother Lode. Its preserved western appearance provides the setting for movies and ads. San Francisco artists often retreat here. The annual **Music of the Mountains Festival** at the end of June draws big name musicians. Restaurants are diverse, elegant, organic, trendy and expensive. A lively music scene offers everything from folk to blues to classical guitar.

The Chamber of Commerce can provide a self-guided walking tour. Although none of the buildings are particularly interesting in themselves, together they paint a general picture of how a thriving gold rush town must have appeared.

The *National Hotel,* on Broad st., is the oldest continuously-running hotel in the country, as well as a historical landmark. Mark Twain stayed here. The hand painted wallpaper, the old overstuffed furniture, and the polished bannisters give the hotel an authentic feel.

The *Nevada Theater,* just up the street, is the oldest in the U.S., and the place where famous 19th century entertainer Lotta Crabtree made her debut. She grew up in Grass Valley and was taken under the wing of Lola Montez, an early European dance sensation already past her prime. At the age of eight, Lotta was dancing for small local functions. After her debut in Nevada City, she toured the mining towns for years, often in grueling one-night stands, until she finally moved on to San Francisco, then to New York where she earned international fame and made a tremendous fortune.

On Spring street, the **American Victorian Museum**, houses Victorian memorabilia and knick-knacks, as well as an excellent radio station (KVMR, 89.5 FM) and a lively bar. The museum also holds events during the famous, turn-of-the-century style 4th of July celebrations.

Accommodations
Nevada City has a number of quaint B&B inns, but you pay for the charm, with prices ranging from $55 and up. The funky old, *National Hotel* is more moderate ($25 and up). There is a saloon with live music downstairs, tel. 265-4551. Motels are found in Grass Valley and near the highway.

Important addresses and phone numbers

Area Code: tel. 916.
Chamber of Commerce: 132 Main st., tel. 265-2692.
Greyhound: Spring and S. Pine sts., tel. 272-9091.
Gold Country Stage: tel. 265-1411.

Around Nevada City

Grass Valley is located on Route 49 just a few miles south of
Nevada City. Its **Empire Mine State Historic Park** gives a clear
picture of the workings of a major mine. One-and-a+half miles north
of Highway 20, on Empire st. Open daily 9am-6pm until Labor Day,
9am-5pm until March 31st. Nominal admission, tel. 273-8522. This
was one of the largest and richest hard rock mines in the Mother
Lode, and the first electrified mine. The museum has beautiful
gardens and mine buildings and interesting equipment. There are
daily tours and audio-visual programs.

Heading north toward Yuba Pass, Route 49 cuts through some
rugged country. The town of **Downieville**, hugging both shores of the
Yuba River, still preserves the old architecture and narrow winding
streets of the early town. This town was once jammed with miners,
and holds the dubious distinction of being the only gold rush town
where a woman was hanged. Juanita, a Mexican dance hall girl,
stabbed a miner, and although she claimed that she had acted in
self-defence and was with child, she was hanged from hastily-built
gallows.

A turn east at Tyler-Foote Crossing road will lead to
Malakoff Diggins State Historic Park. Here, the world's largest
hydraulic mine blasted away half a mountain and left behind a
huge ugly pit, a monument to human disregard for nature. Nature,
however, smoothed over the scars and shaped and polished the
jagged cliffs into beautiful formations. Hiking trails abound, and there
is a state campground at North Bloomfield, the deserted boom town
that is now part of the park, tel. 265-2740.

Georgetown

Off the section of Route 49 between Auburn and Coloma, Highway
193 heads in the direction of Georgetown and makes a loop back
to the main road. This route is off the beaten track. Some of the
scenery is stupendous, along a winding road that dips into deep
sharp-cliffed gorges.

Georgetown itself extends for only about two blocks, along one
wide street. There are no special sites here. The town, however, in
its unadorned simplicity, is authentic and peaceful. The area has
many cycling routes and hiking trails, and the nearby American
River offers white water rafting. Founded by a group of sailors,
Georgetown was situated near one of the richest lodes. By 1853,
about $2 million worth of gold was found in the area. When the gold

diminished, the town managed to remain stable and even boasted on opera house.

In this tiny place there are two hotels worth mentioning: *The Georgetown Hotel* on Main street dates back to 1896. Rates range from $35-$55, and each room has different decor, often with beautiful antique furniture. There are no private baths, but the claw-footed bathtub traveled around Cape Horn, if that's any solace! Downstairs, the bar is a local hangout, with live music at night, tel. 916-333-4373.

Across Main st. and up a block or so is the *American River Inn*, a restored 1853 inn (the original one burnt down and was reconstructed at the turn of the century). The price, $45-$67, includes full breakfast and use of the pool, sauna and bicycles, tel. 333-4499.

Coloma

Coloma, on Route 49 north of Placerville, is the place where James Marshall first found gold. The area, then called **Sutter's Mill**, was on the south fork of the American River. By the summer of 1848, 2,000 miners were camped on the river banks, and a year later 10,000 were mining here. Coloma was the natural hub of the gold country until the digging center finally shifted away and the town declined.

Today, most of the small town lies within the **Marshall Gold Discovery State Historical Park**. The park includes some old stone buildings, a Chinese store, and a cabin where Marshall lived after he discovered gold. At the river bank is a plaque marking the spot where he supposedly made his first discovery, and nearby stands an exact replica of Sutter's Mill. Across the road is the small and excellent park museum outlining the history before and after the discovery. Open daily 10am-5pm. $2 admission, tel. 622-3470.

On the hill behind the old town is a tall bronze statue of James Marshall, in a heroic pose. From the museum, you can drive your car to the monument or take a one-mile round-trip hike by way of the Marshall cabin. The town swells with visitors around January 24th, the anniversary of the discovery of gold, when the event is re-enacted.

Placerville

Placerville, at the junction of Routes 45 and 50, replaced Coloma as the center of gold country. It became a stop for covered wagons after the Sierra crossing, a supply center for the mining camps, a staging point for expeditions to the Nevada silver mines, and a station on the *Pony Express* line. It also became known as Hangtown, after proving to be an efficient lynching center. Those days are vividly recalled by the dummy hanging from the second-floor of a building on Main street.

Placerville also seems to have inspired early Californian capitalism. Railroad magnates Leland Stanford and Mark Hopkins both worked here as small-time merchants. John Studebaker, the auto industrialist, once worked here as a wheelwright, and meat packer Philip Armour worked as a butcher.

Today, Highway 50 runs along a scenic, rugged route to the Sierras, South Lake Tahoe and Nevada, and Placerville provides a pleasant resting spot. There are reasonable and varied restaurants in the small old town center.

There are many B&B inns in the area, combining history and old-time Victorian luxury. The Chamber of Commerce has a complete list. There are also reasonable, if nondescript, motels on the outskirts of town. Most campgrounds in the immediate area are private. About seven miles (11 km) to the east on Route 50 is the El Dorado National Forest Information Center which can provide a list of nearby campgrounds, some primitive, some more fully equipped, ranging in price from free to $6. Information on camping in the wilderness areas near South Lake Tahoe is also available.

From far and wide, travelers come to *Poor Red's* in El Dorado, famous for its ribs. Several miles south of Placerville, on Main st.

The **Gold Bug Park and Mine**, located on Bedford st., just east of Route 49, is a pretty city park with miles of hiking trails and a real mine. There is a beautiful white-water rafting stretch on the South Fork of the American River from Chili Bar near Placerville, west of Folsom Reservoir. One and two-day trips are offered on this stretch of river, by various rafting outlets. A list is available from the Chamber of Commerce.

The Placerville area is fruit growing and wine country. Visitors can stop in on any number of farms along a route mapped out by the local growers' cooperative. It is a nice way to get a look at the countryside outside the towns and tourist services, and to enjoy apple pie, apple butter and apple wine. Maps of the apple farms and wineries which are open for visits and tasting are available from the local Chamber of Commerce.

In June, there is a professional rodeo and the arrival of the annual Highway 50 wagon train following the route of the old wagon trains from Carson City, over the Sierra Nevada to Placerville.

Important addresses and phone numbers
Area Code: tel. 916.
Chamber of Commerce: 542 Main st., tel. 626-2344.
Greyhound: 1750 Broadway, tel. 626-1010.
El Dorado National Forest Visitor Center: Highway 50, 7 miles east of Placerville.

Calaveras County

Calaveras County, toward the southern end of the gold country, had two tremendous strokes of fortune: it was situated on one of the richest areas of gold deposits, and it was named in Mark Twains's famous story, "The Celebrated Jumping Frog of Calaveras County". The gold has long since diminished, but the second resource is still being mined.

Twain spent some time at the main hotel in **Angel's Camp** listening to the tales of the miners. His name has become associated with almost everything in the town, and frogs have become the town's symbol. They are painted on the sidewalks, and every year a jumping frog contest is held on the 3rd weekend in May, in which the human owners end up hopping around more than the amphibious contestants. Frogs are available for rent for those who don't bring their own!

At the northern end of town is the local historical museum, which is not really worth visiting, but the counter of the museum serves as a Visitor Center where you can obtain a map with a self-guided walking or driving tour of the Angel's Camp area.

Head northeast up Route 4 for some nice surprises. First there is **Moaning Cavern**, near Vallecito. Although it has been hyped up, it is interesting and it really does moan. If stairways bore you, try rappelling down 180 ft. (61 m) by rope (extra fee). Be aware, however, that 13,000 years ago some didn't make it and human bones have been found at the bottom. Continue along Route 4 to **Murphys**, a cute, tree lined, one-street town. At the *Murphys Hotel* you can see the Ulysses S. Grant Presidential Suite, and the room where Mark Twain stayed.

About 16 miles (25 km) further is **Calaveras Big Trees State Park**, the only spot outside Yosemite or Sequoia National Park where you'll find sequoias. There is a North Grove and a South Grove, with the North Grove at the park entrance and the southern about nine miles (14 km) away. A mile-long trail loops through the northern grove, and a self-guided trail map is available. This park is very family oriented. The Visitor Center, open 10am-5pm daily, offers slide shows, nature exhibits, and schedules of guided walks and campfire programs. The campground ($6) comes complete with bears. Reservations needed for most weekends. P.O. Box 120, Arnold, CA., 95223, or through *Ticketron*. A $3 advanced reservation fee is attached to the camping fee, tel. 795-2334.

The town of **San Andreas** was established by Mexicans in 1849, but they were elbowed out by the Americans, and then the Chinese came, reworking the diggings abandoned by their less patient predecessors.

Only a few of the gold rush buildings remain today. There is a beautiful old courthouse, which houses the Chamber of Commerce, a museum with an interesting collection of artifacts, and the local historical society. It is worth walking around here and showing some curiosity about the region; the staff will reward you with warmth and some unusual local legends.

The cemetery on the western outskirts of town have stones bearing some chilling and pithy epitaphs. Black Bart, the notorious stagecoach robber, was caught, tried and convicted in San Andreas, and purportedly slept in the jail behind the courthouse. Black Bart was quite a character. Failing to find gold legally, he worked as a clerk for a stagecoach company and studied the schedules, routes and drivers until the stagelines became easy prey. Meanwhile, he moved to San Francisco with his newly acquired wealth and became a prominent businessman who hobnobbed with the powerful. When his finances declined, he changed outfits and hit another stagecoach, always polite and gentle and leaving behind a few lines of poetry.

Important addresses and phone numbers
Area Code: tel. 209.
Chamber of Commerce: Old Courthouse Building, 30 N. Main st., San Andreas, tel. 754-3391.

Southern Mother Lode
Columbia State Historic Park has a strange existence. It is a tourist attraction, a state park, and a replica town of days gone by when people sold sarsaparilla and penny candy, but at the same time a real lived-in town complete with courthouse. Even though you know that the guy in the old-fashioned costume does not usually dress like that, and that the blacksmith plies his trade largely for the benefit of tourist, the town is lived in and so well-preserved, that it gives an unmatched feeling for the past. Maps and guides can be obtained at the Visitor Center, tel. 532-4301.

If you want gas, drugstores, cheap stucco motels and other symbols of modernity, then go to Sonora. Further west, off Route 49, is Jamestown, an attractive antique looking town with brightly painted two-story frame buildings. Ride the steam-powered trains at the Railtown 1897 State Historic Park. Fifth ave., off Route 49/108. tel. 984-3953.

You can also try your luck at gold digging by joining one of the teams that leaves Jamestown, headed by geologists and other gold diggers. This special tour does not ensure your discovering gold, however it does mean you will enjoy a unique experience. The length of these expeditions range from a day to a fortnight. For further details, tel. 209-984-4653.

Accommodations
Sonora has no shortage of motels. However, probably the best motel

to check into is built of wood and situated in a natural wood. This is the *Columbia Gem Motel*. The wood cabins on Columbia Hwy, is half-a-mile from the Columbia History State Park. The owners, the Harris', are laden with information and good-will. For further information and reservations, tel. 209-532-45508. Approximately $40 a night.

Important addresses and phone numbers

Area Code: tel. 209.
Chamber of Commerce: 158 W. Bradford st., Sonora, tel. 532-4212.
Tuolumne County Visitors Bureau: 16 W. Stockton st., Sonora, tel. 948-INFO.
Greyhound: 260 E. Nonoway, Sonora, tel. 532-1356.

Lake Tahoe

Lake Tahoe straddles two states and two worlds. Nevada lies along the eastern shore, and California on the western. Also to the west and southwest there are high rugged mountains, snow covered even in the summer. Among these mountains is **Desolation Wilderness** a beautiful area set aside for hikers, where no vehicles are allowed. This is a real wilderness, a hiker's challenge and paradise. Yet within viewing distance of these peaks are the ski lifts, and the strip of motels and restaurants, and the flashing lights of the casinos of Stateline, the tiny resort on the Nevada border, literally across the street from California.

Tahoe itself is truly a jewel in the wilderness, pristine and immense, 22 miles (35 km) long and 12 miles (19 km) across. The lake was formed by faulting and uplifting of the Sierra Nevada block, as well as by later damming by lava, and sculpting and gouging by glaciers. The waters are incredibly blue, due to the great depth (averaging 1,000 ft./340 m), the purity of the water, and the clarity of the atmosphere. The water is clear enough to see down to 120 ft. (40 m).

In 1859, with the discovery of silver at Comstock Lode in northern Nevada, loggers clear-cut the surrounding forests, hauled them over the eastern crests, and floated them by flume to the mining communities. Vast areas of woodland were slashed and razed, but, amazingly, the forests regenerated themselves.

However, about a century later came another onslaught against the ecologically delicate lake. The natural beauty of the predominantly private shoreline was spoilt by the building of resorts. Waste was dumped into the lake, seriously damaging this mountain gem. Steps were rapidly taken to save the land that remained, and to limit and control continuing development.

Today, the area abounds with reserves to explore. Tahoe is a point upon which everyone converges: hikers, boaters, canoeists, revelers, skiers or gamblers. It is one of the prime vacation spots in the country. Recently, it has turned into a year-round resort, with extensive skiing facilities drawing the crowds in the winter.

The quietest period is early fall, when it is too cold and rainy for boating, swimming and most hiking, and too early for the fresh snows. Prices fluctuate not only between seasons, but during the week as well. Even during the off-season, the resort fills up on weekends, because it is so accessible and convenient to major urban centers. The endless row of hotels at South Lake Tahoe is packed over weekends, even in autumn, but during the week in the off-season, Tahoe is a vacationer's market. Visitors can choose among the motels, with rooms that might cost less than $20 per night to luxury resort facilities. As for eating, the casinos on the Nevada border offer great bargains similar to those in Reno and Las Vegas, though more limited. Great buffets are served for a few dollars and up.

How to get there

The two main approaches to Lake Tahoe from the California side both stem from Sacramento. Route 50 heads east through Placerville, and up through the Sierra foothills along an old covered-wagon trail, toward the lower end of Tahoe. The road is wide, but not a super highway. It is mind boggling to imagine covered wagons crossing this serpentine pass. I-80 climbs up to Truckee, north of Lake Tahoe, and over Donner Pass.

The **Lake Tahoe Airport**, located, near South Lake Tahoe, is served by *AirCal* and *Pacific Coast*. *PSA* periodically offers special packages including airfare, lodging, car rental and ski tickets, through PSA Great Escape Vacations. Shuttles run from Reno's airport, with its national carriers to Tahoe's resorts.

The *Amtrak* station at Truckee is on the *California Zephyr* line between San Francisco and Chicago. No tickets are sold at that station; make reservations, board the train, and pay the conductor. *Greyhound* also serves Truckee.

Tahoe Area Regional Transit runs buses between Incline Village in Nevada at the northest end of the lake, to Tahoma about halfway down the western shore. Buses also run between Tahoma and South Lake Tahoe. At the southern end of the lake, a bus serves key recreation sites between the town of South Lake Tahoe and the Forest Service Visitor Center at the southwestern tip.

Although the western shore of Lake Tahoe can be quite hilly, the area around South Lake Tahoe is a beautiful area for bicycle riding. It is a popular means of local transportation and rentals are readily available.

Several companies operate commercial boat cruises, combining travel and pleasure. They sail between the north and south shores of the lake, hit the casinos, and also dock near the ski resorts. The Chamber of Commerce can provide company names and addresses.

Accommodations

The hotels and motels are lined up almost side by side all along Highway 50 through South Lake Tahoe. At Stateline on the Nevada side are the casino-hotels. During the week visitors have their choice, but during weekends, even during the off-season of early fall, all these lodgings may be jammed, and prices are higher too.

Generally, the lodgings tend to be cheaper further away from the border casinos. The various casinos offer free shuttle service to the motels on the California side.

One interesting lodge, far away from the hubbub of South Lake Tahoe, is the *Strawberry Lodge*, a refurbished pine and rock structure. The area is surrounded by thick pine forest, the atmosphere is warm and friendly. The lodge is adjacent to hiking in Desolation Wilderness. There is a restaurant on the premises. Rates begin at $33 per night for a double. P.O. Box 1075, South Lake Tahoe 95705, tel. 659-7200.

Also at South Lake Tahoe, there is a thriving rental business in condominium time sharing. These arrangements sometimes work out more economically than resorts. Most units have some sort of kitchen facilities, and can often be divided among two or more parties. For information, call Security Timeshare Marketing: tel. 544-5611.

There are about seven state parks in the Tahoe region. The ones on the rim of the lake can be crowded through the summer. Parks further away, such as **Donner Memorial State Park**, tel. 525-7277, or **Grover Hot Springs**, tel. 831-0494, are usually less crowded. Both are set in beautiful scenery. State parks range in price from $3 to $6. The central state park office for the area has details on the parks.

The huge **El Dorado National Forest**, bordering Lake Tahoe on the west, has numerous campsites, ranging in price from free to $9 per night. On Route 89 north of Truckee, there are less crowded campgrounds along the road.

Food

The best eating in South Lake Tahoe is found in the casinos of Stateline. Although the choice is more limited than at the major resorts, there are excellent buffets here. All-you-can-eat breakfasts begin at 99 cents, lunches cost only a few dollars, and sumptuous

Lake Tahoe

prime-rib buffets go for as little as $5.95, but there are lines during prime hours.

What to see

Emerald Bay, towards the southern end of Route 89, is a stunning sight when first glimpsed from the road. It is a popular spot for overlooks and walks down the cliffside to the shore. Trails lead along the beautiful rock shoreline, down from the **Emerald Bay Overlook** (closed when icy) to **Vikingsholm**, a reproduction of a Norse fortress, which is open for guided tours during the summer June-Sept. 10am-4pm. Small admission, tel. 914-541-3030. Both parks have camping facilities, but campgrounds are continually crowded during the summer.

Across the road from Emerald Bay is a parking area for the short, steep hike to the footbridge above the cataracts of **Eagle Falls**. If the snow has cleared, you can continue on the same trail about one mile to **Eagle Lake.**

South of Emerald Bay, the Lake Tahoe Visitor Center, operated by the USFS, offers nature talks by ranger and self-guided tours on the flora and fauna of Lake Tahoe. "The Trail of the Washoe" exhibit shows how the lake's local Indians lived off the land for thousands of years with little impact on the environment. Open daily in summer, tel. 573-2600.

The Forest Service and State Parks operate tours throughout the baronial estates that graced the southern lakeshore at the turn of the century. The **Valhalia Estate** and **Baldwin Log Cabin** host concerts, ranging from chamber music to bluegrass, in the summer. Check with the Forest Service Visitor Center for schedules, or call tel. 916-544-5050.

CALIFORNIA

Lake Tahoe has a tremendous concentration of ski resorts, including the famous **Squaw Valley**, site of the 1960 winter Olympics. Between them, the resorts provide a variety of runs, as well as several hundred miles of cross country trails. Most of the ski resorts are clustered along the western shore of the lake. Several of them offer shuttle connections to hotels and resort areas. In February, the annual winter carnival of **Snowfest** fills the lakeshore resorts with concerts, dances, theater, parades and skiing exhibitions, tel. 583-7625.

The aerial tram ride at the **Heavenly Ski Resort**, south of Stateline, off Route 50, climbs to an elevation exceeding 8,000 ft. (2,720 m), offering a breathtaking view of Lake Tahoe and the Sierra Nevada. There is also a restaurant at the top with great views, a wonderful place for late Sunday brunch. Tram tickets cost $9 for adults, $5 for children age 12 and under, tel. 583-6985.

To sail on Lake Tahoe, you must either hire a boat or join an organized sail on the pleasure boat the *Tahoe Queen*, which sails several times a day during the summer, on a two-hour route. You can also board the boat for a dinner-dance in the evening. The boat is also operative during winter and spring, though at greater intervals. Boarding is at Sky Run Marina, at the Stateline casinos. The scenery viewed on this tour is much more spectacular than anything seen through the boat's glass bottom. $12.50 per adult. $4.50 for under 11-year-olds. For details and reservations, tel. 916-541-3364.

A little further south of the lake is the **Grover Hot Springs State Park**, surrounded by hiking trails and abruptly rising peaks, and containing two deliciously hot pools. Camping is available 3 miles (5 km) west of Markleeville, which is on Route E1. From Lake Tahoe, take Route 89 south to Route 88, skirt east to Woodford, and then south on E1 for the turnoff to the park at Markleeville. During summer season, open daily 9am-9pm. $1 adults, 50 cents age 17 and younger, tel. 694-2248.

The **Desolation Wilderness**, looming west of the South Lake Tahoe region spans both slopes of the Sierra Nevada. It embraces 10,000 ft. (3,400 m) high peaks, glacial valleys and over 100 lakes, and draws enough hikers and campers to necessitate the rationing of camping permits. The adjacent **Mokelumne Wilderness** is smaller, less crowded, and still rugged. Check with the Forest Service Visitor Center for maps, details and weather conditions in both areas.

Truckee is a small mountain town right off I-80, spruced up for tourists but not overdone. With its original buildings and wooden sidewalks, it maintains the ambience of an old frontier town. There are a few nice restaurants and cafés. The information center is located in the train station, on the southern end of the main street just beyond the traffic light, tel. 587-2757. Just north of I-80, off the Truckee exit, is a Forest Service Information Center, with details on camping and hiking throughout the immense **El Dorado National Forest**. It covers all the territory along the western shore of Tahoe and further west into the Sierra peaks, including the stunning Desolation Wilderness, and stretches down into the foothills.

At **Donner Lake**, just west of Truckee, the famous Donner party encamped during a terrible Sierra winter in 1846. Their story is one of poor judgement, misfortune, heroic struggle and grim survival. A group of almost 90 people headed west in the summer of 1846 in wagons, under the leadership of two brothers, George and Jacob Donner. By the time they reached the vicinity of Reno, in October, the party was already fraught with tension and bickering due to a serious mistake in routing. They had lost wagons and much cattle. After receiving some relief from one of their members who had crossed the pass earlier to Sacramento, they rested for a week and began the climb over the Sierras. The delay was a fatal mistake, for the snows fell early and heavily. The party was trapped near the lake, huddled in makeshift cabins and brush tepees, while the land lay buried under 22 feet of snow. On improvised snowshoes, a party of 15 hiked west to seek help. Only seven lived, reduced to cannibalism to survive. A relief party reached the others at the lake only in February. The survivors were eating oxhide and bones, and there were more signs of cannibalism. The last survivors were saved only in April. 42 of the 89 members died before reaching their destination.

The cannibalism caused much controversy, and in one case there were even accusations of murder. A museum at **Donner Memorial State Park**, at the southeast corner of Donner Lake, presents the tragic story. Open 10am-6pm daily. Nominal admission.

Donner Lake can provide a pleasant alternative to lodging around Lake Tahoe, especially during the summer. The accommodations at Donner Lake tend to be less expensive than at Tahoe, and the facilities of the lake itself less crowded. Cabins are available with both weekly and nightly rates.

Important addresses and phone numbers

Area Code: 916.
South Lake Tahoe Chamber of Commerce: About 2 miles west of the stateline on Route 50, tel. 541-5255.
North Lake Tahoe Chamber of Commerce: Lighthouse Center, Tahoe City, tel. 583-2371.
Truckee-Donner Chamber of Commerce: tel. 587-2757.
National Weather Service: tel. 447-6941.
U.S. Forest Service: tel. 544-6420, 541-0209 (south shore); tel. 583-3642 (north shore).
California State Parks: tel. 525-7232.
Nevada State Parks: tel. 702-831-0494.
Coast Guard: tel. 583-4433.

*C*ALIFORNIA

Greyhound: 1099 Park ave., tel. 544-2241 (South Lake Tahoe); tel. 587-3882 (Truckee).
Tahoe Area Rapid Transit: tel. 583-2371.
South Tahoe Area Ground Express (STAGE): tel. 573-2080.

Toward Reno

California shares much of its long eastern border with Nevada. In the north, the border runs right through the Sierra Nevada and splits Lake Tahoe down the middle. There are ski resorts on both sides, protected wilderness tracts on the Californian side, and casinos on the Nevada side, literally a few steps across the stateline in some cases. If driving to California along I-80, the main cross-country route, Reno makes a convenient and popular stop. It is often used as an entertaining stopover point heading to or from California. Reno is the commercial and cultural center of northern Nevada's vast territory. At the eastern base of the Sierras, it is at the starting point for one of the main passes over the crests, in pioneer days as well as today. In addition to its casinos, Reno has cheap food and lodging which make it a tempting rest point before crossing the mountains, or a base for trips into the Sierras.

The casinos are the big attraction. At night, sitting on its high, open plateau beneath the shadowy mountains, Reno resembles an electric Emerald City, but in downtown itself, the waves of lights lose their dazzle. Reno, which calls itself "The Biggest Little City in the World" has neither the glamour and overwhelming excitement of Las Vegas, nor the rustic charm of one of the small mountain casino resorts.

Reno is served by *Greyhound* and *Trailways*. The *Chicago-San Francisco Amtrak* line runs right through the city. Regional and national carriers use Reno's airport.

The intersection at Virginia and 2nd st. forms the center of the casino area. Many of the casinos are housed in the large and blazing downtown hotels, as in Las Vegas. These include *Harrah's*, *MGM Grand Hotel*, *The Sahara Reno*, *Circus Circus*, *Mapes* and others. There are restaurants, coffee shops, bars and casinos open all night.

Reno, like Las Vegas has an abundance of inexpensive accommodation and fantastic dining deals. As long as the gambling impulse is under control, this is a penny-pincher's paradise. Even during the summer season, good rooms can often be found for $16-$20. There are plenty of blazing motel signs along the central strip, and spread out along the roads connecting to I-80. Many of the motels offer coupons, distributed by the casinos and redeemable for cash, free cocktails, turns on the slot machine, etc.

Breakfast buffets start at about $2, lunch buffets slightly higher. The various dinner buffets, offering immense spreads, start at about $4. Lunch buffets often have almost the same selection, at a lower price.

Important addresses and phone numbers

Area Code: 702.

Commission on Tourism: Capitol Complex, Carson City, 89710. Brochures and information on the entire state available upon request by mail.

Reno/Tahoe Gaming Academy: An initiation into the mysteries of the gambling games, and tours of the casinos, tel. 348-7403.

Reno International Jazz Festival: Held in April and often featuring big names in jazz, tel. 786-5409.

A glimpse through the trees, Lake Tahoe

Yosemite

In 1851, Indians used to raid the White settlements in the central valley and then disappear into the Sierra Mountains. A force led by Major James Savage followed their trail through the foothills and into the high mountains and suddenly came upon an immense valley carved from rock that stunned him with its beauty and grandeur. Amazingly, Yosemite had remained undiscovered by White explorers until then. It was clear that the valley would never be the same again. The almost magical valley, with its sheer granite cliffs, its high falls and its sculpted domes, immediately attracted those who were overwhelmed by its beauty, and those who wanted to use, exploit and "improve" it. Although the boundaries of the park are secure today, the debate over its future continues as the valley fills up every summer with campers and trailers, resembling an L.A. suburb that has been transplanted into the wilderness.

Just a decade after its discovery, the need to preserve the wonders of this ice-carved valley was recognized, and in 1864 Yosemite became the nation's first state park, and initiated California's direct involvement with the protection of its natural areas. However, the protection was far from inviolate, and in 1890 the area was placed under federal jurisdiction, and guarded by the U.S. army. The army dealt with law-breakers forcefully. When stockmen allowed their sheep to continually strip the hillsides of vegetation, with the excuse that they could not control their flocks, the army drove the sheep across the mountainous area and released them, and the stockmen suddenly discovered new ways of controlling their sheep.

It was John Muir, a Scottish immigrant, who spearheaded the fledgling conservation movement. He also founded and headed the Sierra Club, and most especially fought for the protection of Yosemite. As a young man, he wandered through America on foot and stopped when he reached the Sierras. He knew the Yosemite Park intimately, and collected an enormous amount of data about the area. Geologists doubted that glaciers had formed Yosemite Valley, but Muir set out and discovered glaciers in the area, and also the scars of ancient glaciers. He was known to explore the rim of the valley overnight carrying no more than a notebook, a tin cup and some tea.

Muir began to write of the Sierras, with great eloquence and literary style that captured the public's attention. He purposefully and incessantly used his pen to prod the public into political action to protect Yosemite and other wilderness areas in the Sierras. He became a powerful force, with contacts in high places, and personally led President Theodore Roosevelt through the back country of Yosemite, the two men camping out in four-foot snow drifts. Muir convinced Roosevelt that large tracts of forest land should be protected from foresters. The fledgling Sierra Club, under Muir's leadership, became a forceful voice for preservation, and is now one of the most powerful groups in the entire American conservation movement.

Muir's greatest political defeat also involved Yosemite. North of Yosemite Valley, and clearly within the park boundaries, was the **Hetch Hetchy Valley**, second only to Yosemite itself in the unique beauty of its sculpted canyon. The city of San Francisco decided to build a dam here, although for a slightly greater investment a site could have been chosen elsewhere. The battle reached the Roosevelt Administration and the Congress. The President supported the plan to build the dam within the boundaries of the park, despite Muir's objections. The hard-fought battle tore a gap within the conservation movement, between those who wanted to manage resources with planned and multiple uses, and those who wanted to preserve the area exactly as it was (a rift that continues today within California and across the country). The battle dragged on for twelve years, until Congress finally approved the dam's construction, and building commenced in 1913. Muir was crushed by the defeat and the loss of the canyon, and died a year later. But the battle over Hetch Hetchy made a powerful impact and contributed directly to the creation of the National Park Service in 1916, which solidified the parks' existence and helped formalize their boundaries.

How to get there

Yosemite National Park is located in the Sierras almost due east from the Monterey Bay area, across the San Joaquin Valley and beyond the foothills. No major freeway leads to its gate. Route 99, running north-south along the eastern edge of the valley, is the closest freeway to the west, and the point from which several local highways split off for Yosemite. There is no easy way to travel the length of the Sierras without leaving them and following the foothills or even returning to the flat central valley itself. Even in the foothills, only small winding roads zigzag along the length of the hills.

Route 120 leads from Manteca in the northwest to the northern entrance to the park. Route 41 comes from Fresno in the southwest, skirting the region of the Mariposa Grove, and Route 140 goes directly east from Merced to the Yosemite Valley. This is the main entrance to the park. Route 120, to the north of the Yosemite Valley continues east into the high country of the Sierras, where the peaks are the most rugged. This beautiful road passes through Tuolumne Meadows, which is the junction and center for backpackers tackling some of the lovely high country trails, and continues to the steep Tioga Pass and down to I-395. Route 120 is closed in the winter.

YOSEMITE NATIONAL PARK

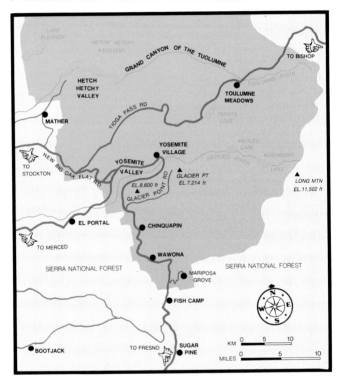

As can be seen on the map, from Yosemite southwards to Sequoia National Park, this is the only highway that traverses the sharply ridged spine of the Sierras.

Public transportation to Yosemite is non-existent. The closest is the private bus line, the *Yosemite Transportation System (YTS)*, tel. 373-4171, which makes connections with commercial bus terminals in Lee Vining, Fresno and Merced, and with the *Amtrak* stations in Merced and Fresno. To Fresno and Merced a one-way fare hovers around $15. To Lee Vining it's over $30. Fast one-day tours are also available from San Francisco, but don't blink or you'll miss something.

Hitchhiking within the park is quite acceptable. People who might not normally assist hitchers are willing to do so here, as it is clear

Yosemite — the valley

that many hikers are making their way to trailheads at the beginning or end of a hike.

When Yosemite Valley is congested, a car can be as much of a liability as in an urban downtown, but you can take advantage of the *Valley Shuttle*. Leave your car at the campground, or in the Curry Village parking lot. Some of the buses are double-deckers, which are a novelty if you haven't been to England. Some areas are open only to shuttles or to bicycles. Bicycles can be rented for about $10 per day. There are some beautiful rides on the valley floor; the path to Mirror Lake is a particularly recommended.

Accomodations

With very few exceptions, all eating and lodging concessions are run by the *Yosemite Park and Curry Company*. Reservations for private accommodations are made through one central office: *Yosemite Park and Curry Co.*, Yosemite National Park, 95389, tel. 209-252-4848 or tel. 255-8345.

The greatest number and variety of lodgings are concentrated in the valley, but each of the regional centers of the park also provides private lodging. Tuolumne Meadows has tent-top cabins, a central dining lodge and drive-in and walk-in campgrounds. White Wolf, on the same road, has cabins and tents. Both facilities are open only in the summer. Wawona has lodges and the old *Wawona Hotel*.

Reservations for all Curry accommodations are essential in summer and are recommended all year round. A deposit of one day's rent must be paid in advance.

The *Ahwahnee Hotel* in the valley is a massive edifice of stone and timber, the kind of place where you want to sit by a roaring fire with a glass of sherry while recounting your tale of survival in a blizzard. Rooms start at over $100 per night, and there are also two-story cottages. *Yosemite Lodge* is a more standard hotel with moderate to high-moderate prices. *Curry Village* is a sub-division with canvas roofs. The concrete-and-canvas Housekeeping Camp units have double beds and wood burning stoves and cost a slightly more than the Curry Village tents. They are open in the summer only.

The Upper River, Lower River, North Pines, Lower Pines, and Upper Pines campgrounds are all drive-in areas, costing $7 per night, at the east end of the valley, and comprise one giant trailer city. Reservations are required in advance for summer spots, but occasionally you can find someone willing to share a space, for partial fee payment. These sites are like parking lots covered in pine needles.

Do not, however, consider the option of snoozing in your car along a dirt road or putting your sleeping bag down somewhere in the valley, because you will probably be caught and fined.

Two walk-in campgrounds in the valley often have space until late in the day, but don't rely on it during high summer season. Backpacker's Camp is located just behind the North Pines Campground, near Mirror Lake. Toward the western end of the valley is Sunnyside, used primarily by climbers, who tend to keep themselves apart. A few nights spent listening to them and you'll either be determined to scale El Capitan or equally determined never to climb a ladder again. Both campgrounds cost $2.

Motels, lodges and private campgrounds are also found in the small towns on the fringe of the park: in Lee Vining east of Tioga Pass, El Portal along Route 140, and Oakhurst along Route 41. Backcountry camping is free along the numerous mountain trails, but a wilderness permit is required. Even for backcountry hiking, reservations are recommended because the trails have quotas, and certain quotas fill up fast. Apply for a permit at the Yosemite Valley Visitor Center or at a ranger station. You may be asked for a rough itinerary. Some campgrounds have bear-proof lockers.

There are drive-in campgrounds, heavily frequented by trailers, along the main highways throughout the park. Some on the outer periphery may have available spots early in the day as people leave. During the summer, it is wise to make reservations for these spots too. Two campgrounds in Yosemite Valley and one in Wawona remain open the year round.

*C*ALIFORNIA

Activities, services, general information

The *Yosemite Guide*, a free newspaper, is your key to current park information. It contains a current listing of all interpretive programs, facilities and services, general information, and feature articles. The guide is available at entrance stations, ranger stations, and visitor centers. Current road, weather and camping information is available by telephone. Consult the Yosemite Guide for numbers.

Special information for disabled visitors, and wheelchair-emblem placards for vehicles for special driving privileges are available on request at entrance and information stations.

Printed information in Spanish, Japanese, German, and French is also available on request.

The *Yosemite Road Guide* is a descriptive booklet keyed to numbered posts along park roads. It can be purchased at most information stations and gift shops in the park.

Numerous publications about the park are available at outlets throughout the park or by writing to Yosemite Natural History Association, Box 545, Yosemite National Park, 95389.

Every Visitor Center and some of the ranger stations conduct local programs of campfire evenings, general and specialized walks such as early morning bird-watching and late night star gazing.

The park can be divided into three basic parts: the gently sloping west, with its groves of sequoia trees; Yosemite Valley, which is both the most beautiful and the most overcrowded, and the spectacular, jagged peaks of the high country, with Tuolumne Meadows as the central base. Within these areas is a remarkable range of terrain and animal life.

Western Area

There are three groves of sequoia in Yosemite. **Tuolumne** and **Merced Groves** are located just inside the entrance along route 120. Near the southeast entrance off route 41, is the **Mariposa Grove**, which is the largest, and the one with major interpretive services. Visitors park their cars and board free trams, which are accompanied by guides and circle through the grove. Included among the trees here is the Grizzly Giant, about 2,700 years old. A tunnel cut through one of the trees, as a novelty, destroyed the shallow root network over the years, and a heavy snowfall finally toppled the tree. There are gentle trails, a small museum in a cabin, and plenty of opportunities to approach the trees directly.

Along Route 41 on the way to the Yosemite Valley, **Wawona** is a business and service center, as well as a restored historical village where frontier crafts are practiced and demonstrated. Stagecoach rides are available here. There are interpretive programs in the evening. Gasoline is also available. The old, rambling building just south of the junction is *Wawona Hotel*, built in 1875 and still operating today. Food and lodging are available at the *Wawona*.

The one and only turnoff for the **Glacier Point Overlook** is also on Route 41, at Chiquapin Junction, and it's a detour well worth taking. On the way to Glacier Point is the **Badger Pass Ski Area** (the road beyond this point is closed during the winter). From the edge of a sheer rock cliff dropping 3,200 ft. (1,088 m) to the valley floor, the view from Glacier Point is vast and fantastic. All the major features along the valley walls are clearly visible, and form an unusual perspective. Backing it all are the snow-covered peaks of the high Sierra. Bus tours from the valley floor reach this point. The Panoramic Trail is a beautiful trail of several miles from this point to the Yosemite Valley floor. The eight-mile (13 km) trail offers a pleasant and not very strenuous hike.

The best way to do this hike is to leave your car in the valley, hitch up to Glacier Point, and then start hiking downhill. This will bring you to the top of Nevada Falls, and then past Vernal Falls. The descent past misty and verdant Vernal Falls leads to the valley floor, where a shuttle bus can take you to back to your car.

The Valley

From naturalist John Muir to photographer Ansel Adams, artists, writers, and nature-lovers have been enchanted by Yosemite Valley. This glacier-carved canyon along the Merced River, with its sheer granite walls and bulging outcroppings, its sculpted domes and waterfalls plunging from hanging valleys, is one of the great natural wonders of the world. Over two million visitors visit Yosemite a year, and many of them never realize that the seven-mile (11 km) valley is but a small sliver of the 1,200-square mile park.

Half Dome and **El Capitan** are probably the two best-known monoliths along the valley floor. Master mountain climbers try their skills on the sheer cliff of El Capitan. Half Dome can be reached by good hikers via the easier rear route, the last section with the aid of cables embedded in the rock. The top is wider than its seems from below, and offers incredible views. The waterfalls yield their greatest flow around May when swollen with melted snow. The greatest of the waterfalls is **Yosemite Falls**, plunging through two falls over 2,400 ft. (816 m). The other major falls are **Ribbon**, **Bridalveil**, **Nevada** and **Vernal Falls**. Vernal Falls and Nevada Falls are accessible from the Happy Isles Nature Center at the far eastern end of the valley, along the steep, slippery Mist Trail. At the top, trails head towards Half Dome, Tuolumne Meadows and Glacier Point.

The valley can be a depressing place. It became so overdeveloped by the 1970s that the Park Service began to impose certain restrictions. The rows of trailers in the campgrounds, with two antennas and blasting radios, seem incongruous with the surrounding beauty, and many of the stores and tourist facilities

El Capitan

seem inappropriate to the character of the park. In recent years, the Park Service has closed some tennis courts, re-directed traffic, and introduced a campground reservation system for the valley, but with two million visitors a year, the valley can be awfully crowded, and may make you want a vacation from your vacation.

Nevertheless, you should not miss the opportunity to explore and enjoy the valley, as there is an enormous amount to discover, but do not forget to explore further in the huge park area beyond the lip of the valley.

The valley is the center of everything in the park. Here you can rent horses, take climbing lessons or sit on the porch of the luxurious but rustic *Ahawanee Hotel*. In the mosaic of meadow and woodlands in the west, immerse yourself in spring's wildflowers.

Yosemite Valley has a comprehensive system of interpretative programs, and every visitor center in the park conducts local programs too.

The Valley Visitor Center, located just west of Yosemite Village, provides an interesting introduction to the natural and human history of the valley and park. The **Indian Cultural Museum**, and the **Indian Village**, behind the Visitor Center, commemorate the local Indians who dwelled in this valley for thousands of years, living by hunting game and collecting acorns. At the eastern end of the valley, accessible by shuttle, is the **Happy Isles Nature Center**, named for the tiny islands formed by the confluence of the Merced River and Illouette Creek. Several heavily-wooded acres provide exhibits and information on the park's features, and a ranger can answer questions. This is also the starting point (or end point) for the trail to Vernal Falls, Half Dome and Glacier Point.

Tuolumne Meadows

Tuolumne Meadows is the center for Yosemite's high country, and a base for motorists, day-hikers and overnight trekkers. The alpine meadows, the lakes and granite slopes in this area form some of the most stunning scenery in the High Sierra, and it is easily accessible from Tuolumne by even a short hike.

Tuolumne Meadows, the largest sub-alpine meadow in the Sierras, teems with wildflowers and wildlife in early summer. To the east, on Route 120 is the eastern entrance to the park, beyond Tioga Pass, which is about 10,000 ft. (3,400 m) high. Tuolumne Meadows is a hub for a network of short and long trails following the High Sierra watershed and penetrating into some of the wildest sections of Yosemite. The famous **Pacific Crest Trail** (called the John Muir Trail at this section) passes through here. Many hikers use this as a starting point or endpoint for hiking one section of this trail. Ambitious and experienced hikers can follow this trail south all the way into the Sequoia National Park. There is a beautiful but well-trodden overnight hike from here to Yosemite Valley. Another beautiful route for good hikers follows the Tuolumne River into the appropriately named Grand Canyon of the Tuolumne. Horses can be hired here.

One of the best times to visit Tuolumne, as with the whole park, is early fall, before the November snowstorms. At these heights, the aspens, willows, pines and other deciduous trees create a stunning autumnal collage. There are fewer guided activities after Labor Day, but enough to keep the eager visitor busy, and the additional bonus of having no crowds. Lodging, camping and motels in Lee Vining are more easily available.

Eastern Slope

East of the high bulwark of the Sierras is a vast area of arid plateaus, twisted volcanic formations, and islands of forest and greenery. The main route along the eastern slope is I-395. South of the Tioga Pass in Yosemite, no road crosses the spine of the Sierras to the separate, other-worldy eastern terrain. About 30 miles (50 km) north of the Tioga Pass, off 395 to the east, is **Bodie**, one of the few remnants of the little-known gold rush on the eastern slope of the Sierras. Once boasting a population of 12,000, some 65 saloons, and an average of one murder a day, Bodie is now a genuine ghost town, preserved by the state park system in its state of natural decay. Pick up a visitors brochure at the ranger's house on Green st.

Due east of Lee Vining is **Mono Lake**, haunting and moon-like. The lava-strewn islands are the remaining signs of ancient volcanic explosions from the depths of the lake. The tufa spires add to the strange appearance. It is possible to canoe among them, and to take ranger-guided walks through this unusual landscape. The remnant of an ancient inland sea, Lake Mono has no outlet. The beaches around the lake are eroded pumice. The lava-strewn islands constitute the state's largest rookery for California's gulls.

For years, statewide environmental and local interests have battled L.A., which since 1941 has diverted water from four of the five streams that feed the lake, using the water for its own municipal supply. That water, combined with water from the Owens Valley, south of the lake, is diverted to Los Angeles by aqueduct and constitutes the bulk of the city's water supply. The stream diversions lowered the level of the lake over the years, threatening brine shrimp in the lake and the California gulls that feed on them, although the recent rainy years have helped to raise the water level somewhat.

Mono Lake is managed by the Bureau of Land Management. Information on the lake and on tours can be obtained from the Lee Vining Information Center on I-395, as well as at the Bakersfield District Headquarters of the Bureau of Land Management: 800 Truxton, Room 302, Bakersfield, 93301, tel. 805-861-4191.

Half-an-hour's drive south of this unearthly feature are the very earthly pleasures of **Mammouth Mountain**, a popular ski resort in alpine woods style, which is one of the largest in the country. In addition to the downhill ski slopes there is an extensive network of cross-country trails, and hiking trails leading into the high country's **John Muir Wilderness**. The ski season is unusually long, lasting occasionally to the Fourth of July.

Majestic heights — the Half Dome

For information on Mammouth's ski conditions, call the 24-hour Snowline: tel. 619-934-6166. Mammouth has a wide range of accommodation and restaurants. For the Chamber of Commerce, call tel. 619-934-2712. The ranger station's Visitor Center, tel. 714-934-2505, can give details on the many camping grounds in the area.

Mammouth is located on Route 203, the gateway to some of the **Inyo National Forests**, scenic forested backcountry. Campgrounds open in late April or early May and stay open after Labor Day, until the first snows close them. Most cost from $4-$6. As in most popular resorts, the prices here are a bit higher than surrounding areas, with motel rooms starting at about $30 and up.

Devil's Postpile National Monument also lies on Route 203. The 60-foot (20 m) columns, resembling a giant pipe organ, were created 900,000 years ago as molten lava poured from the earth's crust. At Rainbow Falls, the San Joaquin River plunges 140 ft. (48 m) over lava ledges. **Oh! Ridge** (no, that's no typo) provides a spectacular view of June Lake, as well as something just as rare in these parts: a campground that is not always full. In the summer, a shuttlebus operates from Minaret Summit to the monument. The monument is administered by the Sequoia/Kings Canyon office, at Three Rivers, 93271, tel. 565-3342.

Mono Lake

Bodie — a genuine ghost town

The scrubby bristlecone pines, oldest organisms in the world, grow in the bare, exposed terrain of the White Mountains. The sequoias are mere babes in the woods compared to the gnarled and grizzled bristlecones, which are more than 4,000 years old. The oldest, the Methuselah Tree, is 4,700 years old, already ancient at the beginning of the common era. Some of the fallen trees date back an incredible 9,000 years. The bristlecone pine forest is reached by taking Route 395 to Bigpine, about 15 miles (25 km) south of Independence. Head east on Route 168 for 13 miles (20 km), to Westgard Pass, then 10 miles (16 km) north on White Mountain rd. Contact the Inyo County Park Department for information: tel. 619-878-2411. No gas, water, or commercial services are available in the forest itself. Evening ranger programs are held. There is an information station in the forest.

The North Coast: Mendocino and the Redwood Country

Mendocino Coast

Occasionally the suggestion arises, even in the state legislature, that the northern section of California secede from the state. The barbed joke hints that this is a different world up here, more attuned in geography, resources, climate, society and mentality to Oregon and the Pacific Northwest. Spanish influence barely reached here: no missions, no Spanish names, no red-tile roofs and white-washed adobe. The tiny coastal villages seem to have been transplanted from New England, where many of the early settlements' founders originated.

This is the land of lumber. The acreage of towering trees, redwoods especially, but Douglas fir and others as well, seems endless. Since the days of the earliest White settlements, the lumber industry dominated the region's economy, followed by fishing, ranching and other activities. The lumbermen cleared the slopes rapidly and the two thousand year old redwoods were suddenly threatened with extinction. But the lumber industry itself has fallen on hard times, and is no longer the king it once was. The vast network of lumber operations and mill towns has shrunken over the years. The coast is dotted with the debris of that earlier age; barren stump-studded slopes, abandoned installations and mill towns.

Except for the quaint village of Mendocino, and the line of redwood parks to the north, there are few well-known tourist sights in this neck of the woods. However, if you are a beach-stroller, bluff-climber, tide pool prober or lighthouse-lover, a hunter of driftwood, taster of wine, and fanatic for New England you will find this area fascinating. The pace up here is slow, easy and deeply relaxing.

Fog blankets the Mendocino coastline in summer, and storms pound it in winter. During the tourist season, from Memorial Day to Labor Day, the nights can be cool and damp. The fog is not constant, but when it drifts in, it can drip down your neck and moisten your clothes. You can almost bottle it.

In June, you'll witness the colorful explosion of azaleas and rhododendrons. October may surprise you with balmy days. But winter, stretching to April or even May, creates a world of grey sea along grey cliffs, and foghorns bleating through grey fogs under grey clouds.

How to get there

By car, head north from San Francisco, inland along Highway 101 or on Route 1 along the coast. Route 101 is faster but misses the coastal rollercoaster road of Highway 1. Several roads connect the two parallel highways, offering the chance to see the beautiful diversity of this countryside, and still make good time.

Greyhound runs along Route 101, serving Ukiah and Willits. *Greyhound* operates a line from Eureka as well, north toward Arcata and south toward Fort Bragg. A regular run between Fort Brag and Santa Rosa stops at Mendocino. The *Mendocino Transit Authority (MTA)* operates a coastal van between Eureka and Sonoma, which stops at junctions with links to the transportation systems of Sonoma County.

What to see

Heading up 101 brings you to Mendocino's well-known wine country. The many valleys, ridges and mountains divide the region into a patchwork of "microclimates", creating individuality and variety between the valleys, and great diversity among the grapes and wines produced there.

The wineries are clustered in several areas. The southern inland valley around Hopland, on Route 101, is fringed by vineyards. There are wineries at either end of town, with tasting rooms. For those with a more proletarian palate there is also the **Mendocino Brewing company.**

Further north, in the deep valley surrounding Ukiah, are more wineries, as well as restaurants and motels. For an especially lovely drive off 101, turn northwest on route 128 just north of Cloverdale. This two-lane country road glides through the gently folded, green and golden hills of the Anderson Valley, toward the coast. Between Booneville and Navarro the wineries are scattered, some with picnic areas, and there are stores along the way to pick up picnic fixings.

Driving north up the coastal Route 1, the first town along the Mendocino coast is **Gualala**, an old lumbertown transformed to a more tourist oriented center. The non-profit Gualala Arts organization presents the "Art in the Redwoods" festival in August. Store fronts in **The Gallery** center proffer some fine craftwork, paintings and sculpture. North of Gualala, the coastal road undulates past jutting cliffs, headland, coves, islands, slivers of beach, salt marshes and rare, fragile patches of giant dunes. Take your time here to relax and take in the scenery.

Don't miss a visit in the historic old and elegant **Miland Hotel** on HWY 1, north of Gualala which was built at the beginning of this century.

Four miles (6.5 km) north of Gualala is **Anchor Bay,** which offers restaurants and Bed & Breakfast nooks. Protected on the north and south by jutting land masses, the coast here is sunny when the rest of the earth disappears in fog. Ten miles (16 km) further north is **Point Arena**, with its lighthouse dominating the nearby bluff. It is accessible and can be climbed. Open 11am-2:30pm daily, admission $1.00, tel. 707-882-2777.

Mendocino, the muted jewel of this coast, began with the inauspicious name of Meiggsville. In the 19th century Harry Meiggs came seeking a wrecked cargo of Chinese silk. He ended up founding the area's first sawmill. Although Meiggs headed on to establish a rail system through the Andes, the logging industry remained and prospered. Meiggsville became Mendocino, a logger's town of saloons, hotels and brothels, all built in the gabled and turreted style of an old New England village. Today, it appears much the same, minus the brothels.

Be sure to take the self-guided walking map in the beautiful restored **Kelley House Museum**, 45007 Albion st., tel. 937-539, and wander around the charming streets.

It is a quiet isolated village of artists, artisans, fishermen and small tourist oriented shops, but it keeps its dignity and charm.

The stark headland cliffs, just beyond town, which form Mendocino Headlands State Park are breathtaking. A walk along the cliffs on a foggy day, followed by a soak in one of the local hot tub establishments and a drink in a wood-paneled bar, makes for a beautiful day.

The Visitor Center for Mendocino Headlands State Park, at the Ford House on Main st., provides maps and information. Open Thurs.-Fri. noon-5:30pm, Sat.-Sun. 10am-5:30pm, tel. 937-5397.

The **Mendocino Art Center** is the town's cultural and artistic center. 45200 Little Lake st. Open daily 10am-5pm, tel. 937-5818. The influx of artists and the educational programs give the town a cosmopolitan touch. The center's gallery is open all week, and there is a Sunday afternoon concert series.

For the kind of tiny town resort it is, Mendocino's food and lodging are reasonably priced, and most things here are done with care and quality.

Russian Gulch State Park lies just north of Mendocino, with its carved and pockmarked headland. It is a pleasant hike up Russian Gulch Creek to the waterfall. Further to the north, **Van Damme State Park** is known for its pygmy forest of waist high conifers. The trees are stunted by poor soil but manage to hang on. Admission $2 per day.

Fort Bragg is a lumbertown of about 5,000, and a dirty industrial smudge it is, contrasted with the immense greenery around it, but it has reliable, reasonably priced standard motels, as well as a few nice B&B lodges. Fort Bragg and Eureka have plenty of cheap eateries, as do some of the smaller mill towns along the coastal route. On North Harbor dr. several seafood restaurants offer reasonably priced delicious meals, serving the morning's catch hauled to Noyo Harbor by the local fleet.

South of Fort Bragg, the **Mendocino Coast Botanical Garden** encompasses 14 acres of shady glades in dazzling color. 18220 Route 1 at Route 20. Open daily 8am-5:30pm, tel. 964-4352. Route 20 itself provides a scenic and direct connection between the coastal road and 101, Fort Bragg and Willits. There's hardly a town to be seen, only endlessly stretching forests, with some camping spots. Here, the logging trucks on the road may determine your speed on the narrow winding road.

An interesting option is to take the Skunk Train (so named for the smell of the early engines), along a 100-year old rail route, hewn through the mountains to haul lumber. An open-air car allows you to take in the wind and scenery. The 7-hour round trip from Fort Bragg includes an hour stop in Willits. A shorter ride chugs to the old logging town of Northspur. Fare for the full trip is $20, and $10 for ages 5-11. The depot is on Laurel south of Main st., tel. 964-6371.

Redwood Country

I see that you're a logger, and not just a common bum, 'cause nobody but a logger stirs his coffee with his thumb.
American Folk Song

North of Fort Bragg, Route 1 veers inland at Rockport and joins Route 101 at Legget. North of Legget along the highway begin the parks of towering redwoods.

Today's redwood stands comprise less than 10% of the vast acreage of these trees that once thrived on the California coast. Of those surviving, slightly more than 50% are protected, and the greatest concentration of these trees, including some of the tallest, grow along this section of the coast. They are of tremendous girth, towering well over 300 feet (120 m; the length of an American football field), and sometimes grow so closely together that their hefty trunks appear to form a solid wall. Here the world is immersed in shade, fog, and lush luminous greenery. In some areas the line between the protected forest and the shorn earth is stark and clear, and the scarred, denuded land extends literally to the edge of protected groves.

What to see

Coming from the south, **Richardson Grove State Park**, tel. 247-3318, is the first redwood park, about eight miles (13 km) south of Garberville. One of the smaller redwood parks, it nevertheless has some stunning groves. It is very popular, and its three campgrounds are often full in the summer. The interpretive center has regular ranger programs and guided hikes.

North of Garberville is the **Humboldt Redwoods State Park**. The largest redwood park in the region, it links together several separate groves, and contains the famous **Avenue of the Giants**, along which most visitors to the park pass. From the south, the route begins about six miles (10 km) north of Garberville. This 33-mile (62 km) stretch of road parallels Route 101 and the south fork of the Eel River. It passes through lush and misty pockets carpeted with ferns and moss, while the endless walls of redwoods on either side cast everything in deep, cool shadow. **Rockefeller** and **Founder's Grove** are the best known groves. They encompass some of the tallest of the redwoods, and there is a pleasant nature trail at Founder's Grove. The Visitor Center explains the natural history of these groves, and schedules campfire programs and guided hikes from July to Labor Day. For information on park activities, call tel. 946-2311.

Garberville itself is home to a string of bars, standard motels and the elegant and expensive *Benbow Inn*, which in its heyday gave shelter to such luminaries as Herbert Hoover and Spencer Tracy.

Garberville is also the reputed center for the local marijuana industry. This is no small honor, for marijuana has become one of California's biggest cash crops, though the travel brochures don't boast of this. These coastal hills and valleys form the center of the high country.

In the 60s and 70s, when thousands of young emigrants from the urban mainstream headed for the hills seeking a simpler, home-spun way of life, they brought their smoking habits with them. Garden plots of home-grown crops turned into a cottage industry, and sophisticated techniques and experimentation improved the quality and potency. Markets developed in the cities, especially as the American government squeezed or threatened to squeeze the Mexican sources. In the isolated hills and valleys marijuana fields proliferated. Local authorities even distributed instructions for the hiker who stumbled upon a marijuana plot during a stroll. They launched raids and employed helicopters and advanced infrared spotting techniques. Some of the local growers, who have been transformed from rebels into hip entrepreneurs, guard their investments with armed sentries and guard dogs.

Parallel to the stretch of redwood parks, the coast extends toward **Cape Mendocino**. No roads run along the length of this rough coastline, but various inland roads reach the coast. The towns in this region, which is known as **"The Lost Coast"**, were once thriving fishing, lumber and mining communities, but were bypassed by the port at Eureka and the layout of the highways.

From South Fork on Route 101, take Mattele rd. west toward **Petrolia**, for a worthwhile excursion. The area is not frequented by crowds, and the beauty is pristine and primitive. The road skirts the **Kings Range National Conservation Area** (primitive campgrounds are available, with no registration needed), then passes through Petrolia, and later hugs the headlands. There are stretches of black beaches here, where one can enjoy the silence and solitude. Further along is the little doll-house town of **Ferndale**. The restaurants here are reasonably priced, the shops unusual, and the home-made candies delicious. The **Ferndale Museum** at Shaw and 3rd gives a vivid glimpse of North Coast history. Open May-Oct., Tues.-Sat. noon-4pm; Oct-May, same hours, but closed Tues. Small admission. Tel. 786-4466.

Eureka (population of 25,000), on Humboldt Bay, is a typical lumbertown: from its trucks to its smokestacks to the lumberjack breakfast specials. The industrial rumbling and dirt contrasts sharply with the rambling and intricate old Victorian buildings which bear witness to the old lumber kingdoms.

The prime example of this style from an opulent past is the **Carson Mansion** at 2nd and M st., near the refurbished business district. Nearby is the **Clarke Museum** with its collections from local Indian and pioneer culture, and an exquisite marble exterior. 240 East st. Open Tues.-Sat. 10am-4pm. Admission free, tel. 443-1947.

Fort Humbold sits on a hill, overlooking the bay. The museum and logging exhibits give some feel for the rough and simple lifestyle of a typical 'jack. 3431 Fort ave. off Route 101. Open daily 9am-6pm, Admission free, tel. 433-4588, or tel. 433-7952.

Arcata, 10 miles (16 km) to the north, houses **Humboldt State University**, and has a few fancy cafés and restaurants. The university's **marine laboratory**, at Land's End, in the fishing village of **Trinity**, hosts self-guided tours among the aquariums which display local and rare anemones, mollusks, crustaceans and fish. Open Mon.-Fri. 8am-5pm, Sat.-Sun. noon-5pm during the school year. Admission free, tel. 677-3671.

If you are planning to enter the Arcata-to-Ferndale annual Kinetic Sculpture Race in April, remember that all entries must be amphibious and human-powered.

The **Redwood National Park** merges with three state parks — Jedediah Smith, Prairie Creek and Del Norte — to form a contiguous 30-mile (48 km) strip of protected redwood land, between Crick and Crescent City. In most areas the park parallels Route 101 on both sides of the road, and the drive through is beautiful in itself. The parks include a shoreline of beautiful duned beaches, rocky coves and bluffs. There are pull-offs and parking areas which afford access to easy strolls and various groves. The **Tall-Tree** grove can be reached by an 8-mile (13 km) hike or by shuttlebus in the summer. Sections of the park clearly show how real and immediate the threat to the redwoods is; the earth has been stripped right up to the park border.

The trails in the park make good day trips or single over nighters, but are not so suitable for extensive backpacking. There are nature trails at the Lady Bird Johnson Grove and Lagoon Creek, and one near the Prairie Creek headquarters for both sighted and blind people. Prairie Creek, closer to the ocean than some of the other parks, is especially luxuriant in ferns, lichens, moss and other plant cover. In **Jedediah Smith**, canoes and organized kayak trips glide aong the Smith River in summer.

The **National Park Headquarters** in Crescent City provides information for the state parks as well as the national park. 2nd and K sts. Open weekdays 8am-5pm, and until 7pm in the summer, tel. 464-6101. The **Prairie Creek headquarters** on Route 101 in Crick has exhibits and information. Open daily 8am-5pm, until 8pm in summer, tel. 488-2171.

Accommodations

The Mendocino area contains many B&Bs, some built in a distinctly New England style. Prices range from moderate to expensive, and facilities from rustic to luxurious. This is really the land of B&Bs. They fit in perfectly with the tone of the countryside, whereas regular motels spoil the country atmosphere.

There are some motels around, however. They can be found in Fort Bragg and Eureka. In the Eureka area, the average motel price is lower than in more southern parts, starting from $16-$20.

Mendocino Inns: tel. 961-0140. Central referral service for several Mendocino inns.

Mendocino Hotel & Garden Cottages: 45080 Main st., Mendocino, tel. 937-0511; or tel. 800-352-6686. A well-known hotel in a beautiful setting, with rooms and cottages ranging from $38 to $200, singles and doubles.

Benbow Inn: 2675 Benbow rd., just south of Garberville, tel. 923-2124. Has remained a pocket of rustic elegance for many years. Expensive, but it may be just right for a special occasion.

Camping

From the Mendocino area north to the Oregon border, state parks with camping facilities are plentiful along the beaches and in the region of the major redwood groves. Many have drive-in campgrounds, while others have more primitive walk-in campgrounds, and campgrounds primarily for hikers and cyclists.

In the Mendocino area, *Russian Gulch State Park*, tel. 937-5804 is particularly beautiful. *MacKerricher State Park*, three miles north of Fort Bragg, is popular tel. 964-9112 or tel. 937-5804. State parks in the vicinity of Avenue of the Giants tend to fill up quickly.

For State park information in the Mendocino/Fort Bragg region, call tel. 937-5804. For state park camping information in the Redwood National Park area, call the office in Crick: tel. 488-2171.

A youth hostel run by the AYH is located in Arcata: *The Arcata Crew House Hostel*, 1390 I st., tel. 822-9995.

Food

Brannon's Whale Watch: 45040 Main st. Entered through an old whale-watching tower, this spot is popular for lunch and breakfast. The upstairs view will encourage you to linger over another cup of coffee.

The Cheese Shop: Little Lake and Lansing, Mendocino. The atmosphere many be rural but the selection is fit for a gourmet, with everything needed for a picnic on the headlands.

Seagull Inn Cellar Bar: Lansing and Ukiah st., Mendocino. The beautiful bar is actually upstairs. Locals and visitors drink and listen to the live music.

Cap'n Flint's: 32250 North Harbor dr., Noyo Harbor, Fort Bragg. A popular local seafood restaurant. Reasonably priced.

Samoa Cookhouse: 445 West Washington st., Eureka. This was a genuine lumbercamp cookhouse. The dinners would fill even Paul Bunyan.

Important addresses and phone numbers

Chambers of Commerce:
Fort Bragg: 332 N. Main st., tel. 964-3153.
Ukiah: (serving Mendocino as well) 495 E. Perkins st., tel. 462-4705.
Eureka Visitor Bureau: 121 F st., tel. 443-5097.
Mendocino Transit Authority: 241 Plant rd., Ukiah, tel. 462-1422.
Greyhound:
Ukiah: 7370 S. State st., tel. 462-3682.
Fort Bragg: 140 E. Laurel, tel. 964-0877.
Eureka: 1603 4th st., tel. 442-0370.
Redwood National Park Headquarters: 2nd & K st., Crescent City, tel. 464-6101.
State Parks:
Mendocino/Fort Bragg area: tel. 937-5804.
Redwood National Park area: tel. 488-2171.

Shasta and Lassen

The northern border region of California is rugged, isolated and stunning. It is a different world up here. The mountain scenery is as gorgeous and overwhelming as in the Sierras though geomorphologically quite different, and here there are no crowds. Enormous amounts of snow fall on the foothills of Cascade Range, which extends all the way up to Washington. Valleys of fertile volcanic soil are filled with flowers in spring. There are high, semi-arid plateaus, black twisted volcanic formations, and bubbling sulfuric pools. The long Central Valley, which extends southwards as far as Bakersfield, reaches its northern limit around Red Bluff and Redding at the southernmost peaks of the Cascades.

To the north and west of Lake Tahoe, the Sierra Nevada seem to merge with the Cascades, but in fact they are two distinct ranges. The peaks of the Cascades in California — Mt. Shasta, Mt. Lassen and the others — were shaped by volcanic action, and the formation of this mountain landscape is by no means complete. Some frozen lava flows in the north are only 500 years old, and in the Lassen area, there was volcanic activity as recently as 1915.

There are some quaint old mining and logging towns which have been spruced up a bit for tourists. The 1849 gold rush extended this far north, and in fact there were several major finds here. The main attractions in California's far north are the wonderful natural formations, and the recreational opportunities which they afford. The main recreation areas are Whiskeytown-Shasta-Trinity National Recreation Area, Mt. Lassen Volcanic National Park and Lava Beds National Monument. Surrounding each of these protected areas are huge tracts of national forest land.

I-5 is the main traffic artery penetrating the northern mountains, coming from the Central Valley and continuing into the central valley of Oregon. In the Lassen-Shasta area, along the I-5 route are the two main towns in the region; **Red Bluff** and **Redding**. Red Bluff is indeed located on a red bluff above the Sacramento River. Between these two towns, a visitor can find most of the basic amenities necessary. There are good reasonably priced restaurants as well as the usual fast-food stands, and several basic reasonably priced motels. For forays into the backwoods, stock up here on neccessities — the range is broader and prices lower than in the national parks or small mountain towns.

A popular circular route passes through both the Mt. Lassen and Mt. Shasta regions. Follow I-5 north beyond Redding and through the

Shasta Dam, Shasta Lake and Mt. Shasta

national recreation area, to the town of **Mt. Shasta**, which is situated on the foothills of the massive mountain of the same name. The town is small, with some motels, restaurants and grocery stores, and serves as a re-entry point for serious climbers and backpackers who roam the national forest which includes Mt. Shasta (the mountain, not the town), or who try to scale the peak itself (this is only for experienced climbers). From this point, Route 89 heads east, and then curves south toward Mt. Lassen. Several small towns are connected by this highway. South of Lassen's national park, Route 36 turns west toward Red Bluff and I-5. A glance at the map will show that, in addition to this basic loop, there are numerous other options for trips in the region.

The **Whiskeytown-Shasta-Trinity National Recreation Area**, north and west of Redding, is made up of three separate, unconnected units (thus the three-part name). Each area has a lake which is the centerpiece of its recreation activities, and each lake is artificial, created by the damming and channeling of waters for the benefit of Central Valley agriculture. Although the natural water courses were modified, and reservoirs were created in dry valleys, the surrounding areas were protected and reserved for public use. The lakes created by the Central Valley Water Project (launched as a federal work project during the Depression), filled the various dips and folds of the valleys and formed long, winding shorelines filled with coves and peaceful backwaters.

The lakes, especially in the Whiskeytown and Shasta sections, draw armadas of sailboats, powerboats, windsurfers and waterskiers. On **Shasta Lake**, huge houseboats can be rented and navigated at slow speeds along the various byways of the long lake. The **Shasta Dam** itself, at the confluence of the Sacramento, Pit and McLoud rivers, is one of the world's largest, and the centerpin of the Central Valley project. Free tours are given from 9am-6pm daily in the summer.

In the northwestern area of the Trinity section of the recreation area, is the **Salmon-Trinity Alps Wild Area**, an uncrowded and beautiful hiking region.

The Trinity Alps embrace mountain ridges, deep canyons between the Trinity River and Salmon River, and more than 55 lakes. Permits are required for backcountry campers. Be sure to check conditions before hiking in this isolated wilderness, by calling forest service headquarters in Weaverville, tel. 916-623-2131.

The volcanic forces over the ages have given the Lassen terrain an appearance and feel all its own. The park is dominated by **Mt. Lassen**, a plugged volcanic peak. From 1914, eruptions occured intermittently for seven years. The park encompasses a variety of volcanic formations. Its extensive trails wander among hot pools, volcanic peaks and lush valleys enriched by volcanic soil.

Many of the main attractions near the main road are accessible by car or by taking a short walk from the main road. The park's two Visitor Information Centers are located near the northwest entrance, at **Manzanita Lake**, and at the southwest entrance near **Sulphur Works**. The main park road, **Route 89**, arcs around the base of Mt. Lassen itself. The central portion of this highway is closed in winter due to the heavy snows, which can fall as early as October and last into late spring.

The main route to the park follows I-5 north to Red Bluff, and then Route 36 heading east. This road passes park headquarters at

Mineral. Train service is available to Red Bluff. *Greyhound* runs to Mineral. It is advisable to stock up on groceries in Red Bluff or Redding rather than in the park.

Sulphur Works is not a factory but a thermal area of steam vents, irridescent hot pools and bubbling mudpots. It can be reached by a two-mile (3 km) self-guided trail. The **Bumpass Hell** self-guiding trail leads to the largest concentration of hot springs in the park. The round trip is about 2.5 miles (4 km). The trail to the summit of Mt. Lassen is about 2.5 miles in one direction, but do not be misled by the short length of the trail. It is a tough climb along switchbacks to the 10,457 ft. (3,555 m) high peak. Take your time, and bring a sweater and hiking shoes appropriate for snow, even in summer. The view from the top is breathtaking.

Many trails head to the east of the park, which has almost no regular roads. There is a variety of loop-hikes which go past strings of alpine lakes. A segment of the Pacific Crest Trail crosses the park.

There are several main camping areas in the Lassen park. Those near the road are, of course, the most crowded. The walk-in campground at Sulphur Works is near the hot pools and away from the crowds. Back country camping is bountiful and beautiful. Outside the park to the north is a vast expanse of forest service territory, with developed sites as well as plenty of dirt roads and places where people can camp. The towns of Red Bluff and Redding on I-5, both have a wide array of accommodation at reasonable prices. Basic, simple motel rooms are available for $20 per night and sometimes less.

Lava Beds National Monument, located just below the Oregon border in the northeastern portion of California, is known for its strange lava formations, and for the short but dramatic Modoc Indian War of 1872-73.

The sharp craggy landscape is the result of 5 million years of volcanic activity which has continued right up to very recent times. The youngest cinder cones are only 1,000 years old.

The rich volcanic soil supports a complex plant and animal community. For centuries the Modoc Indians hunted in the valleys and mountains, and used the reeds in Tule Lake to fashion their homes and boats.

The Modocs were connected with other Indian bands that lived in the Klamath Basin, which extends into Oregon. As settlers moved into the region, the American government attempted to relocate the various bands on a reservation, including tribes that had been age-old enemies. The Modocs wanted a reservation on their own land, and over a period of years began deserting their assigned reservation, until an army expedition was dispatched in 1872. Under the leadership of a chief named Captain Jack, 52 Indian rebels dug into the natural fortress of the lava beds and caves, and held off over 1,000 soldiers for five months. Gradually the Indian force was whittled down or captured, until finally Captain Jack surrendered. With three other leaders he was hanged, and the surviving remnant of his band was taken to a reservation in Oklahoma.

The main approach to the park is from Route 39 to the east. The monument is about 30 miles (48 km) south of the town of Tulelake, and 58 miles (92 km) from Klamath Falls in Oregon. Public transportation reaches Klamath Falls, where cars can be rented.

A single road runs the length of the park, in a crescent from the northeast to the southeast corner. There is an information kiosk near the northeast entrance, but the main information center is near the southeast entrance.

Black lava flows and various formations can be seen throughout the park. Much of the monument is inaccessible by auto, and more than half is designated wilderness area. Ranging in elevation from 4,000 to 5,700 feet (1,360 m to 1,940 m), the monument is exposed to cold weather and snow during any season.

The park's sites divide roughly into two parts. In the north are historical reminders of the heroic but futile Modoc War, including **Captain Jack's Stronghold** with a self-guiding trail through it. The monument's best known features, the innumerable lava tubes and caves, are concentrated mainly in the south, near the visitor center.

The visitor center presents exhibits on the Modoc Indians. Adjacent **Mushpot Cave** — the only one which is illuminated — offers explanations of the geology. A film is featured here four times daily. The other caves can be explored by flashlight. Flashlights can be borrowed from the visitor center. Guidebooks to the caves are on sale, and plastic helmets can be rented. The **Cave Loop Road**, dotted with caves, begins at the visitor center and is the most accessible and popular area for some easy amateur spelunking.

Daily guided walks, cave trips and campfire programs are available in the summer. During the winter, deer wander into the area in large numbers, and observing them is a popular activity. Situated on the Pacific Flyway, the monument is a fantastic place to observe the migrations of ducks and geese during the spring and fall. They fly by the millions over this territory and often stop here to rest.

The main campground is located at **Indian Well**, near the visitor center. Off-the-road camping is allowed in the **Modoc National Forest**. Free sites are found at the forest service campground of Howard's Gulch, 30 miles (48 km) south on Route 139. Reasonably priced standard motels are found in Tulelake.

*I*_ND EX_

A

Alcatraz, San Francisco..............................100
Angel Island...127
Angels' Camp..159
Ano Nuevo State Reserve...........................118
Aquatic Park,
    San Francisco...99
Arcata..188
Armstrong Redwoods
    State Reserve..140
Auburn...154
Austin Creek State
    Recreation Area....................................140

B

Berkeley..119
Bodega...143
Bodega Bay...142
Bodie..179
Bullfrog Pond..140
Butano State Park.......................................119

C

Calaveras Big Trees
    State Park..159
Calaveras County.......................................159
California Marine Mammal
    Center..126
Calistoga..134
Cannery Row, Monterey...............................58
Cape Mendocino..187
Carmel Bay
    Ecological Reserve..................................54
Carmel Mission...52
Carmel River State Park...............................54
Castro Street,
    San Francisco.......................................108
Civic Center,
    San Francisco.......................................104
Clement Street,
    San Francisco.......................................107
Coit Tower, San Francisco............................98
Coloma...157
Columbia State Historic Park......................160
Crossroads, Carmel......................................54

D

Dancan Mills...142

Davis..151
Del Monte Forest...55
Desolation Wilderness,
    Lake Tahoe...165
Devils' Postpile
    National Monument...............................180
Donner Lake..166
Donner Memorial State Park.......................166
Dowhieville..156

E

Eagle Falls..164
Eagle Lake...164
El Dorado National Forest...........................166
Emerald Bay..164
Empire Mine State Historic
    Park...156
Eureka..188
Exploratorium, San Francisco.....................102

F

Farallon Islands..129
Ferndale...188
Financial District,
    San Francisco...90
Fisherman's Wharf,
    Monterey...58
Fisherman's Wharf,
    San Francisco...98
Fort Bragg..185
Fort Humbold...188
Fort Mason, San Francisco.........................102
Fort Ross
    State Historical Park.............................143

G

Garberville...187
Georgetown..156
Gold Bug Park
    and Mine, Placerville............................158
Golden Gate Park,
San Francisco..110
Grass Valley..156
Grover Hot Springs
    State Park..165
Gualala..184
Guerneville..140

INDEX

H

Haight-Ashbury,
San Francisco................................108
Healdsburg...142
Humboldt Redwoods
State Park.......................................187

I

Inyo National Forests.........................180

J

Japantown, San Francisco...............106
Jedediah Smith....................................189
Jenner..142
John Muir Wilderness.........................179

K

Kings Range National
Conservation Area.......................188

L

Lake Tahoe..161
Lava Beds
National Monument........................194
Limantour Beach.................................130
Lombard Street,
San Fracisco...................................98
Lovers Point..55

M

Malakoff Diggins
State Historic Park.........................156
Mammouth Mountain..........................179
Marin County...125
Marine World/Africa U.S.A................130
Marshall Gold Discovery State
Historical Park................................157
Mendocino..185
Mendocino Coast
Botanical Garden..........................186
Mission District,
San Francisco................................107
Mission San Francisco Solano.........136
Moaning Cavern....................................159
Modoc National Forest.......................195
Mokelumne Wilderness.......................165
Mono Lake..179
Monterey...56
Moss Landing...62
Mt. Lassen..193
Mt. Shasta..192
Mt. Tamalpais State Park..................127
Muir Woods
National Monument........................128

Murphys..159

N

Napa Valley..131
Nevada City..155
Nob Hill, San Francisco.......................93

O

Occidental...142
Oh! Ridge..180

P

Pacific Grove..55
Paraiso Hot Springs...............................61
Petrolia..187
Pier 39, San Francisco........................100
Pier 41, San Francisco........................100
Pinnacles National Monument...........61
Placerville...157
Point Arena...185
Point Lobos State Reserve..................54
Point Pinos Lighthouse.........................55
Point Reyes..128

R

Red Bluff...191
Redding..191
Redwood Country.................................186
Redwood National Park.......................188
Reno...167
Robert Louis Stevenson
State Park.......................................135
Russian Gulch
State Park.......................................185
Russian River Valley............................139

S

Sacramento..145
St. Helena...133
Salinas..60
Salmon-Trinity Alps
Wild Area...193
San Andreas Fault................................129
San Francisco..70
San Francisco Bay................................114
San Francisco Bay and
Delta Model....................................126
San Jose..118
Santa Cruz...63
Sausalito...126
Sebastopol..142
Seventeen Mile Drive............................55
Silicon Valley...118

INDEX

Shasta Dam............................193
Shasta Lake............................193
SOMA, San Francisco............105
Sonoma State Historical
   Park.................................137
Sonoma Valley........................136
Southern Mother Lode............160
Squaw Valley..........................165
Stanford University.................118
Steinbeck Library.....................61
Sutter's Mill..........................157

T
Telegraph Hill,
   San Francisco......................98
Tennessee Valley...................126
Tiburon..................................126
Trinity...................................188
Truckee.................................165
Tuolumne Meadows................178

U
Union Square,
   San Francisco......................92
Union Street,
   San Francisco....................106

V
Van Damme State Park............185
Vikingsholm...........................164

W
Whiskeytown-Shasta-Trinity
   National Recreation Area......193

Y
Yosemite................................170

NOTES

NOTES

NOTES

NOTES

QUESTIONNAIRE

In our efforts to keep up with the pace and pulse of California, we kindly ask your cooperation in sharing with us any information which you may have as well as your comments. We would greatly appreciate your completing and returning the following questionnaire. Feel free to add additional pages. A complimentary copy of the next edition will be sent to you should any of your suggestions be included.

Our many thanks!

To: Inbal Travel Information (1983) Ltd.
2 Chen Blvd.
Tel Aviv 64071
Israel

Name: _____

Address: _____

_____

Occupation: _____

Date of visit: _____

_____

Purpose of trip (vacation, business, etc.): _____

_____

_____

Comments/Information: _____

_____

_____

_____

_____

_____

_____

_____

_____

_____

_____

_____

_____

_____

_____

INBAL Travel Information Ltd.
P.O.B. 39090 Tel Aviv
ISRAEL 61390